Day & Griffin

The Law of
International Trade

Third Edition

Bernardette Griffin BA LLM

Director

The College of Law, Birmingham

Butterworths
LexisNexis™

Members of the LexisNexis Group worldwide

United Kingdom	LexisNexis Butterworths Tolley, a Division of Reed Elsevier (UK) Ltd, Halsbury House, 35 Chancery Lane, LONDON, WC2A 1EL, and 4 Hill Street, EDINBURGH EH2 3JZ
Argentina	LexisNexis Argentina, BUENOS AIRES
Australia	LexisNexis Butterworths, CHATSWOOD, New South Wales
Austria	LexisNexis Verlag ARD Orac GmbH & Co K G, VIENNA
Canada	LexisNexis Butterworths, MARKHAM, Ontario
Chile	LexisNexis Chile Ltda, SANTIAGO DE CHILE
Czech Republic	Nakladatelství Orac sro, PRAGUE
France	Editions du Juris-Classeur SA, PARIS
Hong Kong	LexisNexis Butterworths, HONG KONG
Hungary	HVG-Orac, BUDAPEST
India	LexisNexis Butterworths, NEW DELHI
Ireland	Butterworths (Ireland) Ltd, DUBLIN
Italy	Giuffrè Editore, MILAN
Malaysia	Malayan Law Journal Sdn Bhd, KUALA LUMPUR
New Zealand	LexisNexis Butterworths, WELLINGTON
Poland	Wydawnictwo Prawnicze LexisNexis, WARSAW
Singapore	LexisNexis Butterworths, SINGAPORE
South Africa	LexisNexis Butterworths, DURBAN
Switzerland	Stämpfli Verlag A G, BERNE
USA	LexisNexis, DAYTON, Ohio

A CIP Catalogue record for this book is available from the British Library.

ISBN 0 406 92183 0

Printed and bound in Great Britain by William Clowes Limited, Beccles and London

Visit Butterworths LexisNexis *direct* at www.butterworths.com

Preface

The third edition of this book retains the forms of the second edition dealing with the modes of carriage before the contracts on which they are based, since the latter are difficult to understand without a knowledge of the former. The book still endeavours to maintain a clear and concise approach to this complex area of the law.

However, the book has been updated and includes developments particularly in the area of electronic commerce dealing with the EU Directive on Electronic Commerce 2000, the Electronic Communications Act 2000, and the UNICITRAL Model Law on Electronic Commerce 1996 (as amended in 1998). Other new aspects are discussion of the Council Regulation on Jurisdiction and the Recognition and Enforcement of Judgments in Civil and Commercial Matters 2000, and the Montreal Convention for the Unification of Certain Rules for International Carriage by Air 1999. The second edition was written just before the Uniform Customs and Practice for Documentary Credits 1993 were due to take effect in 1994. This edition incorporates the new rules. The Arbitration Act 1996 is covered and the changes made by this legislation are included. Also, significant cases decided since the last edition have also been referred to in the text.

We wish to express our gratitude to Witherby & Co for permission to reproduce their bill of lading form, to the Institute of London Underwriters for permission to reproduce their cargo clauses, to the Institute of Export for permission to include their definition of an fob contract in the text and to the International Chamber of Commerce for permission to reproduce the UNCTAD/ICC Rules for Multimodal Transport and the Uniform Customs and Practice for Documentary Credits.

We have endeavoured to state the law as at September 2002.

BTG

DMD

Contents

Contents

Chapter 4   Carriage by air and land and sale contracts based thereon   101

Chapter 5   Combined transport   119

Contents

Contents

Contents

Contents

Table of statutes

Page references in **bold** type indicate where the legislation is set out in part or in full. References in this table to *Statutes* are to Halsbury's Statutes of England (Fourth Edition) showing the volume number and page at which the annotated text of the Act will be found.

Table of statutes

List of cases

List of cases

List of cases

xvii

H

List of cases

List of cases

L

M

List of cases

List of cases

U

V

W

Y

List of cases

Chapter 1

The outline of the transaction

THE PROBLEMS OF INTERNATIONAL SALES

The international sales transaction is in essence a sale of goods and presents all those commercial and legal problems inherent in any sale of goods. Its special features arise from the simple fact that seller and buyer are based in different countries. This exacerbates the normal problems to a degree where the parties have, as a matter of course, to make provision in their contract for dealing with them.

Thus any seller is naturally reluctant to part with the control of goods without receiving payment for them unless he can retain an interest in the goods as some sort of security for payment and any buyer is equally reluctant to pay for goods before he has received them unless he can be given some kind of legal right over them. Neither party, moreover, wishes to have capital tied up in goods in transit. In international sales the difficulties of this situation are clearly more pressing than they would be in a domestic sale.

Again, while any seller is likely to be concerned to ensure that he is paid, this concern is increased when the buyer is in another country and another jurisdiction. In the first place, the seller is less likely to be familiar with the buyer, his solvency, creditworthiness and integrity. In the second place, any attempt, should the buyer default, to obtain payment through legal process is likely to be a much more serious matter and, moreover, be a matter for the application of a foreign system of law. For these reasons a seller will often seek to ensure that the contract of sale sets up a system of payment that will give him recourse against a bank in the United Kingdom.

Similarly, the seller in an ordinary domestic sale in the United Kingdom is unlikely to be unduly perturbed at the prospect that a revolutionary junta might seize power and ban all sales or payments. The seller of goods to some parts of the world can have no such assurance, and he has furthermore to be concerned about export and import licences and possibly exchange control regulations. Arranging for payment to be guaranteed by a bank in the United Kingdom is one possible way of avoiding the consequences of some of these risks. Another is to seek the protection of the Government-sponsored Export Credit Guarantee scheme, which provides insurance cover against some of the losses likely to result from political causes.

The goods themselves have to be transported from the seller to the buyer. This is perhaps the most important single factor in the international sale transaction. Indeed, it is its whole purpose and the arrangements for carrying the goods to the buyer assume a far greater importance than they are likely to have in any normal domestic contract; so much so that the type of sale contract which the parties make will be dictated to a very great extent by the type of carriage they envisage for the goods. The mode of carriage they employ will be determined by various factors. The nature of the goods is clearly one of these. Are they, for example, perishable, fragile, valuable or heavy or otherwise awkward to handle? Other factors include the urgency with which the buyer requires the goods and the availability and cost of the various methods of carriage.

Closely related to the question of the carriage of the goods is that of their insurance. Since the goods have to be carried for long distances – and possibly moved from one mode of transport to another – they are at greater risk of loss or damage and buyer and seller will usually require some form of insurance to protect themselves as far as possible from the financial consequences of such loss or damage.

Because of these problems the overseas sale contract involves the making of other contracts, with bankers, carriers and insurers. Nor is this all. In most of these contracts the parties will be acting through intermediaries, such as insurance brokers, selling agents, forwarding agents and loading brokers, and the functions of these agents and their relationships to the principals will often affect the contract they make. Thus what the businessman may see as a single transaction tends to appear to the lawyer as a complex of contracts, each with its own parties and incidents but all related to the central contract of the sale of goods.

Most of these contracts will take the form of, or involve the issue of, some significant documents such as a bill of lading, an insurance policy or a bill of exchange. In many cases legal rights relating to the goods, to their insurance, to their carriage or to payment for them can be transferred simply from one party to another by the delivery, or indorsement and delivery, of these documents. This documentary transfer of legal rights plays a large part in overcoming the problems inherent in the international sale transaction.

Not all the problems, however, are in the sphere of contract. If a dispute arises on the contract it may be necessary to decide whether an English court has jurisdiction to hear the case and, if it has, whether it should apply English law or the law of another country. The law relating to these questions is known as the Conflict of Laws (or Private International Law) and is obviously very relevant in the area of international trade.

THE OUTLINE OF THE TRANSACTION

The sale contract and the parties

The principal parties to the sale contract, the seller and the buyer, will in many, if not in most, cases act through agents. A manufacturer producing goods in the United Kingdom may sell directly to an overseas buyer but exporting is a highly complex operation, requiring highly specialised knowledge of markets, finance, transport, insurance and many other matters and a manufacturer may well prefer not to be involved directly in it. So while many firms, particularly large ones, have their own export departments, others prefer to leave the operations in the hands of firms with specialised knowledge and administrative machinery, usually called 'export houses' or 'confirming houses'. Many arrangements are used. The confirming house may act simply as an agent for the overseas buyer, in which case the contract of sale is made between seller and buyer and the legal status of the confirming house will be governed by the ordinary law of agency. Alternatively, the confirming house may buy from the United Kingdom seller and resell to the overseas buyer, in which case the confirming house is a principal in both contracts and there is no direct contractual relationship between the United Kingdom seller and the overseas buyer.

Two other arrangements are more involved. In the first, the overseas buyer instructs the confirming house to buy the goods, in its own name, from the seller and undertakes to pay to the confirming house the price of the goods and a commission. In this transaction the confirming house has a dual function. In relation to the seller it is a principal and responsible for the performance of the 'buyer' part of the contract, namely, accepting the goods and paying for them. On the other hand in relation to the overseas buyer it is an agent and responsible to the buyer for the performance of an agent's duties.[1]

In the final arrangement, the overseas buyer instructs the confirming house to buy in the buyer's name and 'confirm' to the seller, that is, give the seller its own undertaking that the contract will be performed. Here again the confirming house will be an agent in relation to the overseas buyer and a principal in relation to the United Kingdom seller. The essential difference between this arrangement and the last is that the buyer and seller also have a direct contractual relationship[2] so that the United Kingdom seller could proceed directly against the overseas buyer if, for example, the confirming house refused to pay for goods accepted.

Dealing through a confirming house in his own country has manifest advantages for an exporter. Nevertheless it is also common to employ agents in the buyer's country. These may be simply agents based in the foreign country but may be subsidiary companies of the exporting company.

In the course of the transaction the parties to the sale contract will become involved in the other, related, contracts of carriage, insurance and so on, but the parties to these related contracts, other than the buyer and the seller, do not become parties to the sale contract and will usually be unaffected by its incidents. Thus the carrier of goods may be liable to the buyer if the goods arrive in bad condition because of negligent carriage because carrier and buyer are parties to the contract of carriage, but the carrier would not be liable for the bad condition of the goods under the sale contract or any term implied therein (such as a term relating to merchantable quality) because the carrier is not party to the contract of sale. On the same basis, a bank engaging in contracts with buyer or seller as part of the mechanism of payment for goods will usually expressly dissociate itself from the sale contract or other related contracts.

Forms of overseas sale contracts

The contract of sale will not only specify the goods to be delivered by the seller and the price to be paid by the buyer but will have to cover other

1   *Sobell Industries Ltd v Cory Bros & Co Ltd* [1955] 2 Lloyd's Rep 82.
2   *Teheran-Europe Co Ltd v ST Belton (Tractors) Ltd* [1968] 2 QB 53, [1968] 1 All ER 585.

matters such as the carriage of the goods overseas to the buyer, the insurance of the goods while they are in transit and the machinery that is to be set up for payment. In theory there could be endless permutations of the allocation of cost and responsibility for different elements between seller and buyer. In practice buyer and seller will almost certainly adopt a recognised and established form of contract the incidents of which are well known and by so doing will to a great extent automatically allocate the duties and expenses, since if they adopt such a contract they will be presumed, in the absence of any express term to the contrary, to have adopted all the normal incidents of that type of contract.

Thus in *Carlos Federspiel & Co SA v Charles Twigg & Co Ltd*[3] the defendants contracted to sell a quantity of bicycles to Central American buyers. Bicycles had been crated and the shipping marks put on the crates for despatch to the buyers when the selling company went into liquidation. The buyers claimed the bicycles on the grounds that they had been appropriated to the contract and that property in them had thereupon passed to the buyers. The sale contract had, however, been made on fob (free on board) terms and the normal rule in such a contract is that the property in the goods passes to the buyer as the goods cross over the ship's rail. By using an fob contract the parties had effectively implied an intention that the property was to pass at that time and therefore the argument that it had passed earlier was rejected.

The existence of these established contracts does not remove all doubt about the parties' responsibilities. In the first place there may, as will be seen, still be doubtful points as to the actual legal position with regard to some elements of these contracts. In the second place the parties are perfectly free to depart from an established form in various respects and the legal effect of their so doing may be unclear. Finally, although these contracts have a worldwide recognition in respect of their general nature, different legal systems may take different views as to their legal effects in particular respects.

Attempts have been made to smooth the operations of international trade by establishing agreed rules to apply to overseas sales to the exclusion of municipal laws. Such rules were agreed by a Hague Conference in 1964 and enacted in the United Kingdom as the Uniform Laws on International Sales Act 1967. This Act came into force in 1972 but made the application of the Uniform Laws subject to the parties expressly adopting them. As

3   [1957] 1 Lloyd's Rep 240.

The outline of the transaction

they appear never to do so, the Uniform Laws can, unfortunately, be disregarded as far as English law is concerned. The Vienna Convention 1980, under the auspices of the United Nations Committee for International Trade Law (UNCITRAL), produced a code which may well eventually be accepted.

Much useful work in the standardisation of sale terms has been done by extra-legal agencies, such as trade associations, who produce standard form contracts for their own trades which are in wide international use, and by the International Chamber of Commerce.

The established contracts are distinguished from each other largely by the different stages at which the responsibility for the goods and the expenses associated with it are transferred from the seller to the buyer. (This may be, but will not necessarily be, the point at which the property in the goods passes to the buyer.) The stage at which this transfer occurs must obviously be a significant point in the transit. In consequence the type of contract the parties employ will be dictated by the method of transport that they envisage. For example, under an fas (free alongside ship) contract the seller's responsibilities in connection with the goods will usually cease when the goods are alongside the ship at the port of loading. This contract will obviously only be used when the primary mode of transport is to be carriage by sea. It would not be used if, for example, it were intended that the goods should be loaded (stuffed) into a container which was to be carried on a single road vehicle from seller to buyer. The fact that at some stage the lorry might be alongside a ship that was to carry it with its load for an incidental sea transit would be irrelevant as a point at which to transfer responsibilities.

As well as establishing the allocation of responsibilities between the parties, the choice of a particular form of contract also establishes what the buyer gets for the price that he pays. At one extreme, under the 'Ex-works' or 'Ex-factory' contract, the seller has merely to deliver the goods at his own place of business and all expenses and duties thereafter fall on the buyer, who must make all arrangements for transport. At the other extreme, when goods are sold 'Free delivered' or on similar terms, the seller must make and pay for all arrangements necessary to get the goods to the buyer's place of business. between these two extremes are various forms, not all of which are necessarily export contracts. Of these, the most important are the fob (free on board) contract and the cif (cost, insurance, freight) contract. Under the former, the seller, for the price he is paid, must deliver the goods on board a vessel at the agreed port of loading. Under the latter, the seller must not only ship the goods as above but also arrange for their carriage to the agreed port of discharge and pay the freight[4] and arrange and pay for suitable insurance on the goods and must tender to the buyer all the documents relating to the transaction, namely, the invoice representing the cost of the goods, the insurance policy and the bill of lading which represents the freight. The documentary aspect of the cif contract is extremely important when considering its legal nature. One variant of this contract is the c and f (cost and freight) contract, under which the seller does not have to arrange and pay for the insurance on the goods.

There are various forms of contract used when carriage is to be by road, rail or air.

THE CONTRACT OF CARRIAGE

Carriage by sea

In spite of recent developments in other forms of transport carriage by sea remains the most usual way of transporting goods overseas. In terms of weight, well over 90% of goods are so carried. The importance of the contract of carriage in the international sale transaction lies in the fact that during the transit the goods which are the subject of the sale contract are in the charge of the carrier and his agents and sub-contractors and neither buyer nor seller has any physical control over them. Sea transit may last for several weeks during which time the goods will be subject to the dangers inherent in sea transit. It is important to know, therefore, that liabilities the carrier of the goods is under to seller or buyer, or, as they are likely to be termed under this contract, shipper and consignee, and what contractual rights they may have against him.

The seller (or shipper) will not usually make the contract of carriage with the carrier directly. He will almost certainly employ a forwarding agent (or freight forwarder) to make all arrangements for carriage. Similarly the carrier will normally employ a loading broker to obtain cargoes for him. In some cases the same firm may act as forwarding agent for the shipper and as loading broker for the carrier.[5]

4   'Freight' is the legal term for the charge made for carrying goods and does not refer to the goods themselves.
5   For a description of the relation and function of these agents see *Heskell v Continental Express Ltd* [1950] 1 All ER 1033 at 1037.

The loading broker or other agent of the carrier will sign and hand to the shipper or his agent a document known as a bill of lading. If the goods have been handed to the carrier for shipment but not yet loaded this will be a 'received for shipment' bill of lading. If the goods have actually been loaded on to the ship it will be a 'shipped' bill of lading. This document, which is of the highest importance in international sale transactions, has three functions. It is evidence of the contract of carriage which has been made, it is a receipt for the goods and it is a document of title to the goods. This last quality means that the ownership or possession of the goods can be transferred from one party to another by delivering, or indorsing and delivering, the bill of lading. It can thus be used to deliver or sell the goods while they are at sea, or used as security for a loan. Moreover, under the Carriage of Goods by Sea Act 1992, section 2, the party to whom a bill of lading is transferred will normally have transferred to him not only the legal rights in the goods but also the rights and duties under the contract of carriage, so that he will have all the rights of action against the carrier that the original shipper would have had.

Bills of lading are normally issued in sets, each bill of lading in the set being numbered and each usually being valid, so that a carrier who hands over the cargo to a party presenting any bill of lading from the set will be discharged from further liability.

If a cargo is very large, a shipper may charter an entire vessel, either for a voyage or for a period of time. In this case he is a charterer and his relationship with the shipowner will be governed by the charterparty.

Carriage by air and land

Carriage of goods by air may be arranged for a seller by a forwarding agent but it is also common for a seller to deal directly with an air carrier. The document issued as a receipt for goods consigned by air is the air way-bill or air consignment note. Unlike the bill of lading it is not a document of title. In the United Kingdom the international carriage of goods by air is governed by the Carriage by Air Act 1961 which applies the Warsaw Conventions of 1929 and 1955.

Carriage by road or rail may be an incidental stage of a transit or it may be the primary mode. In an fob contract, for example, the seller might make a contract for the carriage of the goods by road or rail to the docks where he has to deliver the goods on board the ship. In this situation there is no international element in the road or rail carriage. Alternatively the seller may make a contract to have the goods carried for the entire journey by road or rail. International carriage of goods by road and rail is governed by the CMR Convention 1956 and the CIM Convention 1970. The documents issued as receipts for goods carried by road or rail are consignment notes. Like the air way-bill, and unlike the bill of lading, they are not documents of title.

Combined transport

This is also known as Through Carriage, Intermodal or Multimodal Transport. This arrangement is being increasingly used, particularly when cargoes are carried in containers. All carriage, by whatever mode or modes, involved in the transport of the goods from the seller to buyer is undertaken by a 'combined transport operator' who arranges all the stages with the relevant carriers. The combined transport operator may be a carrier himself or may be a forwarding agent. The seller will make only one contract with the combined transport operator for the entire carriage. The document issued as a receipt will be a combined transport document which may or may not be a document of title. This mode of operation presents various legal problems.

THE INSURANCE OF GOODS IN TRANSIT

Goods in transit, particularly by sea, are at risk. Under the contract of carriage the carrier may be liable to the owner of the goods in respect of loss or damage occurring to the goods while they are in his charge but not all loss or damage will be attributable to fault on the part of the carrier or his servants and, even if it is, the carrier may, under the terms of the contract of carriage, be exempt from liability or be liable only to a limited extent. Thus all goods sent overseas will almost certainly be insured. Whether this insurance is effected by the seller or by the buyer will depend on the contract of sale. Under an Ex-works contract, since the seller has only to deliver at his own place of business, there is no reason why he should insure the goods since they will be at the buyer's risk throughout the entire transit. Conversely, in a Free Delivered contract it will usually be the seller who insures. In fas and fob contracts the goods will be at the risk of the buyer from the time that the goods are alongside and on board the ship respectively. It will therefore normally be the buyer who requires the goods to be insured for the sea transit. The parties may agree, however, that the seller shall actually arrange for this insurance as a service to the buyer for which he will charge the buyer. In a cif contract, on the other hand, it is the duty of the seller, as a normal part of the contract, to procure and pay for the insurance and the insurance policy is one of the documents which he must send to the buyer in order to fulfil his contractual obligations.

The form of insurance used when goods are to be carried by sea will be a policy of marine insurance. Such a policy usually covers not only the sea transit but any incidental surface transit from the seller's place of business to the port of loading and from the port of discharge to the buyer's place of business. Policies of insurance on goods to be carried by air are based largely on marine policies, though legally they are not such.

The policy of insurance on the goods will be assignable so that the seller may take out the policy in his own name and later assign it to the buyer, who will then be able to claim under the policy if the goods are lost or damaged after the property in the goods has passed to him. This assignment does not prevent the insurer from employing against the buyer any defence he would have had against the seller such as a right to avoid the contract because of misrepresentation.

The insurance document usually employed in an overseas sale transaction will be the policy, but certificates of insurance, issued by the insurer, a broker or the seller himself, may also be employed. As a general rule, under a cif contract the policy itself must be tendered to the buyer.

PAYMENT ARRANGEMENTS

As mentioned earlier, the arrangements made in the sale contract for payment will reflect the reluctance of the seller to part with goods without receiving payment, or security for payment, and the reluctance of the buyer to pay without receiving the goods or an adequate interest in them. Where the parties have knowledge of and confidence in each other payment may well be made simply and directly by banker's draft or by mail or telegraphic transfer, whereby the buyer instructs his bank to arrange for the seller to receive payment from a bank in the seller's country.

Usually, however, arrangements will be more elaborate and will be based on the contractual documents. These documents, as has been seen, can be transferred so as to pass to the transferee all the rights involved in the contracts. Thus possession of a bill of lading may give the holder not only the ownership of the goods to which it relates but also rights of action against the carrier. Possession of the insurance policy will give him the right to claim against the insurer for any loss of or damage to the goods which is covered by the policy. The documents, in fact, stand for the goods and can be sold or pledged as the goods and so can be used as security for payment. Thus various arrangements can be made for payment to be made against presentation of the documents. The party making the payment, whether the buyer or some agent of the buyer, such as a bank, will, in exchange for payment, receive the security of the rights represented by the documents. One of the most common and useful arrangements of this nature is the documentary credit, also sometimes called a banker's commercial credit. Under this arrangement the buyer instructs a bank in his own country (the issuing bank) to open a credit in favour of the seller with a bank in the seller's country (the correspondent bank). The seller may draw on this credit only on presentation of the documents specified by the buyer when the credit was opened. Thus the seller can be assured of payment by a bank in his own country and the buyer is assured that the seller will not be paid until he has handed to the bank the documents representing the goods. The correspondent bank has the security of the documents for payment by the issuing bank which will in turn have this security for payment by the buyer. Since the bank is interested in the documents as a security and not in the goods they represent, it will refuse to accept documents which do not meet the specifications laid down by the buyer even in very minor respects.

Payment arrangements

Chapter 2
The carriage of goods by sea

CARRIAGE IN A GENERAL SHIP

A general ship is one carrying various cargoes for different shippers. In most cases contracts for such carriage, under English law, will be governed by the Carriage of Goods by Sea Act 1971. This Act incorporates and gives the force of law to the Hague-Visby Rules, an international convention which attempts to strike a balance between the different interests of carriers and cargo owners arising out of the contract of carriage by sea. The Rules are an amended version of the earlier Hague Rules and intended to update and improve the latter, but there is still a large body of world opinion which considers that the Rules, being originally devised by the 'carrying nations' (those with substantial merchant shipping fleets) are too much weighted in favour of the carrier. For this and other reasons, another code, the Hamburg Rules, were drawn up under the auspices of UNCITRAL.[1] This code came into force on 1 November 1992 having collected the required total of 20 ratifications and accessions from different states. Therefore, overall the international situation with regards to the contract of carriage by sea remains a complex area. Many states remain loyal to the Hague Rules, while others have agreed to the Hague–Visby amendments. Some have adopted the Hamburg Rules, while another group is devising rules based upon a contribution of Hague–Visby and Hamburg Rules. The United Kingdom is not a signatory to the Hamburg Rules, and is unlikely to be in the near future.

Since the Hague–Visby Rules are part of English statute law they are subject to the ordinary rules of statutory interpretation. The courts bear in

1   See appendix 4.

mind, however, the needs for uniformity in the application of international agreements. 'As these Rules must come under the consideration of foreign courts it is desirable in the interests of uniformity that their interpretation should not be rigidly controlled by domestic precedents of antecedent date but rather that the language of the Rules should be construed on broad principles of general acceptation.'[2]

The Rules apply to bills of lading relating to the carriage of goods between ports in different states[3] in three different situations; first, when the bill of lading is issued in a contracting state (a state which is a party to the convention), second, if the carriage is from a port in a contracting state and third, when the contract in (or evidenced by) the bill of lading provides that the Rules are to apply or that the law of any state which gives effect to the Rules is to apply.[4] The application of the Rules is extended by the Carriage of Goods by Sea Act 1971, section 1(6)(b) to any non-negotiable document marked as such if the contract contained in or evidenced by it is a contract for the carriage of goods by sea which expressly provides that the Rules are to apply to it mutatis mutandis as if it were a bill of lading.

It should be clear from the above that most cases relating to bills of lading likely to arise in the United Kingdom will be governed by the Rules. There may, however, be cases that are not. If the goods were shipped from a port in a country which was not a party to the convention and a bill of lading were issued there which did not provide expressly that the Rules were to apply, or provide that the law of a country which has adopted the Rules were to apply, it is possible that an English court might apply the rules of the common law to the case. It is therefore necessary to consider those areas where the common law differs from the Rules. Moreover, the Rules are silent on some points.[5] Where this is so the common law must in any case apply.

The contract of carriage will usually be based on the carrier's bill of lading, normally issued after the goods have been loaded on to the vessel. The bill of lading is important in three respects: it represents or evidences the contract of carriage, it is a receipt for the goods and it is a document of title to the goods.

---

2   *Stag Line Ltd v Foscolo, Mango & Co Ltd* [1932] AC 328 at 350, HL, per Lord Macmillan.
3   The Carriage of Goods by Sea Act 1971, s 1(2) extends the ambit of the Rules to cover the United Kingdom coasting trade.
4   Carriage of Goods by Sea Act 1971, ch, art X.
5   Eg as to the effect of a deviation on the contract of carriage.

THE BILL OF LADING AND THE CONTRACT OF CARRIAGE

The carrier or his agent will issue the bill of lading after the goods have been placed on board. It will contain contractual terms but will not necessarily be the contract of carriage, which in normal circumstances will have been concluded between shipper and carrier before the bill of lading is issued.

The terms printed on the bill of lading may well have been incorporated into the contract of carriage by use of some such phrase as 'subject to the exceptions of our bills of lading'[6] or have been implied into the contract by the parties' previous dealings on the bill of lading terms. Nevertheless, the bill of lading, at least as between the carrier and the original shipper, amounts only to evidence of the contract of carriage. In *SS Ardennes (Cargo Owners) v SS Ardennes (Owners)*[7] oranges were shipped in a Spanish port on the understanding that the ship would sail directly to London. The ship called at Antwerp and the consequent delay in arrival at London caused loss to the cargo owner. The bill of lading contained a term which would have permitted the ship to call at Antwerp and the carrier relied on this term. It was held, however, that the bill of lading was only evidence of the contract of carriage and that the cargo owner was entitled to prove that the contract the parties had in fact made contained a term that the voyage would be direct. In *The Heidberg*,[8] Judge Diamond QC said the transferee of the bill of lading does not, however, take precisely the same contract as that made between the shipper and shipowner (of which the bill of lading is merely the evidence).

This is clearly the position as between the original shipper and the carrier, but the bill of lading will usually be transferred eventually by indorsement to a third party, such as an overseas buyer, who will, in most cases, take over the original shipper's rights and liabilities under the contract of carriage. Such a third party may well be unaware of any terms agreed between shipper and carrier which are not set out in the bill of lading and will not be bound by them. As between carrier and indorsee, the bill of lading will in fact represent the contract of carriage even though, as between carrier and original shipper it would have been mere evidence of the contract.

6   *Armour & Co Ltd v Leopold Walford (London) Ltd* [1921] 3 KB 473.
7   [1951] 1 KB 55, [1950] 2 All ER 517.
8   [1994] 2 Lloyd's Rep 287. See also *Cho Yang Shipping Co Ltd v Coral (UK) Ltd* [1997] 2 Lloyd's Rep 641, CA.

Thus in *The Emilien Marie*[9] three bills of lading were issued on the understanding that the third would only be met if sufficient cargo remained. It was held that the indorsee of this third bill was entitled to demand the full quantity.

If an exporter charters a vessel, his contract of carriage will be expressed in the charterparty. When cargo is loaded on to the chartered vessel, a bill of lading will be issued, but as between the shipper-charterer and the carrier the bill of lading will not replace the charterparty as the contract of carriage. It will not even be evidence of it, since the contract is expressly set out in the charterparty. But if this bill of lading is indorsed to a third party his contract with the carrier will be that contained in the bill of lading. He will only be affected by the charterparty if its terms are clearly incorporated into the bill of lading.

It will be seen from the above that the bill of lading has a somewhat strange relation to the contract of carriage. In the hands of the original shipper the bill of lading will merely be evidence of the contract of carriage and if the original shipper is the charterer it will not even be that. However, once the bill of lading has been indorsed to a third party it becomes, for all practical purposes, the contract between third party and carrier. The idea that a party can transfer contractual rights which he does not have is not a common one in English law but no practical difficulties or injustice usually arise since a carrier is, or should be, aware when he issues a bill of lading that he may become bound to a third party on its terms whatever arrangement he may have made with the original shipper.

THE BILL OF LADING AS A RECEIPT

The bill of lading will acknowledge the quantity of goods put on board, their description and their condition. The bill of lading form will usually be completed by the shipper or his forwarding agent and sent to the carrier. As the goods are loaded they will be checked by tally clerks and if the particulars are found to be correct the bill of lading will be signed for the carrier by his agent, the loading broker. Obviously mistakes can occur and it may be that a bill of lading is signed and issued for a quantity of cargo which has not been put on board or for cargo which is other than that

9   (1875) 44 LJ Adm 9. *Leduc & Co v Ward* (1888) 20 QBD 475, 57 LJQB 379, CA, is often cited on this point but the judgments are in fact based largely on the parol evidence rule and on the assumption, no longer valid, that the Bills of Lading Act 1855 had made the bill of lading the contract of carriage.

described in the bill of lading or which is not in the condition in which the bill of lading states it to be. It is necessary to consider the legal aspects of this situation.

Under the Hague–Visby Rules[10] the carrier is bound, on the shipper's demand, to issue a bill of lading which must show, among other things, the leading marks necessary for identification of the goods, the number of packages/pieces *or* the quantity *or* the weight of the goods and their apparent order and condition. This information will be furnished in writing by the shipper, usually on the bill of lading form. The carrier is not bound to show any of this information in the bill of lading if he has reasonable ground to suspect its accuracy[11] or if he has no reasonable means of checking it[12]. The shipper is deemed to have guaranteed to the carrier the accuracy of his information and must indemnify the carrier against any loss or expense suffered by the latter as a result of inaccuracy.

In the hands of the shipper, the statements in the bill of lading are prima facie evidence of the receipt of the goods as described. Thus it is open to the carrier to rebut this evidence by proving that the goods stated were not in fact put on board or that the goods put on board were not as described.[13] As against the shipper this is reasonable since he must be taken to know what was put on board and, as has been said, will in practice have himself furnished the particulars. The indorsee of the bill of lading, on the other hand, has no knowledge of the goods other than that obtainable from the bill of lading. For this reason once the bill of lading has been transferred to a third party acting in good faith no evidence may be brought to contradict the bill of lading statements: they are then conclusive.

It is necessary to look further at the various statements about the goods which are set out in the bill of lading and to consider these points on which the common law differs from the Hague–Visby Rules.

Statement of quantity

Under the Hague–Visby Rules the carrier is obliged only to commit himself to one expression of quantity. If, for example, he states the number of

10   Carriage of Goods by Sea Act 1971, Sch, art III.
11   *The Mata K* [1998] 2 Lloyd's Rep 614.
12   *The Esmeralda I* [1988] 1 Lloyd's Rep 206.
13   *Grant v Norway* (1851) 10 CB 665. See also *Alimport v Soubert Shipping Co Ltd* [2000] 2 Lloyd's Rep 447.

packages he need not also state weight or measurement or may disclaim knowledge of them.[14]

At common law the carrier need not state any quantity. In practice, of course, he will, since the bill of lading would otherwise serve little purpose, but it is common to add words indicating that weight, quantity etc are 'not known and noted only for the purpose of calculating freight' or 'as declared by shipper but unknown to carrier'. If the carrier inserts a clause in the bill of lading to the effect that weight/quantity is unknown, the carrier is not, in fact, making any representation, and, therefore, article III r 4 as to prima facie evidence does not apply: *The Atlas*.[15] If a bill of lading to which the common law applies does state a quantity without qualifications this statement will, in the hands of the shipper, be merely prima facie evidence of the shipping of the goods described. In the hands of an indorsee, however, the statement will be conclusive evidence, as against the carrier, of the loading of the goods as long as the bill of lading is signed by the master or by any person having the express, implied or apparent authority of the carrier to sign bills of lading. In the case of a received for shipment bill of lading the statement will be conclusive evidence of the receipt of the goods by the carrier.[16]

Statement of condition

Bills of lading usually contain the printed words, 'Shipped in good order and condition ...'. At common law, in the hands of the shipper, this statement is not even prima facie evidence of the condition of the goods when shipped. It amounts merely to evidence of the condition and if goods arrive damaged the onus remains with the shipper to show that the goods were shipped in good condition. The indorsee is in a somewhat better position. If the statement is clear and unqualified by any clause as to bad condition noted on the bill of lading, the carrier will be estopped, as against the indorsee, from denying the truth of the bill of lading statement, provided that the indorsee has acted to his detriment by relying on the statement. In *Compania Naviera Vasconzada v Churchill and Sim*[17] timber was stained with oil when shipped but a 'clean' bill of lading was nonetheless issued to the shipper who indorsed it to a third party. The indorsee sued the

---

14   *Oricon Waren-Handels GmbH v Intergraan NV* [1967] 2 Lloyd's Rep 82.
15   [1996] 1 Lloyds Rep 642.
16   Carriage of Goods by Sea Act 1992, s 4.
17   [1906] 1 KB 237.

carrier in respect of the damage. The carrier was estopped, by the statement in the bill of lading, from denying that the timber was in good condition when loaded and was thus liable to the indorsee for the damage.

On the other hand in *Canadian and Dominion Sugar Co Ltd v Canadian National (West Indies) Steamships*[18] the bill of lading contained the phrase 'signed under guarantee to produce ship's clean receipt', thus clearly incorporating the receipt terms into the bill of lading. The receipt stated, 'Many bags stained, torn and re-sewn'. The bill of lading statement thus qualified did not estop the carrier from proving the condition of the timber when shipped.

A 'claused' bill of lading, that is, one bearing a note by the carrier as to some defect in the condition of the goods, will not normally be acceptable to a third party such as a buyer of goods under a cif contract or a bank which has agreed to pay the seller under a documentary credit on receipt of the documents. For this reason a practice has developed whereby the carrier issues a clean bill of lading for goods shipped in a condition which would normally have resulted in the bill of lading being claused. The shipper, in return, agrees to indemnify the carrier in respect of any loss the latter may suffer as a result of this issue. If the carrier is held liable to an indorsee for the damage not noted, the question arises as to whether or not the carrier can sue the shipper on the indemnity. In *Brown, Jenkinson & Co v Percy Dalton (London) Ltd*[19] it was held that such a contract of indemnity would normally be void on public policy grounds as being in fraud of a third party since both carrier and shipper will be aware that any third party will accept the bill of lading at its face value. Accordingly the carrier will be unable to enforce the indemnity unless, possibly, the arrangement was made honestly as a result of a dispute between shipper and carrier about the condition of the goods,[20] or, presumably, if the carrier had good reason to believe that no third party would be involved.

The condition of the goods noted in the bill of lading is normally the condition on shipment. In *M Golodetz & Co Inc v Czarnikow-Rionda Co Inc, The Galatia*[21] sugar was loaded on to a vessel and then damaged as the result of a fire. A bill of lading was then issued stating in the usual form

18   [1947] AC 46, PC.
19   [1957] 2 QB 621, [1957] 2 All ER 844, CA. See also *Standard Chartered Bank v Pakistan National Shipping Corpn* [1995] 2 Lloyd's Rep 365.
20   Ibid at 633 and 853 respectively, per Morris J.
21   [1980] 1 All ER 501, [1980] 1 Lloyd's Rep 453, CA.

that the goods were shipped in good condition but noting that they had been damaged and discharged. The buyers and two banks refused to accept the bill of lading. The Court of Appeal, upholding Donaldson J, held that the bill of lading was clean (since the goods had originally been shipped in good condition) and that the buyers and the banks should therefore have accepted it. This decision has been criticised for ignoring commercial reality.[22]

Statement of leading marks

Leading marks are the distinguishing marks, code marks, symbols etc placed on the goods or their containers by the shipper. Where the Hague–Visby Rules apply, the carrier can refuse to enter them on the bill of lading unless they are such as should ordinarily remain legible until the end of the voyage.

At common law the carrier is entitled to show that goods shipped were marked otherwise than as noted in the bill of lading as long as the marks in question are not material to the description of the goods. In *Parsons v New Zealand Shipping Co*[23] some carcases of frozen lamb were found on arrival to bear marks different from those in the bill of lading. The marks in question only reflected details in the shipper's storage system and were not related to the quality or description of the carcases. The carrier was thus entitled to prove that the carcases delivered were the ones actually loaded. It appears, however, that the carrier is not bound by any statement as to marks that indicate quality, on the grounds that he is not a judge of quality. In *Cox v Bruce*[24] the bill of lading noted marks which indicated a better quality of jute than that which had been shipped, but the carrier was not estopped by the statement. (The justification for this rule is not easy to see, since the carrier, however justifiably abysmal his ignorance of the finer points of the cargoes he carries, is in as good a position as anyone to see what marks it bears and to know the effect such marks might have on the mind of an indorsee.) The effect of these cases seems to be that at common law the carrier will only be estopped by a statement of leading marks if they are relevant to the description of the goods but do not indicate their quality.

---

22   See eg, Schmitthoff in [1979] JBL 164.
23   [1901] 1 KB 548, CA.
24   (1886) 18 QBD 147, CA.

THE BILL OF LADING AS A DOCUMENT OF TITLE

A document of title is one which the law recognises as representing the goods so that the transfer of the document to a party will vest in that party the ownership or possession of the goods to which the document relates, provided that this transfer of rights was intended by the parties. Some documents of title are so by virtue of the common law's recognition of mercantile usage while others have been made so by statute. The ability to transfer property rights in goods by the transfer of a document is the keystone of international trade practice.

The bill of lading has long been recognised by the courts, following mercantile usage, as having this quality.[1] In *E Clemens Horst Co v Biddell Bros*[2] the buyer under a cif contract was offered a bill of lading but refused to pay until the goods themselves were delivered. It was held that since possession of the bill of lading amounted in law to the possession of the goods the seller was entitled to perform his part of the contract by handing over the document.

While a bill of lading may to this extent be said to be negotiable as long as the goods are in transit it is not a negotiable instrument of the same class as a bill of exchange. The indorsee of a bill of lading, even when he takes it in good faith and for value, will take subject to equities, that is, he will acquire only such rights as were in the transferor, unless the Sale of Goods Act 1979, sections 21–25 apply. These lay down certain situations where a transferee of a document of title may acquire full property rights even though the transferor did not have these rights.[3]

Moreover a bill of lading may not be negotiable in any sense. This is clearly so if it is marked 'Not Negotiable' but there are other cases. By mercantile usage, recognised by the courts, a bill of lading is only normally regarded as negotiable if it states that delivery of the goods is to be made to 'Order or Assigns' of the shipper or consignee.[4] If the document only makes provision for delivery to a named consignee, it is known as a 'straight' bill of lading or way-bill, and lacks the negotiable quality required to qualify it as a document of title.[5] If it is negotiable it may be transferred either by indorsement and delivery or, if it has been indorsed in blank (by the holder

1   *Lickbarrow v Mason* (1787) 2 Term Rep 63.
2   [1912] AC 18, HL.
3   See eg, *Cahn and Mayer v Pockett's Bristol Channel Steam Packet Co Ltd* [1899] 1 QB 643, CA.
4   *Henderson & Co v Comptoir d'Escompte de Paris* (1873) LR 5 PC 253.
5   See *The Chitral* [2000] 1 Lloyd's Rep 529.

signing it without indicating any transferee) it may be transferred by simple delivery.

Even if the bill of lading is negotiable and the transferor has a good title to it, it does not necessarily follow that the delivery, or the indorsement and delivery, of the bill of lading will pass the property in the goods to the transferee. This will only happen when the bill of lading is transferred *with the intention* of passing the property. A seller may, for example, expressly or by implication, 'reserve the right of disposal' of the goods when transferring the bill of lading, which means that the property remains in him, usually until some condition, such as payment, is met by the buyer. (The Sale of Goods Act 1979, section 19 sets out situations where the seller is thus presumed to reserve the right of disposal.) Here there is clearly no intention to transfer the property in the goods by delivery of the bill of lading. A seller may also indorse a bill of lading to his agent in the port of discharge of the goods to enable the agent to deal with the buyer. Again, there is no intention to pass the property in the goods to the agent by this indorsement.

Where the bill of lading relates to goods carried in bulk then, while the cargo on the ship remains in bulk, transfer of a bill of lading in transferable form will not transfer a proprietary interest in the goods.[6] However, the Sale of Goods Act 1979, section 20A introduced by the Sale of Goods (Amendment) Act 1995, enables in respect of all sale contracts made after 18 September 1995 property in an individual share in the bulk to be transferred to the buyer if he has paid the price or part of the price (ie he becomes an owner in the common bulk).

It will be recalled that transfer of the bill of lading may, in addition to passing the property in the goods to the transferee, also pass to him all the rights and liabilities of the contract of carriage as evidenced by the bill of lading. Such a transfer of contractual rights and liabilities was not possible at common law and was originally made possible by the Bills of Lading Act 1855, section 1. This Act, however, made the transfer of rights and liabilities to a holder dependent on his acquiring the property in the goods 'upon or by reason of' the indorsement of the bill to him. Unfortunately there are many situations in which the bill of lading holder acquires the property in the goods before or after the bill of lading is transferred to him[7] or never

---

6   See *Re London Wine Co (Shippers) Ltd* [1986] PCC 121; *Re Goldcorp Exchange Ltd (in receivership)* [1994] 2 All ER 806, PC.

7   As in *The Delfini* [1990] 1 Lloyd's Rep 252, CA.

acquires the property at all.[8] In such cases, because the transfer of the bill of lading was not causally connected with the transfer of property, the bill of lading holder, even when he had suffered loss or damage, had no rights against the carrier.

AN ELECTRONIC BILL OF LADING

Bills of lading have always been issued as paper documents. However, the replacement of a paper bill of lading with an electronic bill of lading seems a sensible step forward in the new electronic commerce world. However, such a system of replacement is not free of problems. A serious problem for an electronic bill of lading is the negotiability of such documents of title. A document of title relies upon the transferability of the document by physical possession. An electronic bill of lading cannot be handled in physical possession with the result that it cannot be produced on delivery, nor endorsed to a new holder. Therefore, this inhibits the capability of it representing a document of title.

Various ways around this problem have been sought. In 1985, a 'bill of lading registry' was suggested by the Chase Manhattan Bank and INTERTANKO, which has established Sea Dock Registry Ltd. Unfortunately this survived just six months. The idea of a registry was further developed by the CMI Uniform Rules for Electronic Bills of Lading adopted in 1990. Also, established in 1996, the UNCITRAL Model Law on Electronic Commerce aims to solve many of the problems affecting the legal effect of electronic documents.

The 'registry' system is designed to be a depository for documents, while the rights to the goods are transferred by the communicating of authenticated messages between the registry and the parties who have an interest in the goods. The registry facilitates the transfer of title from one party to another, cancelling the first party's title at the moment the title is transferred to the new holder. The newest project in this area is called 'BOLERO', whose name stands for Bill of Lading Electronic Registry Organisation. BOLERO is an internet-based system and, therefore, relatively inexpensive. BOLERO builds on the CMI Rules but has established a central registry as the secure third party. BOLERO has a so-called 'Rulebook', agreed to by all parties becoming members. BOLERO has set up an electronic registry for bills of lading called 'the title registry' The registry is a database application. It creates and transfers the rights

8   As in *The Aramis* [1989] 1 Lloyd's Rep 213, CA.

An electronic bill of lading

and obligations relating to an electronic bill of lading. The title registry deals with any change of interest in the goods.

Where the BOLERO system is used, the carrier creates a BOLERO bill of lading, sends the instructions to the title registry and the shipper is logged as holder of the BOLERO bill. If the holder of the bill wishes to transfer his constructive possession to the bill to another, he can make the transfer by attornment. Attornment occurs when the holder sends instructions to the registry that name the new holder. Once these instructions are received the registry sends a message confirming the new holder. It is important to note that when there is a record of holdership, only the record holder can give message instructions to effect the transfer of rights in the goods. The cargo is delivered to the last holder of the bill by the registry giving up the BOLERO bill to the carrier.

BOLERO incorporates security for all transactions. Digital signatures of relevant parties are used and all messages are secure from unauthorised access. In the UK the Electronic Communications Act 2000 regulates the provision of electronic signatures, encryption technology and reliance on third parties such as BOLERO. However, service providers must have a connection with the jurisdiction, ie the service must be provided from premises in the UK or to persons carrying on a business in the UK. This Act, therefore, does support electronic commerce.

The EU Electronic Commerce Directive (Directive 2000/31/EC) deals with certain legal aspects of information society services. The liability of BOLERO or other similar information society service providers is generally set out in rule 4 of the Directive. However, as far as the recognition of electronic documents is concerned, the Directive is not particularly instructive. The Article provides for the conclusion of contracts electronically, although there is no provision for sanctioning the recognition of a contract made and evidenced by an electronic instrument.

The UNCITRAL Model Law on Electronic Commerce (as amended 1998) was created because of the inadequate legislation which existed in relation to international trade and electronic commerce. It covers the main legal issues eg requirements for writing, signature, admissibility and probative value and actions related to contracts of carriage of goods. Its provisions have generally found their way into national laws and the UK Electronic Communications Act 2000 is consistent with the provisions of the UNCITRAL Model Law.[9]

9   Pejovic JBL (September 2001) 484. See Chapter 7 for the new electronic supplement to the UCP 500.

The International Chamber of Commerce has recently launched an e-business tool that provides secure online contracting based on ICC's model international sale contract. It enables the speed and convenience of dealing over the web, rather than transmitting paper documents; tracking of every phase of the negotiation, with revisions preserved under time and date stamps; ability to sign contracts online, using digital ID; secure storage of contracts. Thus, the e-commerce era is moving ahead.

THE CARRIAGE OF GOODS BY SEA ACT 1992

This Act effectively separates the transfer of the bill of lading[10] and the rights and liabilities under the carriage contract from the passing of property in the goods. The lawful holder of a bill of lading (including a received for shipment bill of lading) acquires all the rights under the carriage contract against the carrier.[11] His acquisition of these rights, however, is dependent on his having received the bill of lading under contractual or other arrangements made before the right to possession of the goods ceased to attach to the bill of lading.[12] This provision is designed to protect any genuine party to the sale transaction while excluding the possibility of the transfer of a bill of lading as a mere right of action against the carrier to a person not genuinely concerned in the sale transaction. The Act also protects the rights of a seller who has received the bill of lading when it is returned to him by a buyer who has rejected the goods.[13]

Once a holder has transferred the bill of lading his rights against the carrier cease entirely,[14] but the original shipper, although he loses his rights under the bill of lading, remains liable to the carrier under the carriage contract even after he has transferred the bill of lading.[15]

The bill of lading holder will not be subject to liabilities under the carriage contract unless and until he takes or demands delivery of the goods from the carrier or makes any claim from the carrier in respect of the goods.[16]

10   For the effect of the Act on documents other than bills of lading see under sea way-bill and delivery order.
11   Section 2(1).
12   Section 2(2).
13   Section 2(2)(b).
14   Section 2(5).
15   Section 3(3).
16   Section 3(1).

Thus a person (such as a bank) holding the bill of lading as security will not be liable under the carriage contract unless and until he seeks to realise his security.[17]

The holder of the bill of lading has all rights of suit against the carrier and it is immaterial that he himself may have suffered no loss. He may, therefore, sue in his own name for the benefit of any person who has suffered actual loss.[18] It should also be noted that nothing in the Act prevents the owner of goods who is not party to the contract of carriage from suing the carrier in tort.

OTHER DOCUMENTS

Mate's receipt

Documents other than bills of lading are used in respect of goods carried by sea. One of these is the 'mate's receipt', which may be given when goods are in the custody of the ship but no bill of lading has yet been issued. The document is not normally a document of title although it may be so in some cases by virtue of a local custom.[19] The carrier is not estopped by any statement in the mate's receipt as to quantity or condition. Such a statement is merely prima facie evidence. The holder of the mate's receipt is, however, prima facie entitled to have the bill of lading issued to him.[20] Since the bill of lading will be issued on the basis of the mate's receipt it follows that any defect in the condition of the goods should be noted in the latter document. In *The Nogar Marin*[21] the master issued a clean mate's receipt although the cargo of wire rods was rusty when loaded. The ship's agents consequently issued a clean bill of lading. The master had been negligent and was liable on the bill of lading.

---

17 This provision supplants the rule established in *Sewell v Burdick* (1884) 10 App Cas 74, HL, and renders unnecessary the construction of an implied contract as in *Brandt v Liverpool, Brazil and River Plate Steam Navigation Co* [1924] 1 KB 575, CA.

18 Section 2(4).

19 *Wah Tat Bank v Kum* [1967] 2 Lloyd's Rep 437.

20 *Nippon Yusen Kaisha v Ramjiban Serowgee* [1938] AC 429, [1938] 2 All ER 285, PC.

21 [1988] 1 Lloyd's Rep 412, CA.

Sea way-bill

A sea way-bill is a receipt for goods carried by sea but differs from a bill of lading in that it is not a document of title. It contains or evidences an undertaking by the carrier to the shipper to deliver the goods to an identical person. The shipper may, at any time before the delivery of the goods, change the identity of the person to whom delivery is to be made. The consignee obtains delivery not by presenting the way-bill, which remains in the hands of the shipper, but by production of acceptable evidence of his identity as consignee.

Since the sea way-bill is not a document of title it cannot be used as security. Its chief advantage lies in the fact that it does not have to be transmitted to the consignee to enable him to obtain the goods.

Under the Carriage of Goods by Sea Act 1992 the consignee named in the way-bill will have all rights of suit against the carrier under the contract of carriage contained in or evidenced by the way-bill.[22] It will be recalled that the shipper of goods under a bill of lading who transfers it will by so doing lose all his rights against the carrier.[23] The shipper under a sea way-bill, however, will retain his rights under the carriage contract[1] since the nature of the transaction demands that he shall be able to change the name of the consignee before delivery.

Where payment is to be by way of documentary credit, the sea way-bill is not as acceptable to banks as a bill of lading, because the latter is negotiable and a document of title. However, article 24 of the UCP 500 provides for acceptance of sea way-bills.

As in the case of the bill of lading, the consignee under a sea way-bill will only assume the liabilities under the carriage contract if he takes or claims the goods or makes a claim against the carrier. If the transport document is a sea way-bill the Hague–Visby Rules do not apply but may be expressly incorporated.

Delivery orders

An exporter who ships a bulk cargo and receives one bill of lading in respect of it, or an indorsee of this bill of lading, may afterwards, while the

---

22   Section 2(1).
23   Page 21 above.
1   Section 2(5).

goods are in transit, sell various unascertained portions of this cargo to different buyers. He clearly cannot transfer the bill of lading to all the buyers and must find some other way to satisfy each buyer's demand for some document evidencing his right to the goods he has bought which will enable him to collect or resell them. In such cases a delivery order may be used. 'Delivery order' is not a precise term and the legal status and effect of such a document will depend on its nature and the circumstances in which it is issued.

A delivery order is usually a document addressed by the owner of goods to a party such as a carrier or warehouseman who has custody of he goods, ordering him to deliver them to or hold them for a holder of the order. (Under the Sale of Goods Act 1979, section 29(3) a seller is not deemed to have delivered goods in such circumstances until the party having custody of them as 'attorned' to the buyer, that is, acknowledged that he holds the goods on the buyer's behalf.) The term 'delivery order', however, may also be used to describe a document issued by the custodian of the goods promising to hand them over on production of the document.

A delivery order is not a document of title unless proved to be so by reason of mercantile custom as was the case in *Merchant Banking Co of London v Phoenix Bessemer Steel Co*[2] in respect of certain orders regularly used in the iron trade.

The importance of the nature of a delivery order in a particular case is well illustrated by the case of *Colin and Shields v Weddel & Co.*[3] A contract for the sale of hides c and f Liverpool provided that the seller should tender, among other things, a bill of lading and/or a ship's delivery order and that if a bill of lading were not supplied the buyers should be put in the same position as if it had been. The hides were shipped in error to Manchester, and there unloaded and sent by barge to Liverpool. The sellers tendered a document signed by the carrier and addressed to the master porter at a Liverpool dock ordering him to deliver the hides to the buyers. At this time the hides had not reached Liverpool. The sellers contended that this document satisfied the requirements of the contract. The Court of Appeal, upholding Sellers J, disagreed. Since the goods were not in the custody of the maser porter he could not attorn to the buyers and if the goods had never arrived at Liverpool the document would have been worthless. In addition, the order, since it was addressed by the carrier

2   (1877) 5 Ch D 205.
3   [1952] 2 All ER 337, [1952] 2 Lloyd's Rep 9, CA.

to the master porter, gave the buyers no rights against the carrier and therefore did not put the buyers in the position they would have been in had a bill of lading been tendered.

Under the Carriage of Goods by Sea Act 1992 the person to whom delivery is to be made under the order will have all rights of suit against the carrier under the contract of carriage.[4] He will also be subject to liabilities under the contract once he had demanded or received delivery or made a claim against the carrier.[5] When, as will often be the case, the goods to which the delivery note refers form part of a larger bulk, the rights and liabilities will apply only in respect of that part.[6] As in the case of the sea way-bill the rights of the original shipper are not affected.

THE CARRIER'S RESPONSIBILITIES UNDER A BILL OF LADING

The detailed discussion of the responsibilities of a carrier under the contract of carriage in respect of the ship and the cargo is properly the province of works on the carriage of goods by sea, but since the buyer of goods under an international sale contract will in many cases have transferred to him rights against the carrier in these matters and may have to rely, in the event of loss of or damage to the goods, on these rights it is necessary to examine them briefly.

The common law implies three undertakings by the carrier into a contract of carriage by sea. These terms may be excluded by express terms in the contract. The common law rules differ in these matters from the Hague–Visby Rules. The three terms relate to the seaworthiness of the vessel, to deviation from route and to delay.

Seaworthiness

When goods are to be carried by sea the fitness of the vessel which is to do so is obviously a matter of concern to any person having an interest in the goods. At common law it is an implied term of a contract of carriage that the ship shall be seaworthy. A ship is not seaworthy if it has a defect which a prudent owner would have required to be rectified before sending

4   Section 2(1)(c).
5   Section 3(1).
6   Section 3(2).

the ship to sea.[7] This requirement is absolute; the ship must be seaworthy and it is not enough that every effort has been made to make it so.[8]

The ship must be seaworthy in two respects. It must be fit to sail on the particular voyage or a particular stage of the voyage and it must be fit to receive the particular cargo. As regards the ship itself, unseaworthiness can take many forms. It may be a physical defect, such as inefficient engines but it may also take the form of incompetence on the part of the crew. In this respect the ship must be seaworthy when it sails and there is no breach of the term if it is so but becomes unseaworthy while on the voyage. An example of unseaworthiness in the second respect is *The Maori King (Cargo Owners) v Hughes*[9] where a ship was held to be unseaworthy in respect of a cargo of frozen meat because refrigeration equipment was defective. In this respect the ship must be seaworthy when the cargo is loaded and there is no breach of the implied term if it becomes unfit for the cargo after the cargo has been loaded.

The implied term as to seaworthiness may be expressly excluded but the courts, as is usual in cases of exclusion clauses, will apply the *contra proferentum* rule and the exclusion will be effective only if it is clearly and unambiguously expressed. Thus in *Nelson Line (Liverpool) Ltd v James Nelson & Sons Ltd*[10] the implied term was held not to be excluded by a clause stating that the carrier was not to be liable for any damage 'capable of being covered by insurance'.

The legal effect of a breach of the term will depend on the effect of the breach on the contract. If the breach results in unseaworthiness which is such as to frustrate the commercial purpose of the contract of carriage the cargo owner will be entitled to repudiate the contract. If it is not so serious he must rely on an action for damages.[11] Under a contract for carriage in a general ship the cargo owner will normally be in the latter position unless he is the original shipper.

If there has been a breach of the implied term, the carrier will not be precluded from relying on a clause absolving him from liability for some cause of loss or damage unless the loss or damage was actually caused by the

7   *McFadden & Co v Blue Star Line* [1905] 1 KB 697 at 706.
8   *Steel v State Line Steamship Co* (1877) 3 App Cas 72, HL.
9   [1895] 2 QB 550, CA. See also *The Star Sea* [1997] 1 Lloyd's Rep 360, CA (incompetence of master).
10   [1908] AC 16, HL.
11   *Stanton v Richardson* (1874) LR 9 CP 390. Cf *Hong Kong Fir Shipping Co v Kawasaki Kisen Kaisha* [1962] 2 QB 26, [1962] 1 All ER 474, CA.

unseaworthiness. In *The Europa*[12] a ship collided with a dock and a waterpipe in the ship was broken. Water escaped into the upper section of the cargo space and damaged cargo there. This water would normally have drained into the bilges but, because of defective piping, in fact drained into the lower cargo space and damaged cargo there also. A clause in the contract absolved the carrier from liability for loss or damage caused by collision. The ship was certainly unseaworthy by reason of the defective piping but this had no effect on the upper cargo, which would have been damaged by the collision in any event. The lower cargo, however, was damaged as the result of the collision only because of the unseaworthiness. The carrier was therefore not liable for the first damage but was liable for the second.

It is convenient at this stage to consider the requirements of the Hague–Visby Rules as to seaworthiness. Article III(1) makes the carrier liable, before and at the beginning of the voyage, to exercise due diligence to make the ship seaworthy, properly man, equip and supply the ship and make the cargo spaces fit and safe for the reception, carriage and preservation of the goods. This description of seaworthiness is in effect identical with that applied by the common law. It is important to note, however, that the burden on the carrier is only to *exercise due diligence* to make the ship seaworthy; the requirement is not absolute, as at common law.

The duty to exercise due diligence is not a light one. In *Riverstone Meat Co Pty Ltd v Lancashire Shipping Co Ltd*[13] damage was caused to cargo when water entered the cargo space because of negligent work by a fitter employed by a ship repairer. It was held that the carrier himself could not in these circumstances be considered to have used due diligence.

If due diligence has not been used to make the ship seaworthy the carrier will be liable for any loss or damage resulting from the unseaworthiness even though the primary cause of the loss or damage was one for which the carrier would not otherwise be liable under the Rules. In *Maxine Footwear Co v Canadian Government Merchant Marine*[14] employees of the carrier negligently used an acetylene torch to thaw frozen pipes. The ship caught fire and had to be scuttled. Under article IV(2)(b) of the Rules

12 [1908] P 84.
13 [1961] AC 807, [1961] 1 All ER 495, HL. See also *The Kapitan Sakharov* [2000] 2 Lloyd's Rep 255 (shipment of undeclared dangerous cargo in sealed container): *Dow Europe v Novoklav Inc* [1998] I Lloyd's Rep 306.
14 [1959] AC 589, [1959] 2 All ER 740, PC.

the carrier is not normally liable for loss or damage caused by fire unless he himself has been at fault. The events, however, demonstrated a failure to use due diligence to make the ship seaworthy and the cargo owner whose goods had been damaged was accordingly entitled to recover from the carrier.

Deviation

There is an implied undertaking at common law in any contract for the carriage of goods by sea that the vessel will not unreasonably deviate from the agreed route or, if there is no agreed route, from the usual route or, if there is no usual route, from the direct route. Since the undertaking is implied it can be excluded by an express term in the contract. As with the implied term as to unseaworthiness, any exclusion must be clearly and unambiguously expressed if it is to relieve the carrier from liability and the courts have regard to the purpose of the parties in making the contract of carriage. Thus they have held that a term permitting calls at ports other than the destination port must be taken to refer only to such ports as lie in the ordinary route.[15]

There is no breach of the term if a ship deviates on reasonable grounds as, for example, to avoid dangerous weather or to save life at sea, although deviation to save property at sea is not a permitted deviation at common law[16] as it is under the Hague–Visby Rules. An involuntary departure from the route is not a deviation.[17]

The importance of the term for the cargo owner lies in the legal effect of a breach of the term by the carrier. Any voluntary and unjustified deviation is a fundamental breach of the contract of carriage. In consequence, the cargo owner is entitled to repudiate the contract and, if he does so, the carrier will lose the benefit of any immunity in the contract protecting him from liability for loss or damage except those available to a common carrier and even the common carrier's defences will only be open to him if he can prove that the loss or damage would have occurred even if there had been no deviation.[18] An outstanding example of the strictness of the rule is the

15   *Leduc & Co v Ward* (1888) 20 QBD 475, 57 LJQB 379, CA.
16   *Scaramanga v Stamp* (1880) 5 CPD 295, CA.
17   *Rio Tinto Co v Seed Shipping Co* (1926) 42 TLR 381.
18   As in *Internationale Guano en Superphosphaat-Werken v Robert Macandrew & Co* [1909] 2 KB 360.

case of *Joseph Thorley Ltd v Orchis Steamship Co.*[19] A vessel carrying goods from Cyprus to London deviated, at the beginning of the voyage, to ports in the Eastern Mediterranean. When the vessel arrived at London the cargo was damaged by the negligence of the stevedores unloading it. When the cargo owner sued in respect of this damage the carrier pleaded a clause in the contract absolving him from liability for any such damage. It was held that because the vessel had deviated the cargo owner was entitled to repudiate the contract of carriage and the carrier was not then entitled to the benefit of the immunity unless he could show that the damage by stevedores in London would have occurred even if the vessel had not deviated in the Eastern Mediterranean, a demonstration which clearly presented some difficulties.

A cargo owner is not, of course, bound to repudiate a contract in these circumstances. He may waive the breach of the undertaking either expressly or by implication. Any such waiver will not, however, affect the rights of a subsequent indorsee of a bill of lading who takes it without knowledge of the deviation. In *Hain Steamship Co v Tate and Lyle Ltd*[1] there was a contract for a vessel to load sugar at two ports in Cuba and one in San Domingo. Because of a local failure in communications the master of the vessel did not receive instructions to call at San Domingo. He therefore sailed from Cuba intending to return directly to England. When the mistake was discovered he returned to the San Domingo port. On leaving this port the ship stranded and various expenses were incurred in respect of the sugar. The original holders of the bill of lading were aware of the deviation but took no action and indorsed the bill of lading to the respondents, who were unaware of the deviation and who contested their liability to pay the expenses. It was held that there had been a deviation and that though the original holders of the bill of lading might be taken to have waived their rights in respect of it their action could not affect the position of the subsequent indorsees.

Under the Hague–Visby Rules[2] any deviation in saving or attempting to save life or property at sea or any reasonable deviation is not deemed to be an infringement or breach of the Rules or of the contract of carriage and the carrier is not liable for any resulting loss or damage. Immunity under the first head is also available to the carrier by virtue of article IV(2)(1). The Rules do not define 'any reasonable deviation'. In *Stag Line Ltd v Foscolo*

19   [1907] 1 KB 660, CA.
1   [1936] 2 All ER 597, 55 Ll L Rep 159, HL.
2   Art IV(4).

Mango & Co Ltd[3] Lord Atkin said, 'The true test seems to be what departure from the contract voyage might a prudent person ... make ... having in mind all the relevant circumstances existing at the time including the terms of the contract and the interest of all parties concerned, but without obligation to consider the interests of any one as conclusive.'

The Hague–Visby Rules are silent as to the legal effect of an unreasonable deviation on the contract of carriage and the position will therefore be as at common law.

A deviation, in addition to being a breach of the contract of carriage by sea, may also amount to a breach of a contract of sale by a seller who has agreed, expressly or by implication, that the goods will be carried on a particular route. The legal effect of such a breach would, of course, be a matter to be decided under the law on the sale of goods.

It should be noted that US courts employ the word 'deviation' in a very wide sense to mean any serious breach of the contract of carriage which would entitle the cargo owner to repudiate the contract, such as unauthorised deck stowage.

Delay

At common law there is an implied undertaking by the carrier that the voyage will be carried on without undue delay. In many cases delay will amount to deviation.[4] The Hague–Visby Rules are silent on this matter.

Care of the cargo

At common law the position of a shipowner appears to be that he is either a common carrier or in the same position as a common carrier. He is basically liable for loss of or damage to the goods in his custody, irrespective of fault, unless the loss or damage was caused by act of God, act of the Queen's enemies or inherent vice of the goods. This basic position has been modified by statute and by inserting express contractual terms to relieve the carrier from liability for loss or damage arising from specified causes. This practice of wide exclusion of liability eventually led to the Hague Convention and the Hague Rules, which gave the carrier immunity

3   [1932] AC 328 at 343, HL.
4   *The Patria* (1871) LR 3 A & E 436.

from certain specified liabilities but prevented him from excluding others. Unfortunately, the Hague Rules, and their successors, the Hague–Visby Rules, lay down no single basis of liability: the immunities are founded on the exclusions commonly used in carriage contracts and are rather diverse. (It was for this, among other reasons, that the Hamburg Rules were devised.)

Under article III(2) of the Hague–Visby Rules the carrier must 'properly and carefully load, handle, stow, carry, keep, care for and discharge' the goods. Whether he has done so in a particular case will be a question of fact. The word 'properly' in this context received judicial consideration in *Albacora SRL v Westcott and Laurance Line*[5] where a cargo of salted fish, unknown to the carrier, required refrigeration. The carrier was instructed only to keep it away from engines and boilers. This he did but the fish deteriorated. The House of Lords held that the carrier had carried the goods 'properly'. 'Properly' meant 'in accordance with a sound system', sound in the light of such knowledge as a reasonable carrier would have had about the goods.

The phrase 'the carrier shall ... load' does not impose on the carrier a duty to load in all circumstances. Who is to load will be a matter for each individual contract and may depend on local rules or port customs. It was said in *Pyrene Co v Scindia Navigation Co*[6] that 'the whole contract of carriage is subject to the Rules, but the extent to which loading and discharging are brought within the carrier's obligations is left to the parties themselves to decide'.

The carrier's immunities

Under the Hague–Visby Rules the carrier will not be liable for loss of or damage to the cargo caused by the events below.[7] It should be recalled that these immunities will not avail the carrier if he has not exercised due diligence to make the ship seaworthy and the loss or damage was caused by the unseaworthiness.

(a) Act, neglect or default of the master, mariners, pilot or the servants of the carrier in the navigation or in the management of the ship. While few problems have arisen concerning 'navigation', difficulties have arisen on

5   [1966] 2 Lloyd's Rep 53.
6   [1954] 2 QB 402, [1954] 2 All ER 158.
7   Art IV(2).

what is meant by 'management of the ship'. It does not include care of the cargo, which is a separate duty. Since in a sense the care of the cargo is an essential part of the management of a cargo vessel it is hardly surprising that cases have arisen where the distinction has caused difficulties. Such a case was *Gosse Millerd Ltd v Canadian Government Merchant Marine Ltd*.[8] A ship suffered damage during a voyage and repairers had to be given access to the holds. Hatch covers were removed and temporary coves used to protect the cargo. One of these was not replaced by repairers and rainwater entered the hold and caused damage to a cargo of tinplates. It was held that the failure correctly to replace the cover was negligence in the care of the cargo and not in the management of the ship. The carrier was therefore not protected by the immunity.

(b) Fire, unless caused by the actual fault or privity of the carrier. This immunity is also granted the carrier by reason of the Merchant Shipping Act 1979, section 18 which, however, applies only to British ships and goods on board them.

(c) Perils, dangers and accidents of the sea or other navigable waters. These are dangers to which sea transit is particularly prone, such as stranding, storms, collision and seawater damage. To come within the immunity it must be shown that the loss or damage was caused by something more than the ordinary action of wind and waves. There must be an element of fortuity about the event and it must not be some occurrence which in the ordinary course of events should have been foreseen and guarded against. The carrier may be protected by this immunity even though the peril of the sea was not the immediate cause of the loss or damage. In *The Thrunscoe*[9] ventilators were closed during a storm to prevent seawater entering cargo spaces. Cargo was damaged by overheating through the consequent lack of ventilation. The loss was held to have been caused by a peril of the sea.

On the other hand in *The Torenia*[10] a vessel developed an uncontrollable leak on a voyage from Cuba to Denmark and sank with its cargo. Though a peril of the sea was an operative cause of the loss the most significant cause was corrosion which had existed at the outset of the voyage and which could have been discovered by due diligence. The vessel had thus been unseaworthy and the carrier could not claim the benefit of the immunity.

8   [1929] AC 223, HL.
9   [1897] P 301. Cf *Canada Rice Mills v Union Marine and General Insurance Co Ltd* [1941] AC 55, PC.
10 [1983] 2 Lloyd's Rep 210.

(d) Act of God. This is any natural event for which no human agency is responsible and against which precautions could not reasonably have been taken. Thus a carrier could not plead Act of God when a ship went aground in a fog, since human agency was necessary to steer the ship on to the shoal.[11]

(e) Act of war. This is any direct hostile act resulting from war. War probably includes civil war and does not necessarily involve an official declaration of war.

(f) Public enemies. The nature of these is unclear, though most authorities instance pirates.

(g) Arrest or restraint of princes, rulers or people or seizure under legal process. The phrase 'princes, rulers or people' in effect means 'established governments' and the immunity covers cases of government action such as embargoes, import bans, quarantine restrictions and the like. The limits of the scope of this immunity are shown by the case of *Ciampa v British India Steam Navigation Co*[12] where a ship sailed from Mombasa, a port where plague was endemic, to Naples, where lemons were loaded for London. The ship called at Marseilles, where the authorities ordered it to be fumigated because it had called at Mombasa. This process damaged the lemons. The carrier argued that the damage had been caused by restraint of princes but Rowlatt J held that the carriers knew that the fumigation at Marseilles would be inevitable in the circumstances and the exception could not avail them since they had in effect deliberately subjected the cargo to the treatment by taking it on board at Naples knowing that the ship had called at Mombasa and was bound for Marseilles.

In *The Good Friend*[13] the authorities at the port of destination prohibited the unloading of the vessel because it was infested with insects. The immunity did not apply because the insects had been present when the voyage had begun and the vessel had therefore been unseaworthy.

(h) Quarantine restrictions. In view of the preceding immunity there appears to be no reason for the appearance of this as a separate immunity as far as English law is concerned.

(i) Act or omission of the shipper or owner of the goods, his agent or representative.

11   *Liver Alkali Co v Johnson* (1872) LR 7 Exch 267.
12   [1915] 2 KB 774.
13   [1984] 2 Lloyd's Rep 586.

(j) Strikes or lockouts or stoppages or restraints of labour from whatever cause whether partial or general.

(k) Riots or civil commotions. A civil commotion has been said to be an intermediate stage between a riot and a civil war.[14]

(l) Saving or attempting to save life or property at sea. This immunity clearly overlaps article IV(4). See p 33, above.

(m) Wastage in bulk or weight or any other loss or damage arising from an inherent defect, quality or vice of the goods. This exception, which in the common law is known as 'inherent vice', covers any loss occurring through some natural defect or quality in the goods themselves, as, for example, acid in fertilisers eventually rotting the bags in which they were packed.[15] The immunity will naturally not avail the carrier if the damage, though arising from the nature of the goods, was caused by bad stowage.

(n) Insufficiency of packing. This immunity, like the previous one, will not apply where there has been bad stowage.

(o) Insufficiency or inadequacy of marks.

(p) Latent defects not discoverable by due diligence.

(q) Any other cause arising without the actual fault or privity of the carrier or without the fault or neglect of the agents or servants of the carrier. ... The carrier will be able to claim the benefit of this immunity only to the extent that he can prove the absence of fault, privity or neglect. In *Leesh River Tea Co v British India Steam Navigation Co*[16] damage resulted to cargo as a result of the theft by stevedores of a storm valve cover plate. The carrier was entitled to the benefit of the immunity since a stevedore, although he may for some purposes be an agent of the carrier, is not so when he commits, as here, an act entirely outside the scope of his agency.

Discharge of cargo

As with the loading, the responsibilities in connection with the discharge of the cargo will be allocated by the contract of carriage and by the rules

---

14 *Bolivia Republic v Indemnity Mutual Marine Assurance Co Ltd* [1909] 1 KB 785, CA.
15 *Internationale Guano en Superphosphaat-Werken v Robert Macandrew & Co* [1909] 2 KB 360.
16 [1967] 2 QB 250, [1966] 2 Lloyd's Rep 193, CA.

and customs of the port concerned. If discharge is the responsibility of the carrier he must, if the Hague–Visby Rules apply, carry it out properly and carefully, subject to the immunities in the Rules.

There is no general duty on a carrier to inform consignees that the ship is ready to unload their goods[17] but such a duty may be imposed by the contact of carriage or by the usage of a port. Bills of lading normally contain an item 'Notify Party'. Where the name of a consignee is entered under this head the carrier must notify him of the arrival.[18]

Limitation of liability

It has long been a practice of carriers to limit by contract the sum they have to pay in the event of being liable for loss of or damage to a cargo unless a higher value of the cargo is declared on shipment and any required extra charge paid.[19] Such express limitation is valid at common law. The original Hague Rules[20] laid down a maximum liability of one hundred pounds. Depreciation of the currency made this figure unrealistic in spite of various extra-legal agreements under which carriers undertook to accept higher limits. Article IV(5) of the Hague–Visby Rules set the limit at '10,000 gold francs per package or unit or thirty gold francs per kilo of the gross weight of the goods lost or damaged whichever is the higher'. This gold or 'Poincaré' franc was not a unit of currency but a notional unit of gold[1] whose value was stated from time to time by the Department of Trade. The Poincaré franc has in turn been replaced as the unit of account by the special drawing right (as defined by the International Monetary Fund), effected by the Merchant Shipping Act 1981, section 2(4). The prescribed limitation amounts are 666.67 units of account per package or unit or two units of account per kilo of the gross weight of the goods lost or damaged, whichever is the higher.

The limitation does not apply if the nature and value of the goods are declared to the carrier on shipment and inserted in the bill of lading. Such

17 *Nelson v Dahl* (1879) 12 Ch D 568, CA.
18 *E Clemens Horst Co v Norfolk and North American Steamship Co* (1906) 11 Com Cas 141.
19 See eg, *Nicholson v Willan* (1804) 5 East 507.
20 Carriage of Goods by Sea Act 1924, Sch, art IV(5).
1 65.5 milligrams of gold of millesimal fineness 900. This unit was adopted to tie liability to gold values and thus avoid the effects of currency depreciation, an attempt which vagaries in the gold market have frustrated. See the method employed by eg, the Hamburg Rules, p 50, below.

a declaration is only prima facie evidence of nature and value and is not binding on the carrier. The limitation has posed problems when goods have been 'consolidated'. If, say, a container containing 1,000 boxes has been lost overboard, the question of whether each box or the container was the 'package or unit' is clearly important. The Hague–Visby Rules deal with this problem by laying down that the container or other consolidation unit is to be considered as the package or unit for this purpose unless the contents are separately enumerated in the bill of lading.

In *The Esmeralda I*[2] a full container load (FCL) of boxes of cutlery was locked and sealed with the carrier's seal at the seller's place of business. When the container was opened at the buyer's premises 118 were missing of the 437 boxes allegedly loaded. The bill of lading was marked 'FCL/FCL' and noted that the quantity and contents were furnished by the shipper and could not be checked by the master. It described the goods as 'one 20–foot container said to contain 437 cardboard boxes'.

It was established that the first 'FCL' of the mark meant that the shipper wished to ship whatever the container would hold and the second 'FCL' that it was for the consignee to unload the whole container. In all the circumstances it was held that the container was the 'unit of package' for the purposes of the limitation.

However, in the case of *The River Gurara*[3] a vessel sank with a total loss of cargo. Many of the containers had been filled privately by the shippers and were covered with bills stating that they were 'said to contain' a given number of items such as pallets, crates, cartons and bags. So the question was whether the cargo owners' right of recovery was limited to £100 per container or £100 per individual item listed on the bill. The Court of Appeal held that the parcels and not the containers constituted the relevant unit but the bill of lading was not conclusive and it was for the cargo owner to establish by extrinsic evidence the number of parcels loaded.

The limitation will not apply if it is proved that the damage[4] resulted from an act or omission of the carrier done with intent to cause damage or recklessly and with knowledge that damage would probably result.

2   [1988] 1 Lloyd's Rep 206.
3   [1998] 1 Lloyd's Rep 225.
4   Art IV(5)(e) mentions only 'damage', not 'loss or damage'. The French version similarly has 'dommage' instead of the usual 'perte ou dommage'. The potential importance of the omission is amply demonstrated by *Fothergill v Monarch Airlines* [1980] QB 23, [1979] 3 All ER 445, CA.

Another statutory limitation on a carrier's liability is imposed by the Merchant Shipping Act 1981, which limits the aggregate liability for damage to goods to 1,000 gold francs for each ton of the ship's tonnage.

Variation of liability

Under article III(8) of the Hague–Visby Rules the carrier may not by the contract exclude or limit his liability other than as allowed by the Rules. Should he purport to do so the exclusion or limitation will be void but the validity of the contract will not otherwise be affected.[5] The carrier may increase his liabilities by contract but any such extension must be set out in the bill of lading.

Limitation of action

Under the Limitation Act 1980 the normal period within which an action in contract must be brought is six years after the cause of action arose. A shorter period may be agreed by contract. Article III(6) of the Hague–Visby Rules sets a limit on actions within its scope of one year from the time when the goods were or should have been delivered. It was held in *The Merak*[6] that instituting proceedings under an arbitration agreement is equivalent to bringing an action for the purpose of this rule. In *The Captain Gregos*[7], the strictness of the rule was emphasised in that the cargo owner will be discharged of all liability under the Rules unless the cargo owner brings his action within one year of his loss.

Third parties and the contract

Article IV, rules 2–4 provide protection for persons whom the carrier employs in the performance of his duties, when sued by the cargo owner, for example, for negligent damage to the cargo. Such servants and agents of the carrier can plead the protection of the maximum limits of liability and other defences which the carrier could have pleaded under the Rules had he been sued. However, this protection may not be extended to independent contractors.

5   *The Hollandia* [1983] 1 AC 565, [1982] 3 All ER 1141, HL.
6   [1965] P 223, [1965] 1 All ER 230, CA.
7   [1990] 1 Lloyd's Rep 310, CA.

In *Scruttons Ltd v Midland Silicones Ltd* [8] a drum of chemicals was damaged by stevedores. A clause in the bill of lading (the 'Himalaya' Clause) extended the carrier's immunities and limitations to stevedores among others. It was held that the immunities and limitations could not benefit the stevedores since they were not parties to the bill of lading contract in which the term was contained. The House of Lords accepted, however, that there might be circumstances where the stevedores could be held to be parties to such a contract. Such a situation was held to be the case in *New Zealand Shipping Co Ltd v AM Satterthwaite & Co Ltd* [9] when the court was prepared to construct a unilateral contract between the cargo owners and the stevedores. This circumvention of the doctrine of privity of contract met with a cool reception in the courts of most common law jurisdictions [10] but was restated and reinforced by the Privy Council in *Port Jackson Stevedoring Pty Ltd v Salmond and Spraggon (Australia) Pty* and by the Court of Queen's Bench in *Raymond Burke Motors Ltd v Mersey Docks and Harbour Co.* [11]

The case of *The Pioneer Container* [12] which dealt with the law of bailment has been used to by-pass the doctrine of privity of contract. The contract of carriage provided for the sub-contracting of carriage 'on any terms'. The Privy Council held that the terms of the contract of carriage could be relied upon by a sub-contractor, as sub-bailee, including the exclusive jurisdiction clause. In *The Mahkutai* [13], Lord Goff looked at the privity of contract issue and Himalaya clauses, and expressed a view that the agency and bailments principles should be used to accommodate commercial needs.

The Contracts (Rights of Third Parties) Act 1999, which came into effect on 11 May 2000 attempts to assist the third party dilemma. A third party is entitled to enforce a contractual provision in his own name where either the contract contains an express term to that effect [14] or where the contract purports to confer a benefit on a third party [15] unless in the latter case, it is clear on a true construction of the contract that the contracting parties did not intend the third party to have a personal right to enforce such a

8   [1962] AC 446, [1962] 1 All ER 1, HL.
9   [1975] AC 154, [1974] 1 All ER 1015, PC.
10   For a review see Davis and Palmer [1979] JBL 337.
11   [1980] 3 All ER 257, PC and [1986] 1 Lloyd's Rep 155 respectively.
12   *KH Enterprise (Cargo Owners) v Pioneer Container (Owners), The Pioneer Container* [1994] 1 Lloyd's Rep 593, PC.
13   [1996] 2 Lloyd's Rep 1, PC.
14   Section 1(1)(a).
15   Section 1(1)(b).

benefit.[16] Here, the right of enforcement is dependent on the third party being expressly identified in the contract by name, class or description. However, there is a proviso in section 6(5)(a) relating to contracts of goods by sea which states that the statutory right to enforce a contractual provision is not intended to confer positive rights on a third party, its effect being expressly restricted to enabling a third party to avail himself of an exclusion of limitation of liability provision in such a contract.

THE SHIPPER'S RESPONSIBILITIES

Freight

The shipper naturally has obligations under the contract of carriage. In the first place he is liable to pay the freight. In normal modern practice, freight will be payable in advance and will not be recoverable even if ship and cargo are lost at sea.[17] Even though the ordinary freight is payable in advance, extra freight may become payable. If the cargo cannot, for some sufficient reason, be discharged at the appointed port, the carrier may have to take it to some other port, in which case 'back freight' becomes payable. Under the Carriage of Goods by Sea Act 1992, section 3(1) the liability to pay any freight may pass to the indorsee of the bill of lading but the liability also remains, by virtue of section 3(3), with the original shipper. The carrier has a lien on the cargo for freight, which will continue until the lien is waived or the carrier parts with the actual or constructive possession of the goods.

A cargo owner who has a claim against a carrier for loss of or damage to goods cannot deduct the amount of his claim from any freight due, but must pay the freight and bring an action in respect of the loss or damage.[18]

Dangerous goods

At common law there is an implied undertaking by a shipper that he will not ship dangerous goods without expressly informing the carrier of their nature unless the carrier knows, or should know, that the goods are

---

16 Section 1(2).
17 Contracts of carriage by sea involving freight are expressly excluded from the operation of the Law Reform (Frustrated Contracts) Act 1943.
18 *Dakin v Oxley* (1864) 15 CBNS 646.

dangerous.[19] In The *Giannis NK*[20] it was stated that 'Goods of a dangerous nature' in rule 6 mean goods which either actually cause physical damage or which pose a threat of physical damage to the ship or to the other cargo on board. Inflammable, explosive or corrosive goods are obviously dangerous goods in this sense but goods may be 'dangerous' other than through their physical qualities. In *Mitchell, Cotts & Co v Steel Bros & Co*[21] a cargo of rice was shipped for carriage to Piraeus. At the time the discharge of rice there was only possible with the permission of the British Government, a fact known to the shipper but not to the carrier, who could not reasonably be expected to know it. It was held that in the circumstances the rice was 'dangerous goods' and the shipper was liable to the carrier for delay caused by the shipment. In *Mediterranean Freight Services Ltd v BP Oil International Ltd, The Fiona*[22] a carrier was not entitled to invoke the indemnity under article IV, rule 6 if he was in breach of his obligation under article III, rule 1 to exercise due diligence to make the vessel seaworthy and that was a total or partial cause of the loss.

Under the Hague–Visby Rules, article IV(6) the carrier or his agents may, if dangerous goods have been shipped without their knowledge and consent, land, destroy or render them harmless without compensation and the shipper remains liable for all damages and expenses incurred as a result of the shipment. Even though the goods have been shipped *with* the carrier's knowledge and consent they may, if necessary, be similarly treated without the carrier becoming liable except in general average if this applies.

GENERAL AVERAGE[1]

In most cases loss or damage occurring to ship or cargo will be what is known as particular average, that is it will affect only one interest and will have to be borne by the owner of that interest, subject to any right of action he may have against a party responsible for the loss or damage. However, in the peculiar circumstances of carriage of goods by sea a situation may arise where, in order to avoid some danger which threatens the whole adventure, expense has to be incurred or loss or damage deliberately inflicted in order to save the ship and its cargo. If, for example,

19   *Brass v Maitland* (1856) 26 LJQB 49.
20   [1996] 1 Lloyd's Rep 577, at 583, CA.
21   [1916] 2 KB 610.
22   [1994] 2 Lloyd's Rep 506, CA.
1   'Average' in this context is from the French 'avarie' meaning loss or damage and has no arithmetical significance.

a ship strands it may be necessary to lighten it by jettisoning cargo, that is, deliberately throwing it overboard, so that the ship can be refloated. Alternatively the ship's equipment may in such a situation be sacrificed or maltreated or extraordinary quantities of fuel consumed. In such a case all the interests, ship and cargoes, will have benefited from the action and will have to contribute, in proportion to their value, to the party who has suffered the loss or damage or incurred the expense. This is a general average contribution. The importance of this rule in the international contract of sale lies in the fact that the buyer of goods who has paid for them and received a bill of lading may find that the carrier will exercise his lien on the goods and refuse to release them on presentation of the bill of lading until a general average contribution has been paid or an undertaking given for its payment. The bill of lading holder, by virtue of the transfer to him of the liabilities under the contract of carriage, will be liable to pay this sum although in normal circumstances he will be the holder of an insurance policy which covers this contingency.

There is an international code on general average, the York-Antwerp Rules 1994. These do not have the statutory force of, for example, the Hague–Visby Rules, but are regularly adopted by the parties to a contract of carriage.

In order to constitute general average, loss, damage or expense must be reasonably incurred in order to avert a danger threatening all the interests involved in the voyage. It must be voluntary and necessary and must be a real sacrifice and not an abandonment of something already effectively lost. The unharmed interests must in fact benefit from the sacrifice; there is clearly no point in a general average contribution unless they are actually saved.

A party cannot claim a general average contribution if he was himself responsible for the danger to avert which the sacrifice was made. Thus the shipper of dangerous goods without the knowledge and consent of the carrier would have no claim to a general average contribution if his goods became a threat to the ship and to other cargoes and were accordingly jettisoned. On the other hand a party may claim a general average contribution in respect of loss or damage incurred by him to avert a danger he has himself brought about if the contract of carriage effectively excludes his liability for so doing. Thus a carrier of goods under a bill of lading subject to the Hague–Visby Rules would be able to claim a general average contribution from cargo owners if he paid for a tug to remove the ship from a dangerous situation into which it had come by reason of the master's bad navigation. This is because the carrier is not liable under the Rules for such a fault on the part of the master.

CHARTERPARTIES

Charterparties, contracts for the hire of an entire ship for a specified voyage or period of time, play an important part in international trade. Commodities such as sugar, oil, grain, ores and coal are almost always carried under such contracts. The law on charterparties is vast, complex and developing and in a book of this nature no more than the briefest of surveys is possible, to highlight those features which particularly bear on the sale transaction.

A charterparty is not subject to the Hague–Visby Rules, though these Rules will apply to a bill of lading issued under a charterparty once the bill of lading has come into the hands of an indorsee other than the charterer. The parties are free to make any terms they wish (including a term incorporating the Hague–Visby Rules) but most charterparties contain well-established terms and are standard form contracts agreed by various conferences and known by such code names as Baltime and Gencon. The implied undertakings at common law already discussed as to seaworthiness, deviation, delay and dangerous goods apply to charterparties generally. Other features are determined by the type of charterparty.

Voyage charterparties

The shipowner agrees to provide the ship at the stated port within a specified or reasonable time. His failure to do so will normally give the charterer a right to terminate the contract by virtue of the 'cancelling clause'. The shipowner agrees to carry the goods to the contract destination.

The charterer agrees to provide a full cargo for the ship, to bring this cargo alongside and arrange for it to be loaded in the stipulated time. The shipowner is remunerated in accordance with the quantity of cargo carried. If the charterer does not load a 'full and complete cargo' the shipowner will be entitled to charge 'dead freight' in respect of the deficiency. This dead freight will be noted on the bill of lading issued for the cargo and any holder may be liable to pay this sum.

The high cost and the comparatively short working life of a modern cargo ship make it imperative that it is, as far as possible, working continuously to earn the maximum freight. This means that the time that the ship is idle during loading and discharge of cargo must be kept to a minimum. The charterparty will accordingly lay down a total time, known as the 'lay days', which may be spent on these operations and will normally stipulate an agreed sum of damages, known as 'demurrage', for each day by which the lay days are exceeded. Sometimes the period over which demurrage is payable will itself be specified and for delays thereafter the shipowner will be able to claim 'damages for detention'. The charterparty will give the shipowner a lien on the cargo for demurrage payments, which may therefore have to be paid by a bill of lading holder in order to obtain delivery of goods he has bought.

Time charterparties

The charterer acquires, under this contract, the use of the vessel for a specified period of time and pays 'hire' for this, usually paid monthly during the continuance of the charterparty. A failure by the charterer to pay an instalment promptly will normally entitle the shipowner to withdraw the vessel from the charterer's use.

The charterer undertakes also to engage only in lawful trades and carry lawful goods and to direct the vessel only to safe ports.

As the shipowner receives hire even when the vessel is loading and discharging and irrespective of what, if any, cargo it is carrying, questions of demurrage and dead freight do not arise.

Bills of lading and charterparties

As between charterer and shipowner the contract of carriage is the charterparty. The shipowner will usually issue a bill of lading to the charterer when the latter ships goods but it will, in this context, be merely a receipt for the goods and a document of title. When the bill of lading passes into the hands of an indorsee the position will be different. The Hague–Visby Rules will apply to the bill of lading and the contract between indorsee and shipowner will be on the terms of the bill of lading.

In *The Nea Tyhi*[2] plywood was shipped on a chartered vessel in a Malaysian port for carriage to the UK. The cargo was stowed on deck but the bill of

2   [1982] 1 Lloyd's Rep 606.

lading, which was signed by the charterer's agents, noted 'stowed under deck'. The plywood was damaged by rainwater during the voyage. Since the charterer's agents had ostensible authority to sign the bill of lading, the shipowner was liable to the buyer in respect of the damage since the latter would not have accepted bills of lading showing deck stowage of a cargo of this nature. The question of the balance of rights and responsibilities in such cases was considered by Sheen J.[3]

> [I]f I had to choose whether the shipowner or the endorsee of a bill of lading should be the loser I would have no hesitation in saying that he who contracts with the charterer and puts trust and confidence in him to the extent of authorising the 'charterer' agent to issue and sign bills of lading should be a loser, rather than a stranger. This principle was stated by Holt CJ in *Hern v Nichols* in 1700.

The bill of lading itself, however, may expressly incorporate the charterparty terms[4] in which case the indorsee may be affected by the terms. To be effective, the incorporation must be clear and unambiguous and any term thus incorporated must not conflict with express terms in the bill of lading or, where they apply, with the Hague–Visby Rules. A term commonly incorporated is the 'cesser' clause which purports to free the charterer from liability in respect of the cargo once it has been loaded, in exchange for granting the shipowner the lien on the cargo for demurrage and back freight. Effective incorporation of this term will make the bill of lading holder liable to pay these items to obtain the goods.

The incorporation into a bill of lading of a provision in a charterparty providing that the master shall sign bills of lading 'as presented' does not oblige the master to sign for quantities which he believes have not been loaded.[5]

THE HAMBURG RULES

These Rules were devised at Hamburg in 1978 by a United Nations Convention on the Carriage of Goods by Sea. They have not yet been adopted but will eventually replace the Hague–Visby Rules. The latter, though they date from 1968, are not basically different from the Hague Rules 1921 and have certain disadvantages which the Hamburg Rules are

3   Ibid at 611.
4   A common term is 'All conditions and exceptions as per charterparty'.
5   *The Boukadoura* [1989] 1 Lloyd's Rep 393.

designed to overcome. The Hague–Visby Rules do not lay down a single basis of liability for the carrier but rely on the requirement of seaworthiness and on a number of diverse and overlapping exceptions. The Hague–Visby Rules were not designed to apply to modern methods of through transport. A third disadvantage, in the eyes of many governments, particularly those states with no merchant fleets, is that they are weighted too much in favour of the carrier.

The Hamburg Rules distinguish 'carriers' and 'actual carriers'. The carrier is a party who makes a contract of carriage with a shipper and the 'actual carrier' is any party entrusted, as a result of this contract, with the carriage of the goods. Thus if the shipper makes a contract of carriage with a forwarding agent who is a combined transport operator, the latter will be the carrier. If the carrier then arranges for the sea transit of the goods with a shipowner, the shipowner will be an actual carrier, as will be any other party with whom the shipowner arranges for any part of the sea carriage.[6] The carrier is responsible for the goods for the period during which he is in charge of them at the port of loading, during the carriage and at the port of discharge. His liability during this period is stated by Annex II to the Convention to be based on 'presumed fault or neglect'. Consequently he is liable for loss of, damage to or delay in delivering goods unless he can prove that he or his servants or agents 'took all measures that could reasonably be required to avoid the occurrence and its consequences'.[7] Delay in delivery means a failure to deliver goods within the contract time or a reasonable time.[8]

In case of loss, damage or delay caused by fire the carrier is liable only if it can be proved that the fire was caused by him or his servants or agents or that the loss etc arose from a failure to put out the fire or avoid its consequences. The carrier remains under this liability for the entire carriage whether it is performed by him or by actual carriers, but the actual carrier will be liable for loss etc while the goods are in his charge. In such a case, the carrier and actual carrier will be jointly and severally liable.

If goods are to be carried by a *named* actual carrier, the carrier may expressly exclude his own liability for loss etc while goods are in the hands of the actual carrier, but this exclusion depends on the shipper being able to sue the actual carrier in a 'competent court'.[9]

6   Art 1(1) and (2).
7   Art 5(1).
8   Art 5(2).
9   Art 11(1).

Limitations

The carrier's liability in respect of loss or damage is limited to the value of 835 units of account per package or 'other shipping unit' or 2.5 units of account per kilo of gross weight whichever is the higher.[10] This unit of account is the special drawing right (SDR) of the International Monetary Fund (IMF) and its value will be determined in respect of any particular currency by the IMF's calculation methods. If the loss is caused by delay in delivery, the limitation is two-and-a-half times the freight payable for the goods delayed but not exceeding the total freight under the contract of carriage of goods by sea. The aggregate liability for all loss is limited to the 835 units per package or 2.5 units per kilo. Higher limits may be fixed by the contract.

Action must be brought within two years from the time when delivery is made or should have been made.[11]

Bills of lading

The Rules lay down various items which must be entered on the bill of lading.[12] These include the items required by the Hague–Visby Rules and those which are entered in practice in any case. Exceptional is a requirement that the bill of lading must contain a statement that carriage is subject to the Rules and that the Rules nullify any term derogating from the shipper's or consignee's rights.

---

10 Art 6(1)(a).
11 Art 20.
12 Art 15.

Chapter 3
Sale contracts based on sea carriage

Many of the most important and commonly used sale contracts used in international trade are based on the assumption that the goods will be carried by sea. These are the fas, fob, cif, Arrival, Ex-ship and Ex-quay contracts. Goods sold under other types of contract may, of course, be carried by sea: for example, the overseas buyer of goods under an ex-works contract may arrange for such carriage but this will be irrelevant to the sale contract[1] since the seller is not concerned with the incidents of whatever contract of carriage the buyer may arrange. Since the fas contract has marked similarities to the fob contract it is convenient to consider the latter first.

In order to ensure that the meaning of any trade term is clear, the parties may state explicitly what is meant by a particular trade term, or they may decide to use standard contract forms issued by trade associations, or may make reference in their own conditions of sale to standard trade terms. Examples of the latter are, for example, Incoterms or Intraterms. Incoterms are sponsored by the International Chamber of Commerce under the title of Incoterms 2000. In some countries Incoterms are given statutory force, and in others they are equivalent to customs; but in the UK neither is the case. Intraterms were designed to simplify the language associated with trade terms. Parties may agree to the incorporation of Incoterms into the contract by stating, for example, fob Naples (Incoterms 2000). By stating in the contract that Intraterms are part of it would effectively mean that the interpretation of words in the contract should be construed in accordance with those specified terms.

---

1   Except that the seller may be under an implied obligation to pack the goods for sea transit.

FOB CONTRACTS

The fob contract was described by Devlin J in *Pyrene Co Ltd v Scindia Navigation Co Ltd*[2] as 'a flexible instrument'. It is hardly surprising, therefore, that it is not susceptible of rigid definition. The central idea is clear; the price paid to the seller includes all costs up to the loading of the goods on to an overseas vessel nominated by the buyer; property and risk normally pass to the buyer at this point and all subsequent expenses are for the buyer's account. But the incidents of the contract may be varied in many ways without its losing the essential nature of an fob contract. This may be by reason of express or implied terms in the contract, including terms that the seller shall arrange carriage and/or insurance, but also by reason of rules or customs applying in the different ports involved. The question of whether a contract is or is not an fob contract is not merely an academic one; the answer will determine the parties' responsibilities and rights. Moreover, the fact that the parties have described their contract as 'fob' will not necessarily be conclusive. A court might well examine the contract they have made and come to the conclusion that it is not in fact an fob contract.

Various attempts have been made, by the courts and by academic writers, to subdivide fob contracts into various categories but there is no generally accepted system. Most authorities at least agree on the existence of a 'strict' or 'classic' type but even here there are divergences of opinion. The task of classifying fob contracts is complicated by changes in commercial practice over the last century, particularly through improved communications, so that some earlier definitions and classifications tend to be based on situations which no longer apply. The modern classification made by Devlin LJ in the *Pyrene* case was re-stated by Donaldson LJ in the Court of Appeal in *The El Amria and the El Minia*.[3]

> In the first, or classic type, the buyer nominates the ship and the seller puts the goods on board for the account of the buyer, procuring a bill of lading. The seller is then a party to the contract of carriage and if he has taken the bill of lading to his order, the only contract of carriage to which the buyer can become a party is that contained in or evidenced by the bill of lading which is endorsed to him by the seller. The second is a variant of the first, in that the seller arranges for the ship to come on the berth, but the legal incidents are the

2   [1954] 2 QB 402 at 424, [1954] 2 All ER 158 at 167.
3   [1982] 2 Lloyd's Rep 28 at 32.

same. The third is where the seller puts the goods on board, takes a mate's receipt and gives this to the buyer or his agent who then takes a bill of lading. In this latter type the buyer is a party to the contract of carriage *ab initio*.

A commercial view of the parties' obligations under the strict form of fob contract is given by the Institute of Export.[4]

The seller has:
(1) to make available at the port of loading and to ship free on board goods answering in all respects the description in the contract of sale;
(2) to pay all handling and transport charges in connection with the above operation;
(3) in case of goods from bond or under drawback to complete declarations required by HM Customs and Excise;
(4) to meet all charges arising in connection with the goods up to the time of their passing over the ship's rail.

The buyer has to:
(1) advise the seller in good time on what ship at the port of loading agreed in the contract the seller has to put the goods free on board.
(2) secure shipping space in the designated vessel;
(3) obtain an export licence where necessary (but see p 63 below);
(4) designate an effective ship in time to enable the seller to deliver within the period agreed in the contract;
(5) enter and declare the goods at customs as provided in the Customs Acts, and meet all charges arising from the making of such entry;
(6) make entry and meet charges arising from the upkeep and the conservance of waterways used by the ship in her passage out of the port;
(7) in the event of a breakdown of his arrangement with the ship arrange for substitute vessels with the least possible delay, and pay all additional cost of transport, rent and other charges incurred on account of substitution and/or transfer.

The fob sale is not necessarily an export sale. An exporter who has sold or who wishes to sell goods on fob terms to an overseas buyer may himself *buy* the goods on those terms from a supplier in this country and fulfil his contract with the overseas buyer by delivering to him the documents. In such a situation there are two fob sales: the first by the supplier to the

4   'Export' 1951.

exporter and the second by the exporter to the overseas buyer. The first type of sale may be referred to variously as a 'domestic', 'home' or 'internal' fob contract.

A seller under an fob contract may well undertake to perform duties beyond those required from him under the strict form of the contract. In many cases he will undertake to find shipping space and otherwise arrange for carriage. He may also arrange insurance on behalf of the buyer. Such additional duties will not normally be performed as part of the fob price paid by the buyer but will be invoiced and charged for separately.

A common variation is the sale 'fob stowed' under which the seller is responsible not only for the loading of the goods but for their correct placing in the cargo spaces.

It should be noted that in US usage the term fob is employed in a very wide sense to mean in effect 'delivery to' so that the US equivalent of the English fob would be 'fob vessel'.

The goods

The goods, subject to any contractual stipulation to the contrary, must correspond with any description under which they were sold.[5] This description may relate not only to the goods themselves but to their packing.[6] It may also relate to the shipment of the goods. In *Bowes v Shand*[7] a delivery of rice which had been shipped in February was held not to have satisfied the contractual description of rice to be shipped in March and/or April.

The packing of the goods may be relevant to another implied term in the contract. Since the contract of sale fob clearly envisages carriage by sea then the goods as packed must be fit for such carriage. In *George Wills & Sons Ltd v Thomas Brown & Sons*[8] herrings were sold fob London to an Australian buyer. The packing was inadequate and the herrings deteriorated. The seller was held to be in breach of the implied term that goods must be fit for any purpose made known, expressly or by implication, to the seller.[9]

5   Sale of Goods Act 1979, s 13.
6   *Re Moore & Co and Landauer & Co* [1921] 2 KB 519.
7   (1877) 2 App Cas 455.
8   (1922) 12 Ll L Rep 292. Cf *Kelly, Douglas & Co Ltd v Pollock* (1958) 14 DLR (2d) 526.
9   Sale of Goods Act 1979, s 14(3).

The port of loading

The contract will often state this precisely (eg fob Liverpool) but may give alternatives (eg fob Hull, Grimsby or Immingham) or a range of ports (eg fob Danish port). In these multiport contracts the choice of port, subject to the terms of the particular contract, will normally be the buyer's[10] and he has the corresponding duty of notifying the seller of his choice in good time. The seller is 'not under an obligation to take the goods away from their factory or warehouse and to start them in circulation in the hope or expectation that they may arrive at a place which later the buyers would have said was the place where the buyer's ship was going to be at some particular time'.[11]

If the contract specifies the port of loading or if, in a multiport contract, the buyer has made his choice and informed the seller, then neither party, except by agreement, can claim to be allowed to fulfil the contract by loading or accepting delivery at a different port. In *Peter Turnbull & Co Pty Ltd v Mundas Trading Co (Australasia) Pty Ltd*[12] goods were sold fob Sydney. The sellers then alleged that they could not deliver at Sydney and asked to be allowed to deliver at Melbourne. The buyers refused. In an action for the non-delivery of the goods at Sydney the sellers were held liable and were not excused by the buyers' failure to nominate a ship for Sydney since the sellers' insistence that they could not deliver there made such nomination pointless. The duty to deliver at the agreed port of loading will not be affected by the fact that the seller has undertaken to arrange for the carriage of the goods. The port of loading is of the essence of the contract and is considered as part of the description of the goods.[13]

Conversely, the buyer cannot claim delivery elsewhere than the port agreed in the contract.[14] Neither can he waive his right to have the goods loaded and claim to take delivery of them on the docks[15] though it is not easy to see why he should not waive his contractual rights if by so doing he causes no loss, inconvenience or expense to the seller.

10 *Boyd & Co Ltd v Louca* [1973] 1 Lloyd's Rep 209.
11 *Anglo-African Shipping Co of New York Inc v J Mortner Ltd* [1962] 1 Lloyd's Rep 81 at 92.
12 [1954] 2 Lloyd's Rep 198 (Aust HC) and see *Wertheim v Chicoutimi Pulp Co* [1911] AC 301 at 313.
13 See *Petrograde Inc v Stinnes Handel GMBH* [1995] 1 Lloyd's Rep 142.
14 *Modern Transport Co Ltd v Ternstrom & Roos* (1924) 19 Ll L Rep 345 and *Maine Spinning Co v Sutcliffe & Co* (1917) 87 LJKB 382.
15 *Wackerbarth v Masson* (1812) 3 Camp 270.

FOB contracts

The nomination of the ship

The buyer's duty to nominate a ship is a condition precedent to the seller's duty to load the goods. 'It is the duty of the person who seeks to have the goods to point out the ship or specify the place where they are to be delivered before he can complain that the goods are not on board the ship.'[16] Nevertheless, if the buyer does fail to nominate an effective ship, the seller's remedy is in damages. In *Colley v Overseas Exporters*[17] the buyer under a contract fob Liverpool was remarkably unfortunate in that no fewer than five ships successively nominated failed to arrive. The seller, who had delivered the goods at Liverpool, claimed the contract price and failed to recover it. Since there had, for whatever reason, been no shipment, there had been no delivery to the buyer and the seller could not demand the price but merely damages for non-acceptance of the goods. At this case indicates, the buyer is not committed by a nomination of a particular ship. He may substitute another provided that it will be available for loading within the stipulated period.[18]

It is conceivable that the seller may suffer loss or incur expense if the buyer substitutes another vessel for the first nominated vessel. If, for example, a buyer under an fob contract specifying 'October shipment' were to nominate a vessel for 1 October and then withdraw this nomination and substitute a vessel to load on 31 October, goods delivered to the docks by the seller to meet the first date might deteriorate while they were still at the seller's risk. The basis of any claim that the seller may have against the buyer in this respect is not clear, however.[19]

One solution would be to recognise that the nomination of the vessel really involves two choices by the buyer: of the ship and of the loading date, and that once he has specified the latter he is bound by his choice though he is free to change the former. Alternatively the right of the buyer to substitute could be regarded as subject to an implied undertaking to indemnify the seller against consequent loss. To some extent this is implied by item 7 of the Institute of Export's list of the buyer's duties under an fob contract.[20]

---

16   *Sutherland v Allhusen* (1866) 14 LT 666 at 667, per Pollock CB.
17   [1921] 3 KB 302.
18   *Agricultores Federados Argentinos Sociedad Cooperativa Ltda v Ampro SA* [1965] 2 Lloyd's Rep 157.
19   See eg, *J & J Cunningham Ltd v R A Munro & Co Ltd* (1922) 28 Com Cas 42.
20   Page 53 above.

If the buyer's nomination of a ship is for any reason invalid he may later make a valid nomination and the seller will be obliged to accept this.[21]

'When the seller undertakes to arrange shipping space and carriage in addition to his strict duties, there will obviously be no duty on the buyer to nominate a vessel. This may be so even if the seller merely undertakes to do his best to obtain shipping space'.[1]

Delivery

Assuming that the buyer has nominated an effective ship, the seller's duty is to deliver the goods by putting them on board the ship within the stipulated period. In *All Russian Co-operative Society Ltd v Benjamin Smith & Sons*[2] delivery under a contract fob London was to be made in January. The last part of the cargo was brought alongside the ship a quarter of an hour before the end of the working day on 31 January. The seller was held not to have made delivery within the contract period. The position will, of course, be different if the seller's failure to deliver in time is due to the buyer's late nomination of the ship.[3]

An fob contract will frequently state optional shipment periods, eg 'March/ April shipment' and may state whether the choice within that period is the seller's or the buyer's. If the contract does not, expressly or by implication, allocate the choice it would appear that the choice of the date is the buyer's.[4] If the choice is given by the contract to the seller, he must inform the buyer in good time of his choice so that the buyer can make the necessary nomination of the vessel.[5]

The goods will be at the seller's risk until the appointed delivery time. In *J & J Cunningham Ltd v R A Munro & Co Ltd*[6] the buyers of bran under a contract fob Rotterdam, October shipment, arranged for loading on 28 October. The seller, who had been informed that loading would be 'at the end of October', delivered the bran to the docks for shipment on 14 October.

21   *Modern Transport Co Ltd v Ternstrom & Roos* (1924) 19 Ll L Rep 345.
1   *Handel My J Smits Import-Export NV v English Exporters (London) Ltd* [1957]
     1 Lloyd's Rep 517. See also *Richco International v Bunge and Co (The New Prosper)* [1991] 2 Lloyd's Rep 93.
2   (1923) 14 Ll L Rep 351.
3   *F E Napier v Dexters Ltd* (1926) 26 Ll L Rep 184.
4   *Ian Stach Ltd v Baker Bosley Ltd* [1958] 2 QB 130, [1958] 1 All ER 542.
5   *Harlow and Jones v Panex (International) Ltd* [1967] 2 Lloyd's Rep 509.
6   (1922) 28 Com Cas 42.

The bran deteriorated between 14 and 28 October and the buyers rejected it. It was held that they were entitled to do so.

When the buyer has nominated an effective ship and the seller's failure to ship the goods on time is due to some default of the carrier, it may be that the seller will nevertheless be liable to the buyer for the failure to deliver on time.[7] In such a case the seller would presumably have an action against the carrier.

Under an fob contract the seller completes his duty of delivery by having the goods loaded on to the appropriate ship within the contract period, and the time when the goods actually reach the buyer is irrelevant.[8]

Loading

It is usual to state that in an fob contract the seller is responsible for loading the goods on board the ship and for paying the cost of this.[9] This statement must be regarded with some caution. If, for example, the loading is carried out by the carrier, he will recoup his costs through the freight, which is payable by the buyer. Attempts by buyers to claim from sellers the cost of loading absorbed in freight in this way have been unsuccessful.[10] If loading charges are a separate expense, on the other hand, they may well be paid by the seller.

Loading the goods, or getting them on to the ship, is a separate operation from 'stowing'. Under the strict fob contract the stowage charges will normally be paid by the buyer unless the contract is made 'fob stowed'.

To say that the seller is responsible for loading is not to imply that he or his agents must carry out the task themselves. Who actually loads will frequently be a matter not only for the particular contract but for the regulations and customs of the relevant port. Thus in *Pyrene Co Ltd v Scindia Navigation Co Ltd*[11] Devlin J pointed out, 'It is the practice in the Port of London for all loading to be done by the port authority at the ship's expense. The whole charge, therefore, for loading from alongside is paid by the ship and covered by the freight.' The seller is responsible in the sense that the goods are at his risk until they are loaded and that he will be

---

7   *Pyrene Co Ltd v Scindia Navigation Co Ltd* [1954] 2 QB 402, [1954] 2 All ER 158.
8   *Frebold and Sturznickel v Circle Products Ltd* [1970] 1 Lloyd's Rep 499.
9   See eg, Institute of Export Terms, p 53, above.
10   See eg, *Glengarnock Iron and Steel Co Ltd v Henry Cooper & Co* (1895) 22 R 672.
11   [1954] 2 QB 402 at 425, [1954] 2 All ER 158 at 167.

liable to the buyer for any loss or damage caused by any failure on his part to see that the goods are properly loaded.

The passing of property

The traditional point at which property in goods passes under an fob contract is when the goods cross the ship's rail. This is also the point of delivery. In *Pyrene Co Ltd v Scindia Navigation Co Ltd*[12] Devlin J referred to the 'somewhat absurd spectacle of liabilities shifting uneasily as the cargo sways at the end of a derrick across a notional perpendicular projecting from the ship's rail'. In fact the point at which the property in the goods passes under a particular fob contract will be determined by several factors: by the general law as set out in the Sale of Goods Act 1979, by the terms of the particular contract made by the parties and by whether or not the seller has, or is deemed to have, reserved the right of disposal of the goods.

Since all but a very small minority of fob contracts will be for the sale of unascertained goods[13] the property will, subject to agreement, pass when goods in a deliverable state are unconditionally appropriated to the contract, that is, when particular goods of a kind which and in a condition in which the buyer is bound to accept them are clearly and irrevocably designated as the contract goods by either party with the other's express or implied consent. This point is taken to occur under an fob contract on delivery, since this is 'the last act to be performed by the seller'.[14] The assumption is that at this stage of the operation the seller can no longer withdraw the particular goods and substitute others without being in breach of the contract of sale.

The notion is clearly a legal and not a practical one. In most cases the point at which it becomes physically or commercially impracticable for the seller to substitute other goods of the same kind will occur before, possibly long before, shipment and certainly before the goods cross the ship's rail, but this will not affect the legal view of when appropriation takes place. In *Pyrene Co Ltd v Scindia Navigation Co Ltd*[15] a fire tender, the subject of an fob contract, was badly damaged when it fell back into a lighter from a

12 Ibid at 414 and 164 respectively.
13 Goods which are identified by description only and not as particular items. See Sale of Goods Act 1979, s 61.
14 *Carlos Federspiel & Co SA v Charles Twigg & Co Ltd* [1957] 1 Lloyd's Rep 240 at 255.
15 [1954] 2 QB 402, [1954] 2 All ER 158.

crane before it had passed over the ship's rail. The goods were held to have been the property of the seller at the time they were damaged although the notion that the seller could at this time have halted operations, ordered the tender to be lowered back into the lighter, taken it back on shore, removed it and replaced it by a similar one is clearly ludicrous.

Frequently, moreover, the seller will, expressly or by implication, reserve the right of disposal of the goods, that is, he will make it clear that the property in the goods is to remain in him, irrespective of the fact that the goods have been shipped or even that they have actually come into the possession of the buyer or his agent.[16] He will normally retain this right of disposal until some condition, usually payment of the price, has been met by the buyer. In these circumstances there is no 'unconditional appropriation' of the goods within the meaning of the Sale of Goods Act and the property in the goods will therefore not pass on shipment. In particular, the Sale of Goods Act 1979, section 19(2) creates a prima facie presumption that a seller who takes out a bill of lading in his own name and not in the name of the buyer is deemed to reserve the right of disposal of the goods to which the bill of lading relates. While it has been doubted whether an fob seller can thus reserve the right of disposal without being in breach of the contract[17] the general legal view and certainly the assumption of commercial practice – is that he may do so. But the fact that the seller takes out a bill of lading in the buyer's name does not necessarily create an implication that the seller is *not* reserving the right of disposal. He may do this by other means. In particular, a seller will usually be taken to have reserved the right of disposal when the contract demands payment against the bill of lading[18] but the question can only be settled by reference to the terms of the particular contract made by the parties and all the circumstances surrounding that contract.

The reservation by the seller of the right of disposal does not necessarily leave him free to deal with the goods as he will without regard to the buyer's rights. In *Mirabita v Imperial Ottoman Bank*,[19] where goods which were subject to a seller's right of disposal were sold to a third party after the buyer had tendered payment, Bramwell LJ said:[20]

16   Sale of Goods Act 1979, s 19(1).
17   See eg, Carver *Carriage by Sea*.
18   *Hansson v Hamel and Horley Ltd* [1922] 2 AC 36, HL. The case concerned a cif contract but there is no reason why different principles should apply on this point.
19   (1878) 3 Ex D 164, CA.
20   Ibid at 169.

I think it is not necessary to inquire whether what the shipper possesses is a property, strictly so called, in the goods, or a *jus disponendi*, because I think whichever it is the result must be the same, for the following reasons. That the vendee has an interest in the specific[1] goods as soon as they are shipped is plain. By the contract they are at his risk. If lost or damaged, he must bear the loss. If specially good, and above the average quality which the seller is bound to deliver, the benefit is the vendee's. If he pays the price and the vendor receives it, not having transferred the property, nor having created any right over it in another, the property vests. It is found in this case that as far as intention went the property was to be in the [buyer] on shipment. If the [buyer] had paid, and the defendants had accepted the amount of the bill of exchange, it cannot be doubted that the property would have vested in the [buyer]. Why? Not by any delivery. None might been made; the defendants might have wrongfully withheld the bills of lading. The property would have vested by virtue of the original contract of sale. It follows that it vested on tender of the price, and that whether the vendor's right was a right of property or a *jus disponendi*; for whichever it was it was their intention that it should cease on the buyer's paying the price.

₍On the other hand the assumption that reservation of the right of disposal gives the seller merely some kind of lien must be viewed with suspicion. If this were so the value of the bill of lading as a pledge or as the basis of a documentary credit would be called into question since these transactions necessarily assume that a banker or any pledgee holding a bill of lading can, if necessary, obtain full rights of ownership over the goods in question. In *Stein, Forbes & Co v County Tailoring Co*[2] Atkin J said:

It seems quite plain that the seller or his banker reserved the *jus disponendi*. It was said that the property passed to the buyer on shipment, and the seller only received his unpaid vendor's lien. That view seems to me inconsistent with section 19 of the Sale of Goods Act 1893, and with every business probability.

---

1   It would seem that the word 'specific' here means simply 'particular' and is not
     used in a technical sense.
2   (1916) 86 LJKB 448 at 449.

Risk

The Sale of Goods Act 1979, section 20 lays down a prima facie presumption that the risk of loss of or damage to the goods passes with the property in them. Under an fob contract, however, the risk will usually pass to the buyer on shipment and this will not be affected by the fact that the property does not pass at that time, as, for example, if the seller has reserved the right of disposal. In *Stock v Inglis*[3] sugar was sold fob Hamburg and shipped with other consignments of sugar sold under other contracts. Particular bags were not appropriated to the different contracts, that is, the goods remained unascertained. Under the Sale of Goods Act 1893, section 16[4] property in unascertained goods could not pass until they had become ascertained. The ship and cargo were lost before any appropriation had been made but it was held that the buyer had an insurable interest in the sugar because it had been at his risk since shipment even though property had not passed.

Buyer or seller as shipper

It is often necessary, for various reasons, to decide whether, for some particular purpose, the buyer or the seller is to be considered as the shipper of the goods. The Hague–Visby Rules, for example, are concerned, among other things, with the rights and liabilities of shippers, not with those of buyers and sellers, and various laws and regulations impose duties on or demand payment from a shipper of goods without specifying the status of such a party in any contract of sale. Categorical statements have been made on the assumption that it is possible to decide the question from an examination of the basic elements of an fob contract and in some cases this approach may well be realistic. In an internal or home fob contract, where the seller buys fob at home in order to be able to sell fob abroad, the home seller is most unlikely to be in a position where he has to undertake any of the duties that might fall on a shipper. Where, on the other hand, the seller undertakes all the shipping arrangements it is unlikely that the buyer will be regarded as the shipper. Between these two extremes, however, it is not always easy to decide although certain guidelines exist, the chief of which is to ask whether or not the seller demands payment against the bill of lading.

---

3   (1884) 12 QBD 564, CA.
4   Now Sale of Goods Act 1979, s 16.

In *The Tromp*[5] goods sold under an fob contract were shipped by a party who undertook to indemnify the carrier for giving a clean bill of lading for goods not in good order and condition. In reply to an action by the buyer against the carrier it was argued that the party who had shipped the goods did so as agent of the buyer, since the buyer was the shipper under an fob contract. The court held, however, that the sellers were the shippers in this case (and thus the principals of the agent) largely because they had provided for payment against the presentation of the bill of lading.

Freight and bills of lading

Even though the seller is to be regarded as the shipper under a particular arrangement, it is not his duty under an fob contract to pay the freight unless the particular contract imposes this liability on him.[6] He is therefore entitled to present to the buyer bills of lading marked 'Freight Collect' instead of 'Freight Paid'. The seller in the position of shipper is bound, however, to obtain bills of lading in terms usual in the trade. In most cases this will mean obtaining a shipped bill of lading since a 'received for shipment' bill of lading will not be evidence that the seller has carried out his contractual obligation to load the goods.[7] A mate's receipt, where this is acceptable according to the terms of the contract, will normally be evidence of loading.

Administrative duties and payments

Apart from duties devolving on the parties by virtue of their contractual relations with each other and with the carrier, there is the question of payments and duties imposed by governments and other regulating bodies such as port authorities. While the purely contractual duties can often be allocated by considering the essential incidents of an fob contract and its particular terms, the allocation of this second class of duties is largely a matter of practical convenience. In *Brandt & Co v Morris & Co Ltd*[8] an order had been made by the British Government prohibiting the export without licence of the type of oil which was the subject of the parties' fob contract. The sellers applied for a licence but failed to obtain one until

5   [1921] P 337.
6   *Green v Sichel* (1860) 7 CBNS 747.
7   *Yelo v Machado & Co Ltd* [1952] 1 Lloyd's Rep 183.
8   [1917] 2 KB 784, CA.

after the expiry of the contractual delivery period. The buyers sued for non-delivery. It was held that it was the buyers' duty to obtain the licence, largely on the grounds that it was their duty to find an effective ship, which must mean a ship legally capable of taking the goods out of the country. On the other hand in *Pound & Co v Hardy & Co Inc*[9] the contract was for the sale of goods for the export of which a licence was required from the Portuguese authorities. Because of the destination of the goods, which was known to both parties to the sale, a licence was not forthcoming and the contract could not be performed. The sellers sued for breach of contract by the buyers. It was held that the obtaining of an export licence was, in the circumstances of this case, the duty of the sellers. The decision in *Brandt v Morris*, while it could be justified on its own facts, was disapproved of in so far as it purported to lay down a general rule that it was the buyer's duty under an fob contract to obtain any necessary export licence. Lord Somervell said,[10] 'This is an area in which it is impossible to lay down general rules'. The argument in *Brandt v Morris* that the buyer had to provide an effective ship was countered by the argument that it was just as true to say that the seller must provide effective goods, which must mean goods which can legally be exported. Which party is to obtain any licence will depend on a wide range of factors, including the status of the parties, their possession of the information necessary for any application for a licence and the requirements of the regulation itself. The same factors will operate when the question is of the payment of export duties or other charges.

Payment

The time, means and machinery for payment of the price by the fob buyer will invariably be laid down by the contract and will usually be the subject of a documentary credit arrangement.

FAS CONTRACTS

These have much in common with fob contracts, although they are not used so frequently. The seller fulfils his contractual obligations by delivering the goods alongside the ship nominated by the buyer at the

9   [1956] AC 588, [1956] 1 All ER 639, HL. The case was concerned with an fas contract but the distinction is not relevant to this issue.
10 Ibid at 611 and 650 respectively.

agreed port. Traditionally, 'alongside' means within reach of the lifting tackle which is to load the goods on to the ship and thus may involve the seller in the cost of taking the goods out to a ship in lighters in ports where this is the practice.

The incidents of the contract are like those of an fob contract except that the responsibility for loading and the expense of it are for the buyer. The seller will not be a party to the contract of carriage. The seller under an fas contract, as under an fob contract, may undertake additional duties, such as loading, but this will not affect the basic incidents of the contract.

Property and risk will normally pass when the goods are delivered alongside but the seller may, as in other contracts, reserve the right of disposal of the goods so that the risk alone passes on delivery and the property at a latter stage.

CIF CONTRACTS

cif and fob

Cif contracts are undoubtedly the most important of the contracts based on the carriage of the goods by sea, if not of all sale transactions. The extent to which cif contracts are preferred to fob contracts is determined by various factors. One of these is the availability of shipping and the rates of freight since these will influence a seller's willingness to deliver on cif terms.[11] A more important factor today is government control of economies. Any government concerned about its foreign exchange may bring pressure on its importers to buy fob and employ its national carriers and insurers instead of spending foreign currency reserves on carriage and insurance by foreign firms in the seller's country.[12] The same action, of course, may be taken to protect the national carrying and insurance interests.

It has been seen that at least one type of fob contract, the 'home' or 'internal' variety, need not be an export contract at all, but the cif contract is by its very nature an export transaction, since the carriage of the goods to an overseas destination is an essential feature of the contract.

11   Or his ability to do so. See *Acetylene Corpn of Great Britain v Canada Carbide Co* (1921) 6 Ll L Rep 468.
12   See eg, *Toprak Mahsulleri Ofisi v Finagrain Cie Commerciale Agricole et Financière SA* [1979] 2 Lloyd's Rep 98.

The classical judicial definition of a cif contract was given by Lord Atkinson in *Johnson v Taylor Bros*:[13]

> The vendor in the absence of any special provision to the contrary is bound by his contract to do six things.[14] First, to make out an invoice of the goods sold. Second, to ship at the port of shipment goods of the description contained in the contract. Third, to procure a contract of affreightment under which the goods will be delivered at the destination contemplated by the contract. Fourth, to arrange for an insurance upon the terms current in the trade which will be available for the benefit of the buyer. Fifthly, with all reasonable despatch to send forward and tender to the buyer these shipping documents, namely, the invoice, bill of lading and policy of assurance, delivery of which to the buyer is symbolic of delivery of the goods purchased, placing the same[15] at the buyer's risk and entitling the seller to payment of their price.

This definition assumes that when a contract is made on cif terms the seller thereafter arranges for the shipment of goods in accordance with and as a result of that contract. It is clear that this is not necessarily so. The seller may sell on cif terms goods which he has already shipped or may himself buy goods already shipped and sell them cif. In *Shipton, Anderson & Co v John Weston Co*[16] Greer J said:

> On the cif contract ... the sellers are either to ship the goods in accordance with the contract, or to allocate goods which have been shipped in accordance with the contract. I think it is clear that they may allocate goods which have been shipped by somebody else.

The point arose also in *J H Vantol Ltd v Fairclough, Dodd and Jones Ltd*[17] where it was indicated that a seller under a cif contract might not necessarily be able to plead an export ban as a reason for the impossibility of his performing his obligations since, though shipping the goods was barred, he might be able to perform by buying goods already shipped. Since the seller under an fob contract may also undertake to arrange for the carriage of the goods to the buyer and for their insurance on his behalf, it is necessary to take note of the essential difference between this

13   [1920] AC 144 at 145.
14   His Lordship in fact enumerates five things.
15   If 'same' refers to 'the goods' the position in relation to risk may not be as stated. See p 87 below.
16   (1922) 10 Ll L Rep 762 at 763.
17   [1955] 3 All ER 750, [1955] 1 WLR 1302, CA.

'fob with additional duties' contract and the cif contract. Under the latter, the agreed price includes the cost of carriage and insurance whatever they may in fact prove to be. Should freight rates or premiums rise between the making of the contract and its performance by the seller, his profit on the sale will be reduced; he cannot pass the increase on to the buyer. Conversely, of course, he may gain from a fall in freight rates and premiums. When, on the other hand, the seller under an fob contract arranges for carriage and insurance, their cost is not part of the price. They are services for which he will charge, normally as separate items on the invoice, at whatever rates he actually pays (plus commission if agreed or usual). Wright J thus expressed this feature of the cif price in *Loders and Nucoline v Bank of New Zealand*:[18]

> It is perfectly true that in the contract price there are included both cost, freight and insurance, that is to say, that the seller in consideration of that contract price has not only to provide the goods but he has to ship them at the appropriate port on a vessel under a contract of affreightment on which he is liable and also to provide the insurance; but though these are the obligations of the seller the price in fact is an indivisible price ... The seller must take the risk of what he will have to pay for freight. Whatever he has to pay, that falls on him, and it is for him to determine the total price, estimating it as well as he can.

Another vital distinction between fob and cif contracts relates to performance. In the former, the prime duty of the seller is the delivery of goods on to the ship; in the latter it is the delivery to the buyer of the requisite shipping documents. The importance of the tender of the documents in the cif contract is so great that it has been said that a cif contract is not a sale of goods but a sale of documents relating to them.[19] As will be seen, this statement cannot be accepted as completely representing the true position but it is valuable at least in so far as it emphasises the part played in the transaction by the documents.

Cif and variations

There are some contracts which, mutatis mutandis, will have the same basic nature as a cif contract and which can be regarded as variants of the

18   (1929) 33 Ll L Rep 70 at 73.
19   *Arnhold Karberg & Co v Blythe Green Jourdain & Co* [1915] 2 KB 379 at 388, per Scrutton J.

type. The contract of sale may stipulate for the inclusion in the price of the cost of carriage but leave the insurance for the account of the buyer. This is a c and f (cost and freight) contract. A contract may also be made 'Franco quay' which is like a cif contract except that the seller, for the price, agrees to pay the cost of landing the goods at the port of discharge and to pay any import duties or landing charges. Apart from these established variants it is also possible for the parties to vary the incidents of any cif contract to meet their own requirements. They may, however, vary the incidents of the contract to an extent at which it ceases to be a cif contract at all. If this is the case, the fact that the parties call their contract a cif contract will not prevent a court from holding that they have made some other kind of contract. This may be because their contract lacks some vital ingredient of a cif contract or because it contains terms repugnant to the nature of a cif contract. This is not to say that the parties' own description of their contract is entirely irrelevant to its nature. In *Comptoir d'Achat v Luis de Ridder Ltda*[20] Lord Porter said, 'The description cif must not be neglected.' Nevertheless, it is far from conclusive.

In *The Parchim*[1] the contract, which had at first sight some of the appearances of a cif contract, was described by Lord Parker.

> This, it will be seen, is not an ordinary cif contract. The insurance is separately provided for and the premium is not included in the price, and, although the price includes freight it is only the freight under the charterparty which the buyer is to take over ... As the sum included for freight in the price is a mere matter of calculation and would be payable separately by the buyer and deducted from the price, the price is really for cost only, and the contract has far more of the characteristics of a contract fob Taltal than it has of a contract cif European port.

In *Comptoir d'Achat v Luis de Ridder Ltda*[2] the contract was expressed to be a cif contract. The House of Lords refused to regard it as such since the documents involved were not those which would be required by a cif contract:

> I can see no sufficient reason for supposing either that the delivery order had some commercial value or that [the sellers' agents] undertook personal liability by their indorsement of the document.

20 [1949] AC 293 at 310, [1949] 1 All ER 269 at 275.
1   [1918] AC 157 at 164.
2   [1949] AC 293, [1949] 1 All ER 269.

There was no evidence of commercial value and the document was merely an instruction by one agent of the sellers to another ... The document appears to me to be no more than an indication that a promise already made by the sellers would be carried out in due course, but it in no way increases their obligations or adds to the security of the buyers.[3]

It is possible, nevertheless, for the parties to vary the incidents of a cif contract without transforming it into a contract of some other type, as long as the essential features of a cif contract are left undisturbed. In *Karinjee Jivanjee & Co v William Malcolm & Co*[4] a contract for the sale of sisal cif included the term 'Should the goods or any portion thereof not arrive from loss of vessel or other unavoidable cause, this contract to be void for any such portion'. It was argued that this meant that actual delivery of the goods was essential and that the contract could not therefore be treated as a cif contract. Roche J held, however, that the term was to be construed as meaning only that the sellers would not be bound to tender documents should the goods be lost before they had done so and that the term was thus a mere modification of a normal incident of a cif contract.

If what is otherwise a cif contract contains a term repugnant to the nature of a true cif contract, it does not follow that the contract will, for this reason alone, be held by the courts to be other than cif. In *Law and Bonar v British American Tobacco Co Ltd*[5] a clause in what was expressed to be a cif contract stated that the goods were to be at the seller's risk until delivery. It was held that this clause had no application to a cif contract and that since the contract in question was a cif contract the clause had to be disregarded. In effect the court was prepared to sever the repugnant term.

Whether a contract is a true cif contract or not is clearly a question that can only be answered from the facts of each case. In *Colin and Shields v Weddel & Co*[6] Singleton LJ said:

> [The contract] contains terms both in the typewritten part and in the printed part[7] which are not in accordance with [those] which one

3 Ibid at 310 and 275 respectively, per Lord Porter.
4 (1926) 25 Ll L Rep 28.
5 [1916] 2 KB 605, 85 LJKB 1714.
6 [1952] 2 All ER 337 at 340, [1952] 2 Lloyd's Rep 9 at 15.
7 Confusion about the nature of a contract often arises because the parties have modified a printed form.

CIF contracts

69

finds in an ordinary contract on cif terms. None the less, the contract is on a form which the parties describe as a cif contract. That is a matter for consideration, but one must look at the whole of the contract and its terms to discover what the obligations are.

A sale of documents?

In *Arnhold Karberg & Co v Blythe Green Jourdain & Co*[8] Scrutton J said:

> I am strongly of opinion that the key to many of the difficulties arising in a cif contract is to keep firmly in mind the cardinal distinction that a cif sale is not a sale of goods, but a sale of documents relating to goods. It is not a contract that goods shall arrive, but a contract to ship goods complying with the contract of sale, to obtain, unless the contract otherwise provides, the ordinary contract of carriage to the place of destination, and the ordinary contract of insurance of the goods on that voyage, and to tender these documents against payment of the contract price.

There is no doubt that the seller can perform his obligations under a cif contract merely by tendering the documents to the buyer. In *Biddell Bros v E Clemens Horst Co*[9] Hamilton J said:

> Such [cif] terms constitute an agreement that the delivery of the goods ... shall be delivery on board ship at the port of shipment. It follows that against tender of these documents, the bill of lading, invoice and policy of insurance, which completes delivery in accordance with that agreement, the buyer must be ready and willing to pay the price.

the significance of the tender of the documents can be deduced from the fact that a seller may validly tender documents in fulfilment of his obligations under a cif contract even though the goods have been lost at sea after shipment and both parties are aware of this fact. This was held to be so in *Manbre Saccharine Co Ltd v Corn Products Co*[10] in which McCardie J said:

> All that the buyer can call for is delivery of the customary documents. This represents the measure of the buyer's right and the extent of

8   [1915] 2 KB 379 at 388.
9   [1911] 1 KB 214 at 220.
10   [1919] 1 KB 198.

the vendor's duty. The buyer cannot refuse the documents and ask for the actual goods, nor can the vendor withhold the documents and tender the goods themselves.[11]

Such a tender after loss is not, of course, a mere formality. The transfer of the documents to the buyer will give him all the rights in respect of the goods and the associated contracts. Thus the buyer will, by virtue of the transfer to him of the bill of lading, have all rights of suit against the carrier under the contract of carriage and, by virtue of the transfer to him of the policy of insurance, will be able to claim under it for any loss covered by the policy. A further indication of the paramount importance of the documents is given by the case of *Comptoir d'Achat et de Vente du Boerenbond Belge S/A v Luis de Ridder Ltda.*[12] Grain was sold cif Antwerp and a delivery order and an invoice tendered to the buyers, who paid the price. The House of Lords held that the contract was not, in fact, a cif contract, one of the grounds being that its terms indicated that the buyers must receive the goods themselves, not merely the documents relating to them. The seller, for example, was bound to make good any deficiency between the landed weight and the weight stated in the bill of lading. In a true cif contract the tender of the documents alone should be sufficient performance.

What has been said on the point so far appears to go some way to justifying the dictum of Scrutton J that the cif contract is a sale of documents and not of goods. There are, however, factors that militate against this view. One important objection is the fact that even if the cif seller has tendered valid documents, the buyer will still have the right to reject the actual goods if they do not conform to the requirements of the contract. This could hardly be the case if the seller had already completely performed all his obligations under the contract by tendering the documents. In *Kwei Tek Chao (t/a Zung Fu Co) v British Traders and Shippers Ltd*[13] bills of lading under a cif contract were altered by forwarding agents to make it appear that goods had been shipped at the contract time when in fact they had not. The question arose as to whether the buyers, having accepted the documents in ignorance of the alteration, had any right to reject the goods themselves.

11   Ibid at 202.
12   [1949] AC 293, [1949] 1 All ER 269, HL.
13   [1954] 2 QB 459, [1954] 1 All ER 779. See also *Motis Exports Ltd v Dampskibsselskabet AF 1912 Atieselskab and Atieselskabet Dampskibsselskabet Svendborg* [2000] 1 Lloyd's Rep 211, CA where the bill of lading had been forged and therefore was not treated as a bill of lading.

Because of the alteration of the bills of lading, the tender of the documents was not a valid one but the goods, too, were not in accordance with the contract since they did not correspond with the description in respect of the date of shipment. Devlin J said:[14]

> Here, therefore, there is a right to reject documents and a right to reject goods, and the two things are quite distinct. A cif contract puts a number of obligations on the seller, some of which are in relation to the goods and some of which are in relation to the documents. So far as the goods are concerned, he must put on board at the port of shipment goods in conformity with the contract description but he must also send forward documents, and these documents must comply with the contract.

Moreover, the dictum of Scrutton J in *Arnhold Karberg & Co v Blythe Green Jourdain & Co*[15] was expressly dissented from by the Court of Appeal in the same case.[16] Bankes LJ said:

> I am not able to agree with that view of the contract, that it is a sale of documents relating to goods. I prefer to look upon it as a contract for the sale of goods to be performed by the delivery of documents.[17]

Warrington LJ said:

> [It] seems to me that it is not in accordance with the facts relating to these contracts ... The contracts are contracts for the sale and purchase of goods, but they are contracts which may be performed in [a] particular manner ... that the delivery of the goods may be effected first by placing them on board ship, and secondly by transferring to the purchaser the shipping documents.[18]

Shipment

English law in this area limits the use of the word 'shipment' to the placing of the goods on board a ship, not on any other means of transport. The question arose in *Mowbray, Robinson & Co v Rosser*[19] where the contract

---

14   Ibid at 480 and 790 respectively.
15   [1915] 2 KB 379 at 388.
16   [1916] 1 KB 495, CA.
17   Ibid at 510.
18   Ibid at 514.
19   (1922) 91 LJKB 524.

contained a final date for 'shipment'. The goods were loaded on to railway trucks before this date but not loaded on to the ship until after it. The buyers were held to be entitled to reject the goods; the Court of Appeal did not accept that the earlier loading on to trucks was 'shipment' within the meaning of this contract. This is not, of course, to say that parties might not make a contract which indicated, expressly or by implication, that shipment was to have some meaning other than that of loading on to a ship but the word by itself will presumably be given the limited meaning.

Shipment also means 'putting on board a ship' in the sense that the cif seller, like the fob seller, does not fulfil an obligation to ship within a contract period unless the goods actually are placed on board within that period. Neither does the cif seller fulfil his obligations as regards shipment if he tenders a bill of lading which does not indicate the true date of shipment.[20]

Unless the contract states or implies the contrary, the seller may, as said earlier,[1] perform his obligations not by shipping goods but by procuring and tendering documents for goods already shipped. In both cases, of course, the goods must be of the contract description. This, as in fob contracts, relates not only to the goods and their packing but also to the date of their shipment.[2] It would appear, however, that the seller cannot avoid his obligations in relation to the shipment date by inserting a clause in the contract excluding or limiting his liabilities in respect of the description of the goods. In *Aron & Co v Comptoir Wegimont*[3] goods which should, under a cif contract, have been shipped in October were in fact shipped in November. The buyer's right to reject was denied by the seller on the grounds that the contract contained a clause which stated that any difference between the goods shipped and the contract goods in respect of, among other things, description should not entitle the buyers to reject. While agreeing that the time of shipment was in one sense part of the description of the goods, McCardie J said:[4]

> The express requirement of a contract that goods shall be shipped at a particular period is a good deal more than a mere description of

---

20 *Kwei Tek Chao (t/a Zung Fu Co) v British Traders and Shippers Ltd* [1954] 2 QB 459, [1954] 1 All ER 779; *Suzuki & Co v Burgett and Newsam* (1922) 10 Ll L Rep 223, CA.

1   Page 66 above.

2   See eg, *Bowes v Shand* (1877) 2 App Cas 455, HL.

3   [1921] 3 KB 435.

4   Ibid at 441.

the goods within s 13 of the Sale of Goods Act 1893; it is an express term of the contract independent of that ... It is, I think, a condition precedent.

Appropriation

Appropriation is the act of the seller which allocates particular goods to the contract so as to bind him to deliver those goods and no others. In a cif contract it binds him to deliver the documents relating to those goods. An unconditional appropriation would, unless the parties had agreed otherwise, pass the property in the goods[5] but the appropriation in a cif contract will rarely be unconditional since the seller will, in almost every case, reserve or be deemed to reserve, the right of disposal of the goods. Further, since the property in unascertained goods cannot pass,[6] the seller cannot in any case pass the property in unascertained goods by any appropriation which does not ascertain them. If a seller has shipped goods in bulk and sold unidentified portions to different buyers, he may appropriate a portion to a particular contract but only in the sense that he is thereafter bound to satisfy his contractual obligations from the cargo of that ship and not from that in any other ship.

The point at which appropriation takes place in any particular contract will be determined by the express or implied terms of that contract or by the circumstances in which it was made or performed. In some cases the contract specifically requires the seller to send the buyer a notice of appropriation within a stipulated time. Where this is so, the seller must comply exactly with the requirements of the contract (subject to any latitude allowed by the contract) or the buyer will be entitled to reject the tender of the documents as in *Société Italo-Belge pour le Commerce et l'Industrie SA v Palm and Vegetable Oils (Malaysia) Sdn Bhd, The Post Chaser* where the contract, cif Rotterdam, required the sellers to give notice 'as soon as possible after vessel's sailing'. The sellers received notice from their own sellers but did not transmit this to the buyers for over three weeks. Robert Goff J said,[8]

> [T]he requirement of 'declaration of ship' in the present form of contract constitutes an essential step in the seller's performance of

5   Sale of Goods Act 1979, s 18, r 5.
6   Ibid, s 16.
7   [1982] 1 All ER 19, [1981] 2 Lloyd's Rep 695.
8   At 699.

his contractual obligations. It is, moreover, an important step; because once such a declaration is made, the buyer can then appropriate goods from the ship so declared in performance of his obligations to a particular sub-buyer to whom he has already agreed to sell goods of the same contractual description.

Conversely, the cif buyer must decide promptly whether to accept the notice or not. He has a reasonable time to find out whether or not a sub-buyer is willing to accept it.[9]

In *Kleinjan and Holst NV Rotterdam v Bremer Handelsgesellschaft mbH Hamburg*[10] sellers of sugar-beet pulp cif Rotterdam sent by telex the notice of appropriation required by the contract but sent the name of the wrong ship. They later purported to correct this. Cooke J said:

> [T]he provision requiring the sellers to nominate the ship in the notice of appropriation is an important term of the contract ... The duty to nominate the ship in the notice is the duty of the sellers alone and if a notice reaches the buyers which on the face of it complies with the terms of the contract, the buyers are entitled to treat it as a valid notice subject only to the provisions of the contract itself ... [T]he sellers were not entitled to amend the notice of 5 Feb 1971 by the further notice of 8 Feb and were not entitled to tender shipping documents complying with the amended rather than the original notice ... The buyers might accordingly have declined to accept the documents and pay for the goods.[11]

Where the buyer rejects the first appropriation as invalid, however, the seller may be entitled to withdraw it and make a second. In *Borrowman, Phillips & Co v Free and Hollis*[12] the seller appropriated the cargo of one ship to the contract. The buyer refused to accept this and an arbitrator held that he was entitled to do so. The seller then appropriated the cargo of a second ship. The buyer refused this appropriation on the grounds that he was not obliged to accept the second appropriation in lieu of the invalid first appropriation. This argument was not accepted by the Court of Appeal.

---

9 *Bremer Handelsgesellschaft mbH v Deutsche Conti-Handelsgellschaft mbH* [1983] 2 Lloyd's Rep 45, CA.
10 [1972] 2 Lloyd's Rep 11.
11 Ibid at 20, 21.
12 (1878) 4 QBD 500, CA.

The case may be shortly stated as follows: if [the first ship] was a proper ship, the [sellers] were entitled to tender her cargo; if she was not, they were entitled to withdraw the tender and instead of the cargo of [the first ship] to offer that of [the second ship].[13]

A seller who is in breach of a contractual duty of appropriation may be liable not only for that breach but also for a subsequent failure to deliver. In *Nova Petroleum International Establishment v Tricon Trading Ltd*[14] the sellers nominated the vessel later than was called for by the contract. The buyers did not at this stage terminate the contract but called for delivery within the contract period. The sellers then notified a different time for the arrival of the vessel and the buyers rejected this nomination since it would not allow them to satisfy their sub-buyers. The sellers were held liable in damages for the failure to deliver the goods and not merely for the failure to make a proper nomination.

It the contract does not specifically require a notice of appropriation the point at which appropriation takes place may be in doubt. In *Produce Brokers Co Ltd v Olympia Oil and Cake Co Ltd*[15] Scrutton LJ said, 'The mere shipment of the cargo does not appropriate it to the contract.' On the other hand there seems to be no reason why, in a particular case, shipment should not appropriate the goods. The question can be answered only by reference to the circumstances of each contract. A shipper on a large scale of a common commodity may have made several cif contracts for the sale of his goods and it could be completely impossible to say for which contract any particular cargo was intended on shipment. On the other hand the shipper of goods manufactured by him to the special order of the buyer might well appropriate them by shipping them.

As already noted[16] the seller may tender documents for goods which have been lost or damaged before tender. This is because, as McCardie J said in *Manbre Saccharine Co v Corn Products Co*,[17] 'The contingency of loss is within and not outside the contemplation of the parties to a cif contract.' Can the seller go further, as it were, and appropriate to a cif contract goods which he knows have already been lost or damaged? There are certain judicial indications that he can. In *Produce Brokers Co Ltd v Olympia Oil*

---

13 Ibid at 503.
14 [1989] 1 Lloyd's Rep 312.
15 [1917] 1 KB 320 at 329.
16 Page 63 above.
17 [1919] 1 KB 198 at 203.

and Cake Co Ltd[18] Scrutton LJ doubted the view of the court below in the case that the seller could not do this but it is not clear how far this doubt rested on the facts of the particular case. Assuming, however, that a seller may appropriate lost or damaged goods to a cif contract previously made, can he go further still and make a cif contract with the intention of appropriating to it goods which he knows have already been lost or damaged? The answer must rest largely on the extent to which the cif contract is a contract to deliver goods rather than documents but it appears likely that the seller may validly so make a contract in the absence of such vitiating factors as misrepresentation or fraud on his part.[19]

The documents in cif contracts

These will be the invoice, the policy of insurance and the bill of lading, representing respectively the three elements cost, insurance and freight. In some cases alternative documents may replace the two last and it is of course open to the parties to provide in their contract that other documents shall be tendered in addition.

The invoice

The invoice will debit the buyer with the agreed price of the goods and may set out the cost of carriage and insurance. Contracts frequently state that the invoice is to be in a particular form and contain particular items which the buyer may require for the purpose of complying with revenue and other laws of his own country. If such specifications are not met the buyer will be entitled to reject the documents. Whether an invoice does comply with the contractual requirements will be a matter for interpretation of the contract, which may indicate that a requirement is not essential[20] but while such a requirement might not entitle the buyer to reject the documents, it might well entitle a bank receiving tender under a documentary credit to do so.

Where no particular details are called for by the contract the invoice need only be such as to relate clearly to the contract goods; it need not describe

---

18   [1917] 1 KB 320, CA.
19   For divergent views on this point see Feltham 'The Appropriation to a Cif Contract of Goods Lost or Damaged at Sea' [1975] JBL 273 and *Benjamin's Sale of Goods* (5th edn).
20   *John Martin of London Ltd v A E Taylor & Co Ltd* [1953] 2 Lloyd's Rep 589.

them in detail. An invoice may relate to unascertained goods if, for example, the sale is of a portion of a larger cargo.

If by the contract the buyer is to pay the freight or any other item which under the contract is the responsibility of the seller, the invoice must credit the buyer with the amount he has to pay.[1]

A contract may also call for the sending of a provisional invoice to the buyer, who will usually require this so as to be able to comply with revenue and import laws of his own country. The sending of a provisional invoice is not part of the tender of documents by the seller. The nature of the provisional invoice was described by Lord Wright in *Ross T Smyth & Co Ltd v Bailey, Son & Co:*[2]

> No doubt the provisional invoice is not a tender and cannot be taken to be more than an intimation of the way in which the sellers intend to perform their contract, but it is not necessarily even that. It may be no more than an intimation of the way in which the sellers were willing, as a concession to the buyers, to perform the contract.

The bill of lading

The effect of the transfer to the buyer of the bill of lading was considered in chapter 2. The form and type of bill of lading to be used in a cif contract, as, indeed, in any contract, will be determined by the terms of that contract, including any terms to be implied into it as a result of trade usage or the previous dealings of the parties. Certain general principles will apply, however, when the contract is silent on any point.

In the first place it appears that, subject to any express or implied agreement to the contrary, the bill of lading to be tendered under a cif contract must be a shipped bill of lading. This point was stressed by McCardie J in *Diamond Alkali Export Corpn v Bourgeois.*[3]

> Lord Phillimore in reading the advice of the Privy Council[4] said, 'There can be no difference in principle between the owner, master or agent acknowledging that he has received the goods on his wharf, or allotted portion of quay, or his storehouse awaiting shipment,

1   *Ireland v Livingston* (1872) LR 5 HL 395.
2   [1940] 3 All ER 60 at 71.
3   [1921] 3 KB 443 at 452.
4   In *The Marlborough Hill v Cowan & Sons* [1921] 1 AC 444.

and his acknowledging that the goods have been actually put over the ship's rail.' With the deepest respect I venture to think that there is a profound difference between the two, both from a legal and a business point of view ... If the view of the Privy Council is carried to its logical conclusion, a mere receipt for goods at a dock warehouse for future shipment might well be called a bill of lading.

In practice it is quite common for a cif contract expressly to provide for the tender of a received for shipment bill of lading.

The bill of lading is generally required to have been issued on shipment. The effect of this requirement was explained by Lord Summer in *Hansson v Hamel and Horley Ltd*:[5]

'On shipment' is an expression of some latitude. Bills of lading are constantly signed after the loading is complete, and, in some cases, after the ship has sailed. I do not think that they thereby necessarily cease to be procured 'on shipment'.

The parties may contract on terms that the date shown in the bill of lading is to be considered as conclusive evidence of the date of shipment. In *James Finlay and Co Ltd v NV Kwik Hoo Tong Handel Maatschaffig*[6] the final date for shipment of goods under a cif contract was 30 September. In fact they were shipped on 1 October. The contract contained a term that 'The bill or bills of lading shall be conclusive evidence of the date of shipment.' The buyers resold the goods to sub-buyers on the same terms but when the sub-buyers discovered the true date of shipment they repudiated the sub-sale. It was held that the buyer was not bound, instead of proceeding against the seller, to proceed against the sub-buyers for failure to accept, on the strength of the 'conclusive evidence' clause. The buyer was entitled to consider commercial morality and his business reputation.

Since the seller is responsible for the payment of freight, the bill of lading tendered should be stamped 'Freight Paid'. In *Soproma SpA v Marine and Animal By-Products Corpn*[7] arbitrators had found 'It is common practice in the trade for bills of lading to be marked "Freight Collect" under a c and f contract, and this is regarded as a good tender provided sellers

---

5   [1922] 2 AC 36 at 47.
6   [1929] 1 KB 400, CA.
7   [1966] 1 Lloyd's Rep 367.

either deduct freight from the invoice or tender a freight receipt.' McNair J commented on this finding:[8]

> If this finding means more than that it commonly happens that buyers do not take the objection that a bill of lading in this form is not a valid tender if either the freight is deducted from the price in the invoice or a receipt for freight is tendered, it would ... be a finding which could not be sustainable in law since on the hypothesis stated the documents would be mutually inconsistent.

The bill of lading must show that the goods are to be carried to the agreed destination port and, if the parties have so contracted, by the agreed route. In *Shipton, Anderson & Co v John Weston & Co*[9] a bill of lading giving the carrier very wide liberties to deviate was held to be an invalid tender.

In general terms the bill of lading must be 'valid and effective'. This is not the case where the bill of lading is not transferable on its face, as when, for example, it is marked 'Not negotiable'. Neither is it effective when it is one of a set and another of the set has already been used by a holder to obtain the goods from the carrier.[10] A bill of lading is also not effective if the contract it represents is for any reason void. In *Arnhold Karberg & Co v Blythe Greene Jourdain & Co*[11] goods were sold cif Naples and shipped on a German ship. Though both seller and buyer were British the contract of carriage became void for illegality on the outbreak of war in 1914. The tender of the bill of lading was therefore not valid and effective. As already stated, a bill of lading is still valid and effective although the goods which it represents have been lost after shipment.[12]

The bill of lading must be clean and should not contain forgeries or untrue statements or have been materially altered. In *Kwei Tek Chao (t/a Zung Fu Co) v British Traders and Shippers*[13] the dates on bills of lading were fraudulently altered to give the impression that goods had been shipped within the contract period when they had in fact been shipped later. On the effect of such alterations it was said:[14] 'I think the true view is that we must examine the nature of the alteration and see whether it goes to the whole or

8   Ibid at 387.
9   (1922) 10 Ll L Rep 762.
10 *Glyn, Mills Currie & Co v East and West India Dock Co* (1882) 7 App Cas 591, HL.
11 [1916] 1 KB 495.
12 Page 70 above and cf *Re Weis & Co* [1916] 1 KB 346.
13 [1954] 2 QB 459, [1954] 1 All ER 779.
14 Ibid at 476, per Devlin J.

to the essence of the instrument or not.' Since the holder of a bill of lading is very likely to need to transfer it, the fact that there is an alteration on the face of it may be more important than the nature of the alteration. As Phillimore J said:[15] '[The recipient] is probably dealing largely on borrowed money, and he is possibly buying to sell again. In either case he requires not only documents that would satisfy him but documents which he can compel others to take as being satisfactory.'

In *Procter & Gamble Philippines Manufacturing Corpn v Kurt A Becher GmbH & Co KG*[16] a bill of lading tendered under a cif contract had been wrongly dated. The goods had, however, been shipped within the contract period. The Court of Appeal held that the buyer would have been entitled to reject the documents had he known of the incorrect date, but since he had not, he was entitled to sue for damages only and in fact had suffered no loss.

Even if a bill of lading meets all the requirements outlined above, it does not follow that its tender will be necessarily valid under a cif contract. The purpose of the transfer to the buyer of the bill of lading is to give him not only the property rights in the goods but also all rights under the contract of carriage during the whole time that the goods are at his risk during sea transit. This is usually expressed by saying that the bill of lading tendered must give the buyer 'continuous documentary cover'. A bill of lading which for any reason does not do this will not be a valid tender. In *Hansson v Hamel and Horley Ltd*[17] goods sold cif Yokohama by a Norwegian seller could not be carried directly to Japan from the Norwegian ports of shipment and were therefore taken by one ship to Hamburg where they were transhipped into another vessel for the rest of the voyage. A bill of lading was issued in Hamburg which purported to cover the entire transit. Thirteen days had elapsed between the shipment of the goods at the Norwegian ports and the issue of this bill of lading. The House of Lords, upholding the Court of Appeal, held that the tender of this bill of lading was not valid under a cif contract.

> I am quite sure that, under the circumstances of this case, this ocean bill of lading does not satisfy these conditions. It bears notice of its insufficiency and ambiguity on its face; for though called a through bill of lading, it is not really so. It is the contract of the subsequent

15 *Re Salomon & Co and Naudszus* (1899) 81 LT 325 at 329.
16 [1988] 2 Lloyd's Rep 21, CA.
17 [1922] 2 AC 36, HL.

CIF contracts

carrier only ... [and] the buyer was plainly left with a considerable *lacuna* in the documentary cover to which the contract entitled him.[18]

Substitutes for bills of lading

The parties to a cif contract frequently agree that some other document, such as a delivery order, shall replace the bill of lading. This is necessary when the sale is of an unidentified portion of a consignment covered by a single bill of lading.[19] It is clear that such a substitution may be valid. In *Comptoir d'Achat et de Vente du Boerenbond Belge S/A v Luis de Ridder Ltda* it was said:[20]

> The strict form of a cif contract may, however, be modified: a provision that a delivery order may be substituted for a bill of lading or a certificate of insurance for a policy would not, I think, make the contract concluded upon something other than cif terms but in deciding whether it comes within that category or not all the permutations and combinations of provision and circumstances must be taken into consideration.[1]

There are thus questions. The first, discussed earlier,[2] is whether the documents are such as to prevent the contract from being considered as a cif contract at all. The second is, assuming that the contract is a cif contract, whether the documents represent a valid tender under it. In *Ginzberg v Barrow Haematite Steel Co Ltd and Mckellar*[3] the buyer was anxious to receive the goods. Since it was likely that the bills of lading would not be available until after the ship had arrived, the seller, as agreed, sent a delivery order addressed to the ship's agents with instructions to deliver the goods to the buyers.

McNair J said:[4]

> As it seems to me, the true inference from the facts and the documents in the present case is that the [sellers] intended merely to expedite

---

18   Ibid at 46.
19   See eg, *Cremer v General Carriers SA* [1974] 1 All ER 1, [1974] 1 WLR 341.
20   [1949] AC 293, [1949] 1 All ER 269, HL.
1   Ibid at 309 and 275 respectively, per Lord Porter.
2   Page 68 above.
3   [1966] 1 Lloyd's Rep 343.
4   Ibid at 353.

the delivery for the benefit of the [buyers] ... without in any way departing from the fundamental principles of their cif contract the implementation of which would safeguard them against losing the property in the goods until payment was made.

The policy of insurance

The basic rule in cif contracts is that the seller must tender a valid policy of insurance on the goods to the buyer. In many respects the requirements are similar to those in connection with the tender of the bill of lading and the differences tend to arise because of the peculiar features of each document.

The Sale of Goods Act 1979, section 32(3) demands that where goods are sent by sea the seller should notify the buyer in sufficient time to allow the buyer to take out insurance on the goods. It has been held that this provision does not apply to a cif contract because of its special nature.[5] In general, the contract itself, by its express terms or by implication of trade usage, will lay down the type of policy to be tendered. Subject to this, the following points arise for consideration. In the first place, the seller need not take out the policy expressly for the benefit of the buyer. It is sufficient that it may be assigned to the buyer on tender. The seller will normally wish to cover himself against the risk of loss of or damage to the goods while they are at his risk, which will usually be during the period before shipment. The policy must therefore be capable of being transferred to any other party at whose risk the goods are, or will be, by a simple note of the transfer on the policy itself. If the policy were not assignable in this way the buyer would not easily be able to transfer it should he resell the goods to which it relates. This difficulty does not usually arise with policies themselves, since they are almost invariably assignable, but it may well do so if some document other than a policy is tendered. In respect of such a document it was said in *Diamond Alkali Export Corpn v Bourgeois*:[6]

> Thirdly, I point out that before the buyer could sue at all he would have to show that he was the assignee of the certificate ... In what way can he become the assignee? ... The relevant statutory provision ... says, 'A marine policy may be assigned by endorsement thereon

5   Eg *Law and Bonar v British American Tobacco Co Ltd* [1916] 2 KB 605, 85 LJKB 1714.
6   [1921] 3 KB 443 at 456, per McCardie J.

CIF contracts

or in other customary manner.' This subsection only applies, so far as I can see, to that which is an actual marine policy.

Like the bill of lading the policy tendered must be valid and effective. A policy may be invalid for various reasons. It will, for example, be invalid if the insurer is entitled to avoid it because of misrepresentations made to him or material facts withheld from him before the contract of insurance was made or because of any breach of a warranty after it was made. If, however, the insurer has waived, or is deemed to have waived, any such right to avoid the contract,[7] the tender of the policy will be valid. If a policy is illegal it will not be a valid tender even though it may be the established practice of insurers to honour that type of illegal policy. Of such a policy it was said:

> These two policies are not such as the seller could have tendered to the buyer in discharge of his obligation to insure, nor do they come within the category of policies which are intended to be attached to the documents under a cif (sic) contract. The transaction is the plaintiff's private speculation.[8]

A policy may be effective, and thus a valid tender, even though it does not cover a loss which has actually occurred. If the contract demands a particular form of cover and the seller tenders a policy giving that cover, the tender will be valid although the buyer will not be able to claim on it because the loss has been caused by some peril which the policy did not cover. Thus in *Groom Ltd v Barber*[9] goods were sold cif London on terms which provided for insurance not including war risks. The sale contract also expressly provided that war risks were for the buyer's account. War broke out after shipment and the goods were lost. The buyer declined to accept the policy. It was held that the policy was normal and valid and that the contract term on war risks did not mean that the seller was to insure against war risks and charge the buyer. The buyer was accordingly bound to accept the policy even though it in fact gave him no indemnity for the loss.

Like the bill of lading, the policy tendered must cover the contract goods and no others for the reason given by McCardie J in *Manbre Saccharine Co v Corn Products Co*:[10]

---

7 As in *Cantiere Meccanico Brindisino v Janson* [1912] 3 KB 452, CA.
8 *Strass v Spillers and Bakers* [1911] 2 KB 759 at 773, per Hamilton J.
9 [1915] 1 KB 316.
10 [1919] 1 KB 198 at 204.

Even if the [sellers] had tendered the policies actually held by them I should still have held the tender bad, for they were policies which covered a quantity of goods outside those mentioned in the bills of lading and invoices sent to the [buyers]. In my opinion a purchaser under a cif contract is entitled to demand, as a matter of law, a policy of insurance which covers and covers only the goods mentioned in the bills of lading and invoices ... Unless the purchaser gets a policy limited to his own interest he would become one only of those who are interested in the insurance; and he is entitled in my view, to refuse to occupy a position which may give rise to obvious complications.

The insurance policy must give the buyer the same continuous documentary cover as is required in respect of the bill of lading. In practice, it will usually do so, since the almost invariable custom is to employ a policy containing what is called a 'Warehouse to Warehouse' or 'Transit' clause, which gives protection during the whole of the transit. Even if there appears to be an interruption in the period of cover, it may be that the cover is in fact maintained. In *Belgian Grain and Produce Co v Cox & Co (France) Ltd*[11] peas sold cif Marseilles from Japan were carried on different stages by three different ships. Tender of the policy was refused on the grounds that it covered the goods only in the first two ships. The policy contained, however, a clause extending cover to all situations caused by the carrier's taking advantage of any liberty afforded him by the contract of carriage. As the contract of carriage permitted transhipment of the goods, the policy was in operation throughout the transit.

The policy must be of a type 'usual' or 'current' in the trade. What is usual or current will always be a question of fact, as in *Borthwick v Bank of New Zealand*[12] where the question was as to the usual terms on which frozen meat was insured in the New Zealand meat trade and in *Yuill & Co v Scott-Robson*[13] as to the terms on which live cattle were usually insured. The case of *Groom Ltd v Barber*[14] raised the question of the time at which the terms had to be 'usual'. Did the phrase imply that the policy had to be usual at the time when the contract of sale was made or at the time when the policy of insurance was tendered to the buyer? Atkin J decided that the first interpretation was the correct one. This, however, leaves open the

11 [1919] WN 308, CA.
12 (1900) 6 Com Cas 1.
13 [1908] 1 KB 270, CA.
14 [1915] 1 KB 316.

question of whether the terms must be usual when the policy of insurance is effected.

The extent of the cover given by the policy must, of course, be in accordance with any express requirement in the sale contract.[15]

The policy should cover the goods for their value and include the value of the freight. The value of the goods will be a question of fact.[16]

Substitutes for policies

There will be cases where a seller cannot tender an insurance policy, as, for example, when he has a single policy covering a wide range of shipments. In such a case the contract may expressly provide for some other document to be tendered in place of a policy. Unless the contract does so provide, English law demands the tender of a policy. In *Diamond Alkali Export Corpn v Bourgeois*[17] the seller tendered a certificate of insurance from the insurance company for the shipment. This referred to the policy and purported to give all the rights available under the policy itself. McCardie J held that it was not a good tender. Not only did it not have the recognised and necessary qualities of a policy but it did not state the terms of the policy to which it referred. 'In all the cases a "policy of insurance" is mentioned as an essential document. The law is settled and established.' He went on to say, however, 'It may well be also that the greater part of the difficulties indicated in this judgment can be easily, promptly and effectively met by the insertion of appropriate clauses in cif contracts'.[18]

If another document is, by express agreement, substituted for a policy it must comply with the requirements of the contract and it does not follow that a buyer will be bound by a term in the policy which does not appear in the substituted document. In *Koskas v Standard Marine Insurance*[19] the policy contained a clause making it necessary for the policyholder to give certain notice to the insurer of any loss. The certificate actually tendered purported to contain all the terms in the policy but made no mention of this term. It was held that the buyer was entitled to make a claim under the

15 *Oranje Ltd v Sargant & Sons* (1924) 20 Ll L Rep 329.
16 *Loders and Nucoline v Bank of New Zealand* (1929) 33 Ll L Rep 70.
17 [1921] 3 KB 443.
18 Ibid at 454.
19 (1927) 32 Com Cas 160, CA.

policy although he had not given the stipulated notice. Significantly, Scrutton LJ said in this case, 'The result in this case is, I think, a justification of the rule of English law that a certificate of insurance cannot be tendered as a policy of insurance to satisfy a cif contract.'[20]

'It is possible that the validity of a tender of some document other than a policy may be proved by reference to a trade usage, as opposed to an express term of the contract, but the onus of proof of the existence of such a usage will be very heavy.'[1]

Nevertheless, a substitute for a policy is clearly possible. Indeed, trade would, in modern conditions, be impossible if it were not, but there is no doubt that the courts regard substitutes with a highly critical eye.

Other documents

While the documents so far considered are the essential ones for a valid tender under a cif contract, the contract may require the seller to tender additional ones. Any such documents must conform to the contract specifications or the buyer will be entitled to reject the tender.

One document frequently required by the terms of cif contracts is a certificate of quality. This is usually a signed statement by a person or body, frequently named by the contract, certifying that the goods are of the quality specified by the contract. Frequently the contract will make the certificate conclusive evidence of the quality of the goods.

The effect of a term that a certificate of quality is to be conclusive was well illustrated in *Berger & Co Inc v Gill & Duffus SA*.[2] A contract for the sale of 500 tonnes of beans cif Le Havre contained terms that payment was to be made on first presentation of shipping documents and that a certificate of quality to be issued at the port of discharge was to be conclusive. When the goods reached Le Havre 445 of the 500 tonnes were unloaded; the rest were overcarried to Rotterdam. The sellers presented the documents but the buyers rejected them on the grounds of the absence of the certificate. The sellers then re-presented the documents with a certificate of quality in respect of the 445 tonnes actually arrived but the buyers rejected this. When the balance of the cargo reached Le Havre the buyers

---

20   Ibid at 163.
1   *Wilson, Holgate & Co Ltd v Belgian Grain and Produce Co Ltd* [1920] 2 KB 1.
2   [1984] AC 382, HL.

contended that they were entitled to reject the goods for various reasons including the fact that the certificate of quality related only to the 445 tonnes first unloaded. The House of Lords held that the buyers were wrong to have rejected the certificate. Lord Diplock[3] referred to

> the delay and expense aris[ing] from the refusal of the buyers to comply with and the failure of some of the arbitration and judicial authorities to recognise the obligation, freely negotiated and included in the contract between the parties in the interests of speed, certainty and economy to accept as final the certificate of the expert chosen by the parties ...

A clause as to the conclusiveness of a certificate of quality will not necessarily apply to the condition of goods as opposed to their quality.

In *Cremer v General Carriers SA*[4] a cif contract stated that goods were to be shipped in good condition and stipulated also for a maximum 14% moisture in the goods. It also stated, 'Shipped quality and analysis to be final as per certificate issued by [a named firm]'. Certificates were issued which showed the moisture content of two samples to be 12.77% and 13.24%. The cargo arrived in bad condition because of its excessive moisture content. Kerr J said:

> Generally speaking, if a contract contains distinct provisions relating respectively to quality and to condition, then the parties will be taken to have intended to draw a distinction between these two characteristics. This is so in the present case, with the added factor that the provision relating to quality also contains a conclusive evidence provision by stipulating that a certificate as to quality is to be final. It must therefore be construed restrictively so that full effect must be given to the incorporation of [the clause] which provides distinctly and expressly that shipment is to be made in good condition.[5]

Another document commonly stipulated for is a certificate of origin, which may be required by the buyer either for reasons connected with revenue and import regulations in his own country or to indicate that the consignment is not from a country against which his government is, for example, operating a trade boycott.

---

3   At 388.
4   [1974] 1 All ER 1, [1974] 1 WLR 341.
5   Ibid at 14.

In order to avoid unnecessary difficulties arising from defects in or omissions of documents it is not uncommon to stipulate in the sale contract that if any document is missing or is in apparent contradiction of the contract or contains errors or omissions, the buyer must nevertheless take up the documents on condition that the seller guarantees performance in accordance with the contract. Any such clause will be strictly construed by the courts.[6]

The tender of the documents

The general rule is that the seller under a cif contract must tender the shipping documents to the buyer 'as soon as possible'.[7] This point had been amplified by Brett MR in *Sanders Bros v Maclean & Co*[8] when he said:

> [I]t is obvious the reasonable thing is that [the seller] should make every reasonable exertion to send forward the bill of lading as soon as possible after he has destined the cargo to the particular vendee or consignee. If that be so, the question of whether he has used such reasonable exertion will depend upon the particular circumstances of each case.

If the contract expresses or implies any time limit for tender, the buyer is entitled to reject the documents if they are not tendered within this limit. In *Alfred C Toepfer v Lenersan-Poortman NV*[9] a cif contract stipulated, 'Payment: net cash against documents ... on arrival of the vessel at port of discharge but not later than 20 days after bill of lading.' Bills of lading were issued on 11 December 1974. The documents were tendered in February 1975 but were rejected by the buyers as being out of time. It was held that they were entitled to do so in view of the express clause. The terms of a documentary credit may also lay down a time limit for the presentation of the shipping documents to the bank through which the seller is to be paid.

Under the terms of a cif contract which establishes such a credit, tender of the documents will be required to be made not to the buyer but to the bank

---

6   *SIAT di del Ferro v Tradax Overseas SA* [1980] 1 Lloyd's Rep 53, CA.
7   *Landauer & Co v Craven and Speeding Bros* [1912] 2 KB 94 at 105, per Scrutton J.
8   (1883) 11 QBD 327 at 337.
9   (1978) 122 Sol Jo 417.

CIF contracts

with whom the buyer has arranged for payment to be made to the seller on presentation of valid documents. In such a case, if the tender to the bank is not a good one and the bank refuses to accept the documents, the seller cannot afterwards make a valid tender direct to the buyer. 'Assuming that a letter of credit has been opened by the buyer ... could the seller at his option disregard the contractual letter of credit and present the documents direct to the buyer? As it seems to me, the answer must plainly be in the negative.'[10]

This is not to say that a valid second tender of documents may never be made after an earlier and invalid one. The decision of the Court of Appeal in *Borrowman, Phillips & Co v Free and Hollis*,[11] that a seller could make a second and valid appropriation, would clearly apply to a tender of documents as long, of course, as the second tender was made within any time limit prescribed by the contract and was made to the party prescribed.

The passing of property

The passing of property under a cif contract depends on two things: the general law of the sale of goods and the intentions of the parties as expressed or implied in their contract or manifested in their performance of it. As far as the general law is concerned, property in specific or ascertained goods will pass when the parties intend it to pass.[12] In fact contracts for the sale of specific goods will rarely be made on cif terms. Where there is a sale of unascertained goods the property does not pass until the goods are ascertained. In *Re Wait*[13] the seller bought 1,000 tons of wheat and resold 500 tons to the buyers, who paid the price without receiving any documents. The sellers became bankrupt and the wheat was claimed by the trustee in bankruptcy. The sellers alleged their ownership but since their consignment was an unidentified portion of a bulk it was clearly neither specific nor ascertained goods and the Court of Appeal held that property had thus not passed to the buyers. The buyers' argument that they had acquired an equitable title was also rejected.

Assuming, then, that goods are specific or ascertained, at what stage in the transaction may the property pass? In *Stein, Forbes & Co v County*

10   *Soproma SpA v Marine and Animal By-Products Corpn* [1966] 1 Lloyd's Rep 367 at 386, per McNair J.
11   (1878) 4 QBD 500, p 68 above.
12   Sale of Goods Act 1979, s 17.
13   [1927] 1 Ch 606.

Tailoring Co[14] Atkin J said: 'It seems to me impossible to lay down a general rule applicable to all cif contracts. The overruling question is, "Does the intention of the parties appear in the making and the fulfilment of the contract?" ' Lord Sumner too, in *The Kronprinsessan Margareta*,[15] said, 'The passing of property being a question of intention is ultimately a question of fact.' In spite of these statements there are indications that not all judges would accept that there was no established point at which property passes under a cif contract.

There are, for example, dicta to the effect that property may pass on shipment of the goods. In *Comptoir d'Achat et de Vente du Boerenbond Belge S/A v Luis de Ridder Ltda*[16] Lord Porter said, '[The] property may pass either on shipment or on tender' and in *Biddell Bros v E Clemens Horst* Kennedy LJ said[17] in the Court of Appeal:

> The vendor tenders the bill of lading, with the insurance policy and the other shipping documents ... to the purchaser, to whom from the moment of shipment the property has passed and at whose risk, covered by insurance, the goods were at the time of the loss.

Earlier, he had expressed this idea more fully. After saying that there were two legal results arising out of the shipment he went on to say:

> [T]he property in the goods has passed to the purchaser, either conditionally or unconditionally. It passes conditionally where the bill of lading is made out in favour of the vendor or his agent or representative ... It passes conditionally where the bill of lading is made out in favour of the purchaser or his agent or representative as consignee.

Two elements appear to form the basis of this view: the passing of risk and the form of the bill of lading. As the above dicta indicate, the rationale behind the view that property passes on shipment appears to be the fact that the risk passes to the buyer at that point. This is not necessarily an inversion of the rule that risk passes with property. The view is not that property must pass with risk but that since risk passes with property and risk passes on shipment then property must have passed on shipment since otherwise the risk could not have passed. All the indications are,

14   (1916) 86 LJKB 448 at 449.
15   [1921] 1 AC 486 at 511.
16   [1949] AC 293, [1949] 1 All ER 269.
17   [1911] 1 KB 934 at 959 in a dissenting judgment approved by the House of Lords in the same case.

however, that the view that property passes on shipment under a cif contract is of very doubtful validity. In deciding if it does, the question of whether the bill of lading is taken out by the seller to his own order or to the order of the buyer is clearly of some importance. In *The Kronprinsessan Margareta* Lord Sumner said,[18] 'Again, importance attaches to the fact that the shippers, having loaded the coffee on to a general ship ... took the bills of lading to the consignee's order.' He thought, however, that the retention by the seller of the bill of lading was inconsistent with an intention to pass the property in the goods to the buyer.

The position appears to be that since the time of the passing of the property is a matter for the intention of the parties, it may be possible to infer that they intended the property to pass on shipment and that in making this inference the fact that the bill of lading was made out in the buyer's name or that the seller did not retain the bill of lading will be of importance.

The main argument against the view that property passes with shipment is a practical one. If the property passes to the buyer on shipment what right, other than an unpaid seller's lien, does the seller retain so as to be able to enforce payment? More important, how can the seller finance the transaction if the document which he wishes to use as security cannot serve to give ownership? Lord Wright stated the point clearly in *Ross T Smyth & Co ltd v Bailey, Son & Co*[19]

> The general course of international commerce involves the practice of raising money on the documents so as to bridge the period between shipment and the time of obtaining payment against documents. These credit facilities, which are of the first importance, would be completely unsettled if the incidence of the property were made a matter of doubt.

He went on:

> The whole system of commercial credits depends on the seller's ability to give a charge on the goods and the policies of insurance. A mere unpaid seller's lien would, for obvious reasons, be inadequate and unsatisfactory.

Lord Wright was in that case dealing with a suggestion that the property in the goods passed to the buyer on the appropriation of the goods to the contract by the seller, but the objection is clearly equally applicable to the

18   [1921] 1 AC 486 at 512.
19   [1940] 3 All ER 60 at 68.

suggestion that property passes on shipment. On the question of appropriation he said:

> The notice of appropriation under an ordinary cif contract is not intended to pass, and does not pass, the property. Where, as here, the sale is of unascertained goods by description, there are, at that stage, no goods to which the contract can attach. The seller is free to appropriate to the contract any goods which answer the contract description. This he does by the notice of appropriation which specifies and defines the goods to which the contract attaches. Those thereupon he is bound to deliver and the buyer is bound to accept, subject to the terms of the contract. That, however, does not involve the passing of property.

The argument that the property passes to the buyer on appropriation is based on the provisions of the Sale of Goods Act 1979, section 18, rule 5, that where there is a sale of unascertained goods the property passes when the goods are 'unconditionally appropriated' to the contract by the seller with the buyer's consent.[20] But in the first place the seller under a cif contract will usually make it clear that the property is not to pass until payment and that any appropriation before that will, therefore, not be unconditional and, in the second place, the property in the goods, assuming them to be ascertained, will pass when the parties intend it to pass[1] and their intentions, or, at any rate, the seller's intentions, will almost invariably indicate that the property is to pass at some time other than the time of the appropriation. The appropriation would therefore appear to have little significance in the passing of the property.

In fact the most usual, and certainly the most practical point for the passing of property under a cif contract will be on the tender of the documents to the buyer, against which, by a usual express term, the buyer will be required to pay the price. As Lord Porter said in *The Glenroy (No 2)*,[2] 'It is in terms [a cif] contract and therefore in the normal case the property would not pass until the documents were taken up and paid for.'

But although it is most usual for property to pass on tender of the documents to the buyer, it does not follow that this occurs automatically. Even if the seller hands over the documents to the buyer he may either expressly or by implication reserve the right of disposal of the goods. In

---

20   This consent is normally implied. See eg, *Pignataro v Gilroy* [1919] 1 KB 459.
1   Sale of Goods Act 1979, s 17.
2   [1945] AC 124 at 135.

other words, the intention of the parties remains the true criterion for deciding when the property passes and whether the documents are tendered or retained is only one fact which may help indicate that intention. Roskill LJ said in *Cheetham & Co Ltd v Thornham Spinning Co Ltd*[3] that the question of the passing of the property turned

> not upon the dealing, or rather the absence of dealing, with the shipping documents as such, but upon the question whether the [sellers], by that which they did, divested themselves of their title to what by this time had become specific and ascertained goods. The question of the retention of the bill of lading is, I think, relevant only as showing the intention of the parties at the time.

In *Ginzberg v Barrow Haematite Steel Co Ltd and Mckellar*[4] the sellers sent delivery orders to the buyers because the bills of lading would be delayed and the buyers were anxious to obtain the goods. The buyers actually obtained the goods but it was held that they had not obtained the property in them. McNair J said:[5]

> The true inference from the facts and the documents in the present case is that the [sellers] intended merely to expedite the delivery for the benefit of the [buyers] ... without in any way departing from the fundamental principles of their cif contract the implementation of which would safeguard them against losing the property in the goods until payment was made.

It is no doubt significant that he was also prepared in this case to take into account, as an indication of the sellers' intentions, evidence of their practice of not selling on credit.

Thus if payment has not been made the property will not pass, even though the buyer has actually obtained the goods, if the seller has effectively reserved the right of disposal.[6] Conversely, even though the buyer has paid the price on tender to him of the documents the property in the goods cannot pass if the goods are still unascertained at this time; if, for example, as in *Re Wait*,[7] they are an unidentified portion of a bulk. In

---

3   [1964] 2 Lloyd's Rep 17 at 22.
4   [1966] 1 Lloyd's Rep 343.
5   Ibid at 353.
6   *Ginzberg v Barrow Haematite Steel Co Ltd and Mckellar* [1966] 1 Lloyd's Rep 343; *Cheetham & Co v Thornham Spinning Co Ltd* [1964] 2 Lloyd's Rep 17.
7   [1927] 1 Ch 606, CA.

such a case the property in the goods cannot pass to the buyer until the goods are ascertained which would probably not be before delivery.

Moreover, even if the goods are ascertained and the buyer has received the documents and paid the price, he retains the right to reject the goods if they do not conform to the specifications of the contract and if he exercises this right the property will revest in the seller. In *Kwei Tek Chao (t/a Zung Fu Co) v British Traders and Shippers Ltd*[8] the buyers paid the price against the tender of documents and then discovered that the goods did not conform to the contract. The question arose as to their right to reject, since they had placed the goods in a warehouse and pledged the documents relating to them to a bank. Devlin J suggested[9] that the true view was that:

> what the buyer obtains, when the title under the documents is given to him, is the property in the goods, subject to the condition that they revest if upon examination he finds them to be not in accordance with the contract. That means he gets only conditional property in the goods, the condition being a condition subsequent. All his dealings with the documents are dealings only with that conditional property in the goods ... If the property passes conditionally the only ownership left in the seller is the reversionary interest in the property in the event of the condition subsequent operating to restore it to him.

The implication is thus clearly that any transfer of property under a cif contract, no matter at what point it is deemed to have taken place, must be regarded as conditional until such time as the buyer, expressly or by implication of conduct, clearly and unambiguously accepts the actual goods.

Risk

In most sales of goods the risk will pass with the property in accordance with the Sale of Goods Act 1979, section 20. In cif contracts, however, risk will almost always pass on shipment, irrespective of the time at which the property passes. In *Biddell Bros v E Clemens Horst Co*[10] Kennedy LJ said:

8   [1954] 2 QB 459, [1954] 1 All ER 779.
9   Ibid at 487.
10   [1911] 1 KB 934 at 937.

Two further legal results arise out of shipment. [One is that] the goods are at the risk of the purchaser, against which he has protected himself by the stipulation in his cif contract that the vendor shall, at his own cost, provide him with a proper policy of marine insurance intended to protect the buyer's interest, and available for his use if the goods should be lost in transit.

Where the seller fulfils his obligations under a cif contract by tendering to the buyer documents for goods already afloat when the contract was made, the risk will be regarded as being with the buyer as from shipment.

As already noted,[11] the fact that a loss that occurs is not covered by the insurance policy tendered will not affect the passing of the risk to the buyer unless the contract called for a policy that covered the loss. Since the principle that the risk, under a cif contract, is with the buyer after shipment of the goods, it may be that an express clause in the contract of sale placing the risk during transit on the seller will be at variance with the true nature of a cif contract. In *Law and Bonar v British American Tobacco Co Ltd*[12] the court regarded as repugnant to a cif contract a clause that the goods were to be at the seller's risk until delivery. It is, however, quite usual to find a clause to the effect that a cif contract is to be regarded as void with regard to any portion of the cargo that fails to arrive. While in one sense this clause will mean that any loss will fall on the seller the clause is not regarded as being at variance with the general principle.

Payment

Subject to any agreement to the contrary, the buyer will usually be bound to pay the cif price when a valid tender of the shipping documents is made to him and, as has been seen,[13] he will not be absolved from his duty to pay even though the goods have ceased to exist. Cif contracts frequently employ the phrase 'cash against documents' or a similar expression, but even if no such phrase is expressly employed the presumption that the buyer must pay on tender of the documents is a very strong one and is unlikely to be rebutted by any but the most cogent evidence of an intention to the contrary. It will, of course, be rebutted by an express provision in the contract. One which is in normal use is the stipulation that the contract

11   Page 84 above.
12   [1916] 2 KB 605.
13   Page 70 above.

is to be void if the goods, or any part of them, fail to arrive because the vessel has been lost. In such a case the seller is not bound to tender the documents nor the buyer to pay against them.[14]

All charges due after the arrival of the goods as the port of discharge specified in the contract are, unless the contract or trade or port usage provides otherwise, for the buyer's account. In consequence there is an implied obligation on the buyer to reimburse a seller who pays these charges.[15]

The vast majority of cif contracts made today will establish a documentary credit as the method of payment and will ensure that the seller receives payment of the price on tender of valid shipping documents to a specified bank.

ARRIVAL (EX-SHIP) CONTRACTS

Under the terms of this contract the seller delivers the goods to the buyer from the ship at the agreed port of arrival. The seller's obligations under the contract were indicated by Lord Sumner in *Yangtsze Insurance Association v Lukmanjee*.[16]

> In the case of a sale 'ex-ship', the seller has to cause delivery to be made to the buyer from a ship which has arrived at the port of delivery and has reached a place therein which is usual for the delivery of goods of the kind in question. The seller has therefore to pay the freight, or otherwise release the shipowner's lien and to furnish the buyer with an effectual direction to the ship to deliver. Until this is done, the buyer is not bound to pay for the goods.

The contract is thus of a nature very different from that of the cif contract. The seller is primarily obliged to deliver goods and does not fulfil his obligations by tendering documents. As Lord Sumner also said, 'Again, the mere documents do not take the place of the goods under such a contract. They are not the subject matter of the sale.' In practice the seller may, as Lord Sumner's dictum states, have to provide the buyer with a delivery order or some such document which will enable him to obtain possession of the goods, but the provision of such a document is merely

14   *Karinjee Jivanjee & Co v William Malcolm & Co* (1926) 25 Ll L Rep 28.
15   *American Commerce Co Ltd v Frederick Boehm Ltd* (1919) 35 TLR 224.
16   [1918] AC 585 at 589.

Arrival (ex-ship) contracts

incidental to the seller's primary duty to deliver the actual goods and is not in any way comparable to his duty to deliver shipping documents under a cif contract.

Since the goods are at the seller's risk until delivery – another marked distinction from the cif contract – there is no obligation on him to take out an insurance policy for the benefit of the buyer. In the *Yangtsze Insurance* case,[17] delivery of timber under an ex-ship contract was properly made into the sea alongside the ship where it was consolidated into rafts for taking ashore. During this process it was lost because of bad weather. The buyer claimed the benefit of the insurance policy which the seller had taken out. The Privy Council refused to accept the policy inured from the benefit of the buyer. Insurance for the buyer's benefit was not called for by this type of contract and the policy had been intended to cover the seller's interest only.

The contract may stipulate a particular ship from which the goods are to be delivered and, if so, the buyer will be entitled to reject the delivery of goods from another ship, since such goods will not correspond with the contract description. If the contract stipulates a period during which the ship is to arrive, the buyer will similarly be entitled to reject any tender of the goods from a ship arriving outside this period. On the other hand, in *Neill v Whitworth*[18] the contract stipulated 'Goods to be taken from the quay'. No particular ship was specified in the contract but the sellers later declared two ships from which delivery was to be made. One of these ships stranded and the goods were taken to their destination by rail. Since there was no time limit for delivery and no naming of a particular ship in the contract itself, it was held that the buyers were not entitled to refuse delivery.

Some authorites[19] prefer to draw a distinction between ex-ship and ex-quay contracts. Under this classification the contract described above is known as an ex-quay contract and the ex-ship contract is one that obliges the buyer to pay any landing charges.

FREE DELIVERED

This contract may also be described as 'Delivered Duty Paid' or 'Franco Domicile'. The seller is obliged to pay all charges and expenses up to the

---

17   Ibid.
18   (1865) 18 CBNS 435.
19   Eg the International Chamber of Commerce.

actual delivery of the goods to the buyer's place of business or other agreed point in the buyer's country. Since the goods are at the seller's risk throughout, any insurance he effects will be for his own benefit only.

Chapter 4

Carriage by air and land and sale contracts based thereon

THE INTERNATIONAL CONVENTIONS

International carriage of goods by air and land is governed in the United Kingdom almost entirely by international conventions. Air carriage (including the carriage of passengers and their baggage) is governed by the Warsaw Conventions of 1929 and 1955, both of which now have legal effect by virtue of the Carriage by Air Act 1961 as amended. Road carriage is governed by the Convention on International Carriage of Goods by Road 1956 (CMR), given legal effect by the Carriage of Goods by Road Act 1965 and rail carriage by the International Transport Conventions Act 1983 giving effect to the Convention on International Carriage of Goods by Rail 1970 (CIM).

Most questions of law arising in these areas turn on the interpretation and applicability of the provisions of the various conventions. Not surprisingly, there was an earlier tendency on the part of the courts to take the same approach to this matter as they would have done in the case of an ordinary English statute. The more modern approach to the interpretation of international conventions was indicated in *Fothergill v Monarch Airlines*.[1] The Warsaw Conventions on carriage by air provide that a complainant must, within a specified time, give notice in writing of 'damage' to goods or baggage if he is to be able to maintain an action against the carrier in respect of that damage. The plaintiff noticed and reported damage to his suitcase but did not discover a loss of some of its contents until the specified time had elapsed. He argued, however, that the Convention

---

1   [1981] AC 251, [1980] 2 All ER 696, HL; reversing [1980] QB 23, [1979] 3 All ER 445, CA.

restricted the time for giving notice of 'damage' but said nothing about 'loss'. The majority in the Court of Appeal (Lord Denning MR dissenting) took the view that 'damage' must be construed in its ordinary sense which could not include 'loss'. The House of Lords reversed this decision, taking into account, among other things, the differences between drafting practices in statutes and those in conventions, which may have several authoritative versions in different languages. The literal approach might be suitable for statutes 'but here we are concerned with construing an Act which gives effect to, and actually incorporates, an international convention and for that purpose a strictly literal construction is not appropriate.'[2]

Their Lordships considered it proper, therefore, to consider *travaux préparatoires* and to consult the other language texts of the Convention in order to discover and effect its purpose.[3]

CARRIAGE BY AIR

The amount of cargo carried by air is very small when compared with the vast bulks carried by sea, but is none the less significant. Air carriage is used for small or light consignments when speed of transit is desirable and air cargoes tend to be more varied and more valuable than sea cargoes.[4]

Unfortunately there is no single system of rules for the carriage of goods by air since any one of three possible sets of rules may apply, depending on the positions of the states in which carriage begins and ends in relation to the two Warsaw Conventions.

The original Warsaw Convention 1929 was amended in 1955 and the amended Convention was given legal effect in the United Kingdom by the Carriage by Air Act 1961. But because many states, including the USA, which were parties to the original Convention did not accede to the amended Convention, the Carriage by Air Act 1961, while it repealed the Act which gave effect to the original Convention, nevertheless left the provisions of the original Convention standing to apply in certain cases. Thus either the original or the amended Convention may apply to a contract for the carriage of goods by air. On 28 May 1999, a new Convention to

2   Ibid at 709, per Lord Fraser.
3   On this approach to international conventions see also dictum of Lord Macmillan in *Stag Line Ltd v Foscolo, Mango & Co Ltd* [1932] AC 328 at 350, p 12, above.
4   A very high proportion of reported cases on air carriage of goods concern the carriage – or miscarriage – of gold or jewels.

replace the Warsaw Convention and its many protocols and amendments was signed in Montreal, Canada. The Montreal Convention for the Unification of Certain Rules for International Carriage by Air will be ratified by the UK and the EU. The Convention will come into force once 30 countries have deposited their instruments for ratification. However, presently, the provisions of the Warsaw Convention and the amended Warsaw Convention are still relevant. Further, in some cases neither Warsaw Convention will apply. In such cases English law applies the so-called 'Non-international Carriage Rules'. This term is a misnomer, since 'non-international' merely means 'not international as defined by the Warsaw Conventions' and is more accurately referred to as 'Non-Convention' carriage.

The Warsaw Convention 1929

Application

This Convention, which will be referred to as the 'original' Convention, applies in two situations. It applies when the departure and destination points set out in the contract of carriage are in the territories of two states which are both parties to the original Convention but are not both parties to the amended Convention. It applies also when the contractual departure and destination points are both within the territory of a single state which is a party to the original Convention and not a party to the amended Convention if the contract of carriage designates any stopping place outside the territory of this state. Which states and territories are parties to either Convention is laid down, for the purposes of actions heard in English courts, by various Carriage by Air (Parties to Conventions) Orders. The Convention does not apply to trial flights made with a view to establishing regular lines or to any carriage performed in extraordinary circumstances and outside the scope of the carrier's normal business.[5]

The Convention governs the carrier's liability while the goods are in his charge, whether at an airport or not. It does not extend to any other form of carriage performed incidentally and outside an airport, but if any such carriage is performed for loading, delivery or transhipment purposes, any damage is presumed, subject to proof to the contrary, to have occurred during air carriage.[6]

5   Art 34.
6   Art 18.

The air way-bill

This document is in fact referred to in the original Convention as an 'Air Consignment Note', but the more modern term 'Air Way-bill' is generally used. In contracts made under the Convention the carrier may require the consignor to make out and hand over an air way-bill and the consignor may require the carrier to accept it.[7] Separate air way-bills may be required for separate packages.[8]

The air-way-bill, unlike the bill of lading, is not a document of title. The absence of an air way-bill will not affect the validity of the contract or the application of the Convention but it may prevent the carrier from enjoying the benefit of various exclusions and limitations of liability given by the Convention.[9] The speed of air carriage means that the cargo usually arrives before the consignor could send the consignee the air way-bill so that it cannot play the part in air carriage that the bill of lading plays in contracts for carriage by sea.[10]

Article 8 of the Convention lays down various items that must appear on the air way-bill. Among the more important of these are the nature of the goods, the method of packing and marks or numbers on them; the weight, quantity and volume or dimensions of the goods; the apparent condition of the goods and their packing and a statement that the carriage is subject to the Convention's rules on the liability of the carrier. The acceptance by the carrier of goods without an air way-bill, or with one that omits certain of the required items, results in his being unable to avail himself of the provisions of the Convention which limit or exclude his liability.[11] In consequence of this rule there have been various cases where consignors and others have alleged the absence or inadequacy of these items. Earlier cases showed a tendency on the part of the courts to apply the rules strictly. In *Westminster Bank v Imperial Airways*[12] It was held that the statement in the air way-bill as to the application of the Convention must be explicit and that a vague paraphrase would not suffice. The statement that the carriage was 'based upon' the Convention was unsatisfactory and the carrier accordingly lost the benefit of the provision limiting his liability.

7   Art 5.
8   Art 7.
9   Arts 5(2) and 9.
10   See art 13.
11   Art 9.
12   [1936] 2 All ER 890.

On the other hand, in the later case of *Seth v British Overseas Airways Corpn*,[13] where a cargo of gold on which no declaration of value had been made was lost in transit from London to Zurich, the air way-bill was of a type used by the carrier for both Convention and non-Convention carriage and stated that the carriage was subject to the Convention if it was international carriage. The cargo owners alleged that this was not sufficiently explicit to comply with the requirement. The Court of Appeal held otherwise. Lord Denning MR said:[14]

> Any other result would lead to great inconvenience. It is very desirable that the air transport companies should be able to use one way-bill to fit both international carriage and also non-international carriage. The reason is because it may be beyond the wit of any clerk to know in some cases whether the carriage is international or non-international carriage. If you look at the definition of 'international carriage' in the Convention you will see that it is a most complex definition.

This less formal approach, which takes into account the realities of business, characterises the more recent decisions in this area.[15]

The consignor is responsible for the accuracy of those particulars relating to the goods which he inserts in the air way-bill and is liable for any damage caused by omission or inaccuracy.[16]

The air way-bill is prima facie evidence of the conclusion of the contract of carriage and of its conditions and also of the weight dimensions and packing of the goods and of the number of packages, but statements of quantity and volume are not evidence against the carrier unless they have been checked in his presence and the air way-bill states this, or, in the case of the condition, unless it refers to apparent condition.[17]

The right of disposal

The consignor has a general right to dispose of goods while they are in transit by withdrawing them, stopping them en route or by requiring the carrier to return them to the departure airport or to deliver them to a party

13   Cited at [1966] 1 Lloyd's Rep 323.
14   Ibid at 326.
15   See eg, *Corocraft Ltd v Pan American Airways Inc* [1969] 1 QB 616.
16   Art 10.
17   Art 11.

other than the original consignee at the destination or at an intermediate point. The consignor must pay any expenses incurred by his exercise of this right and cannot exercise it in such a way as to prejudice the carrier or other consignors.[18]

The carrier's liability

The carrier is liable for all loss of or damage to goods in his charge and for damage occasioned by delay unless he proves that he or his agents have taken all necessary measures to avoid the damage or that it was impossible for him or them to take such measures.[19] The effect of the phrase 'all necessary measures' was discussed in *Grein v Imperial Airways Ltd*[20] in which Greer LJ said, 'The effect of this is to put upon [the carriers] the obligation of disproving negligence, leaving them liable for damages for negligence if they fail to disprove it.'

There is a special provision that the carrier is not liable if he proves that damage was caused by negligent pilotage or negligence in the handling of the aircraft or in navigation, provided that in other respects all necessary measures were taken to avoid the damage.[1]

The owner of goods may sue the carrier even though he is not the consignee. In *Gatewhite Ltd v Iberia Lineas Aereas de España SA*[2] the plaintiff brought an action in respect of a cargo of flowers which had perished through delays on the part of the carriers. The consignee was the plaintiff's customs clearing agent and the defendants argued that the plaintiff had no standing in the case. The commercial court held that the plaintiff could sue in his own name. The Convention does not exclude the owner's right to do so and it would be impracticable and unjust to make the owner's recovery of damages depend on the willingness or ability of another party to bring an action against the carrier.

Successive carriers

The carrier with whom the consignor contracts (the 'contracting carrier') may sub-contract the whole or parts of the carriage to other carriers, with

18   Art 12.
19   Arts 19, 20.
20   [1937] 1 KB 50 at 57.
1   This provision, which appears to be modelled on art IV(2)(a) of the Hague Rules, is not present in the amended Convention.
2   [1990] 1 QB 326, [1989] 1 Lloyd's Rep 160.

whom the consignor would normally have no contractual relationship. The Convention therefore lays down that, where a carriage contract is performed by successive carriers, each carrier is deemed to be a contracting party in respect of that part of the carriage for which he is responsible.[3] In this position he is known as the 'actual carrier'. The consignor will have rights of action against the first carrier and against the actual carrier performing when the damage occurred. The consignee will have rights of action against the last carrier and the actual carrier. The contracting carrier remains liable throughout. (The contracting carrier is not necessarily the first or an actual carrier, since he may have sub-contracted all carriage.) All the carriers have the protection of the Convention.

Limitation of liability

The carrier's liability in respect of loss of or damage to the goods or delay in delivery is limited to a maximum of 17 SDRs (Special Drawing Rights) per kilogram or the value declared by the shipper for which any supplementary charge has been paid. The conversion of SDRs into sterling on a particular day is effected by obtaining a certificate relating to the converted sterling value. Any provision in the contract reducing or excluding this liability is void, but this will not affect the validity of the contract or the application to it of the Convention.[4]

The carrier will not be entitled to avail himself of the provisions limiting or excluding his liability if he has caused, or his servants or agents acting in the scope of their employment have caused, the relevant damage by wilful misconduct.[5] The meaning of 'wilful misconduct' was considered in *Horabin v British Overseas Airways Corpn*, in which Barry J said:[6]

> To be guilty of wilful misconduct the person concerned must appreciate that he is acting wrongfully, or is wrongfully omitting to act, and yet persists in so acting or omitting to act regardless of the consequences, or acts or omits to act with reckless indifference as to what the results may be.

3   This rule was formulated by the Guadalajara Convention 1961 and given legal effect by the Carriage by Air (Supplementary Provisions) Act 1962.
4   Art 23.
5   Art 25.
6   [1952] 2 All ER 1016 at 1022.

Carriage by air

He held, moreover, that a series of comparatively minor defaults could not be taken in the aggregate to amount to wilful misconduct. Each act had to be considered by itself.

Limitation of action

Where goods have suffered damage the consignee or other party concerned must give the carrier written notice of it within seven days of his receipt of the goods. If this is done, no action will lie against the carrier unless he has been fraudulent.[7] For the purposes of this rule 'damage' must be taken to include loss.[8]

All rights of action are extinguished unless action is brought within two years of the date of arrival of the goods, the date when the goods should have arrived or the date when the carriage terminated.[9]

The Warsaw Convention 1955

This Convention, referred to as the 'amended' Convention, applies when the departure and destination points set out in the contract of carriage are in the territories of two states which are both parties to the amended Convention and also when both departure and destination points are within the territory of a single state which is a party to the amended Convention if the contract designates any stopping place outside the territory of that state. Flights outside the normal course of the carrier's business are within this Convention but are exempt from some of the provisions relating to air way-bills.

The major points on which the amended Convention differs from the original Convention are set out below.

The air way-bill

The required particulars are much fewer. The air way-bill need contain only the departure and destination points, an indication of any stopping point if this would bring the contract within the Convention and a notice

---

7   Art 26.
8   Carriage by Air Act 1961, s 4A. See also *Fothergill v Monarch Airlines* [1981] AC 251, [1980] 2 All ER 696, HL.
9   Art 28.

warning the consignor that the carrier's liability may be limited if the Convention applies.[10]

The carrier's liability

This is identical with that under the original Convention except that the defence of negligent pilotage or negligence in the handling or navigation of the aircraft is not available to the carrier and that he may by contract provide that he is not to be liable for damage to cargo caused by inherent vice or the nature of the cargo.[11]

Limitation of liability

The levels of limitation are identical but the inability of the carrier to avail himself of them rests not on 'wilful misconduct' but on 'intention to cause damage or to cause damage recklessly and with knowledge that damage would probably result'.[12]

A servant or agent of the carrier may claim the benefit of the limitation clause on the same terms.[13]

Limitation of action

The consignee has fourteen days (as opposed to seven under the original Convention) in which to give written notice to the carrier of loss of or damage to the goods.[14]

Non-convention carriage rules

These Rules are applied, under English law, to contracts for international carriage when neither of the Conventions applies. In essence they are as for the amended Convention except that there is no requirement for an air way-bill and the limitation of the carrier's liability is expressed in SDRs.

10   Art 8.
11   Art 23(2).
12   Art 25. Also, see *Antwerp United Diamonds BVBA and the Excess Insurance Co Ltd v Air Europe* [1995] 2 Lloyd's Rep 224, CA for a consideration of wilful misconduct.
13   Art 25A.
14   Art 26.

IATA conditions

The International Air Transport Association, which has a wide membership among air carriers, produces a standard form carriage contract. This cannot, of course, conflict with the Conventions where these apply, but produces a large measure of uniformity in contracts. These conditions also effectively apply the provisions of the Conventions to non-Convention carriage.

The Montreal Convention 1999

Many of the provisions of the Montreal Convention are the same as those for the amended Warsaw Convention. However, some provisions do make changes, for example, to the relationship between the actual carriers and contracting carriers; the use of the carriers domicile instead of the 'ordinary resident' provision; any dispute arising from the contract of carriage should be resolved by arbitration if the parties agree; and the liability of the carrier for damages providing the event causing the damage took place during the carriage by air.

SALE CONTRACTS BASED ON CARRIAGE BY AIR

There are certain similarities between sea and air carriage contracts in that both are based on a distinctive form of transport only available between special departure and arrival points. Seller and buyer will have their own road access and possibly their own railway sidings, but they are unlikely to own sea or air ports. In consequence, the goods will almost invariably have to be taken to and from the special loading and discharge points by other means of transport and their loading or discharge at these points will be significant stages in the performance of the contract. It is not surprising, therefore, that sale contracts in which the parties envisage the carriage of the goods by air are modelled on the established forms of contract that envisage carriage by sea. Sale contracts 'Ex-works' or 'Free Delivered' can obviously be made in the same way whatever mode of transport is envisaged, but it is quite common to sell goods on such terms as 'fob Hamburg Airport' or 'cif air London'. The analogy must not be taken too far. As one authority has pointed out:[15]

> Despite some superficial similarities, airborne trade markedly differs
> from seaborne commerce in operational speed, geographical span,

15   Pal 'Air Trade Terms' [1973] JBL 9 at 10.

freight rate structure, inter-line co-ordination, loading, stowing and packaging techniques, appropriation of goods to the contract and their checking in transit, carrier's risk and liability, the role of telecommunication, documentary requirements, the degree and scope of standardisation, the methods of export insurance and export finance and in several other technical, economic and procedural facets.

In particular, the fact that an air way-bill is not a document of title, when considered with the speed of air transit, means that a 'cif air' contract does not have, and is extremely unlikely to develop, those qualities which distinguish the cif contract proper, such as its essential documentary nature. Nor, in practice, does it need to, since goods of a type likely to be the subject of sale and resale during transit, particularly commodities, are unlikely to be carried by air.

CARRIAGE BY LAND: ROAD

The CMR Convention 1956

Because Britain is an island carriage by road plays a far smaller part in international trade than carriage by sea or air. Nevertheless, the development of methods whereby loaded lorries can be driven on to ferries for a short sea transit and driven off at the arrival port has increased the importance of international road transport. The law in this area is governed by the Carriage of Goods by Road Act 1965, which incorporates the CMR Convention 1956.[16]

Application

The Convention applies to contracts for carriage by road when the place of taking over goods and the designated place of delivery are in different countries, at least one of which is a party to the Convention.[17] It does not, by virtue of a special exception, apply to carriage between the United Kingdom and the Republic of Ireland. It applies during any period during which the road vehicle with the goods on it is carried by air, sea or inland

16 Signed at Geneva and named from its French title: 'Convention relative au contrat de transport international de Marchandises par Route'.
17 Art 1.

waterway. If it can be proved that any loss, damage or delay was not the responsibility of the road carrier but was due to default in the other mode of transport, then the liability of the road carrier is determined in accordance with the provisions of any convention appropriate to that mode of transport. This includes those cases where the road carrier is also the carrier by the other mode.[18]

The consignment note

This is made out in three copies. The sender retains the first, the second accompanies the goods and the carrier retains the third. It must contain various particulars as to the goods and the transit. The sender is liable for expense, loss and damage caused by the inadequacy or inaccuracy of the information which he supplies. If the note does not contain the required statement that the carriage is subject to the Convention, the carrier will be liable for any loss or damage caused by the omission.[1]

The consignment note is prima facie evidence of the making of the contract and of its conditions and of the receipt of the goods by the carrier. Subject to proof to the contrary, it is presumed that goods were in apparent good condition when the carrier took them over and that the number of packages and their marks and numbers corresponded with the statements in the note. This presumption will not be made in respect of defects as to which the carrier makes a special reservation in the consignment note.[2]

The consignment note is not a document of title. The consignee is entitled to demand the goods and the second copy of the consignment note from the carrier in exchange for a receipt. The Convention provides, however, that a consignee is entitled to sue in his own name in respect of any loss, damage or delay for which the carrier may be liable.

Right of disposal

The consignor has the right to dispose of the goods by asking the carrier to stop them in transit, change the place at which delivery is to be made or deliver them to a consignee other than the one designated in the consignment note. This right ceases once the consignee receives the

18   Art 2.
1   Art 7.
2   Cf the 'clausing' of a bill of lading.

consignment note from the carrier or demands it from him against a receipt. The consignor will be responsible for loss or expense occasioned by his exercise of this right, which must not interfere with the carrier's operations or prejudice other senders or consignees. The right may not be exercised in respect of part only of a consignment.

Successive carriers

Each successive road carrier under a single contract for international road carriage is responsible for the whole operation and each is a party to the contract of carriage. An action in respect of loss of or damage to the goods may be brought against the first carrier, the last carrier or the carrier actually performing when the loss or damage occurred. There are provisions for apportionment of damages between carriers and for their liability in the case of the insolvency of one of them.

The relative status of successive carriers was considered in *ITT Schaub-Lorenz Vertriebsgesellschaft mbH v Birkart Johann Internationale Spedition GmbH & Co KG*[3] which concerned carriage involving several carriers, the final one of whom was not a CMR carrier, since the section of transit for which he was responsible and during which the goods were lost was entirely within the UK. Bingham J said:[4]

> Where there are successive CMR carriers, a CMR carrier successfully sued by the sender or consignee can recover against a CMR carrier responsible for the loss or damage, but that carrier cannot escape liability by showing that he has delegated or sub-contracted performance to a non-CMR carrier who was actually responsible. By art 34 a successor CMR carrier makes himself responsible for the whole operation and he remains responsible for a non-CMR carrier or delegate under art 3.

The carrier's liability

The carrier is liable for loss of or damage to the goods, including loss caused by delay, but not if this is caused by the claimant himself or by inherent vice of the goods or by circumstances which the carrier could not avoid and the consequences of which he was unable to prevent. In

3   [1988] 1 Lloyd's Rep 487.
4   At 493.

GL Cicatello SrL v Anglo European Shipping Services Ltd[5] goods were being transported from Ayr to Salerno when they were stolen by armed robbers between Rome and Naples. The owners alleged that because there was no security device on the vehicle the carrier could not rely on article 17(2). It was held that nothing could have been done to prevent the robbery; therefore, the carrier was not liable The burden of proof that the loss or damage was so caused is on the carrier. In *Michael Galley Footwear Ltd v Iaboni*[6] a lorry carrying shoes from Milan to the UK was left on an unguarded car park while the driver and his assistant went for a meal. Thieves bypassed the alarm system and stole the lorry and its load. The carrier was liable since he could not show that the loss would still have occurred had the driver and assistant taken turns to guard the vehicle.

There are specific defences to the general liability, including the insufficiency of marks on the goods.[7]

Limitation of liability

The carrier's liability is limited to 8.33 SDRs per kilogram of gross weight unless a higher value is declared and a surcharge paid. In addition, the carrier is liable to refund 'carriage charges, customs duties and other charges incurred in respect of the carriage of the goods'. In *James Buchanan & Co Ltd v Babco Forwarding and Shipping (UK) Ltd*[8] it was held that 'other charges' covered excise duty payable by the consignor because the carrier's negligence had led to the theft in the UK of whisky destined for export and in *ICI plc and ICI France SA v MAT Transport Ltd*[9] that it covered a fee for a survey of damaged goods.

The limitation will not be available to a carrier who causes loss or damage by wilful misconduct.[10]

Limitation of action

To maintain an action against the carrier in respect of loss of or damage to the goods, the consignee must give notice or 'reservations' to the carrier

5   [1994] 1 Lloyd's Rep 678.
6   [1982] 2 All ER 200.
7   Arts 17, 18.
8   [1978] AC 141, [1977] 3 All ER 1048.
9   [1987] 1 Lloyd's Rep 354.
10 See *Lacey's Footwear (Wholesale) Ltd Bowler International Freight Ltd* [1997] 2 Lloyd's Rep 369 for the Court of Appeal's discussion of this provision.

at the time of delivery in the cases of apparent loss or damage, within seven days of delivery if it is not apparent and within twenty-one days in the case of loss caused by delay.

The period of limitation of action is normally one year but will be three years if the loss or damage was caused by the wilful misconduct of the carrier.

SALE CONTRACTS BASED ON ROAD CARRIAGE

The chief advantage of road carriage is that it permits door-to-door transport by a single vehicle and contracts envisaging such transport are usually made on Ex-works or Free Delivered or similar terms. In international road carriage, however, a significant point is a national boundary and contracts are frequently made on the terms 'Free Delivered Frontier', the frontier in question being that of the seller's country. Property and risk will pass at this point. There are no special terms implied as to insurance.

CARRIAGE BY LAND: RAIL

The CIM Convention 1970

The carriage of goods by rail has played a very small part in the international trade of the United Kingdom, although rail carriage is frequently used for the carriage to ports of goods to be shipped. However, with the introduction of the Channel Tunnel, the international carriage of goods by rail may play a more significant role. Where the actual rail carriage is international it is governed by the CIM Convention.[11] This has effect in the United Kingdom by virtue of the International Transport Conventions Act 1983. In 1999, the Protocol for the Modification of the Convention Concerning International Carriage by Rail (COTIF) was agreed to by the Intergovernmental Organisation for International Carriage by Rail (OTIF). The Protocol amends and updates some of the current provisions of the Convention. The amended Convention does not come into force until two-thirds of the existing member states of OTIF have ratified the amended Protocol. Reaching the number required is not expected to happen

---

11   Convention Internationale concernant le transport de Marchandises par chemin de fer.

before 2004. The existing Convention will therefore be referred to when looking at carriage by rail.

The Convention applies to the carriage of goods under a through consignment note for carriage over the territories of at least two contracting states on railway lines designated as international.

The transport document is a consignment note. The requirements for the contents of this note are very comprehensive and the procedures connected with it are complex. It is not a document of title.

The rail carrier's liability in respect of the goods is general, but does not extend to loss, damage or delay caused by the wrongful act of the claimant, the inherent vice of the goods or circumstances which the carrier could not avoid and the consequences of which he was unable to prevent. The burden of proof that the loss or damage was attributable to these causes is on the carrier. There are also specific causes of loss or damage for which the carrier will not be liable if he establishes that the loss or damage was attributable to one or more of them, but it is open to a claimant to show that the loss or damage was not so attributable.

There is an overall limitation on the carrier's liability of 17 units of account per kilogram of gross mass short and the refund of carriage charges and other amounts incurred in connection with the goods except in cases of the carrier's wilful misconduct or gross negligence.

The limitation period for actions against the carrier is one year except in specified cases, such as those involving fraud or wilful misconduct by the carrier, when the limitation period is two years.

SALE CONTRACTS BASED ON RAIL CARRIAGE

There are established forms of sale contract assuming that the goods are to be carried by rail, which are not necessarily international contracts. They may be used when through rail transit to the buyer is intended but are used also when the initial stage only of the carriage is to be by rail.

Free on rail (FOR)

This contract is as for the Ex-works contract but the seller bears the additional responsibility for the delivery of the goods into the charge of a railway carrier and pays all the expenses up to this point, including the cost of packing the goods in any particular manner required for rail carriage. All risk and expense after delivery of the goods to the rail carrier are for the buyer's account.

Free on truck (FOT)

This contract is like the 'for' contract except that the seller is additionally responsible for the expense of loading the goods on to the rolling stock.

Chapter 5
Combined transport

GENERAL

The object of this book thus far has been to describe the nature and the legal incidents of the established overseas sale contracts and to show how they are inevitably shaped by the mode of transport which the parties envisage for the goods. (The only exceptions are the Ex-works and the Free Delivered contracts which, since they are based respectively on delivery at the seller's and at the buyer's places of business, do not necessarily imply carriage by any particular mode.) The established contracts assume one contract for carriage by one mode of transport; other modes will be involved but will be incidental only and will not affect the basic contract. Thus, when a sale of goods is made on cif terms, the seller will obviously, in most cases, have to make a contract of carriage in order to get the goods to the docks for shipment but this will be a matter for the seller alone and the terms of the contract that he makes for this purpose and the mode of transport that he employs will be irrelevant to any considerations of the cif contract, which is firmly based solely on the carriage of the goods by sea. Thus under this, and the other established contracts so far considered, there will be, in addition to the main contract, further and separate contracts concerned with the movement of goods over those sections of the transit not covered by the main contract.

It is, however, more convenient in practice to arrange from the outset for one contract of carriage which will cover the entire transit of the goods from seller to buyer. An exporter may, for example, make a single contract with a forwarding agent, or freight forwarder, who will arrange for all carriage by carriers employing various modes of transport. In such a case the forwarding agent may well be himself the first carrier.

The development of such combined transport agreements has been accelerated by the developments in modern carriage methods, notably the development of container transport. The packing, or 'stuffing' of a cargo or different cargoes into a single modular box which can form a single lorry load, railway wagon load or standard unit of shipping or aircraft space obviously increases the speed of transit, reduces handling costs and gives increased protection to the goods transported since it can be transferred from one mode of transport to the other in a single operation. There are other methods of 'consolidation' of cargo. Goods are frequently collected into loads on pallets so that they can be moved as a single unit by a forklift truck. Goods may be stowed in a lighter which can be towed out to a ship and lifted, lighter, goods and all, and stowed as a unit in the ship (Lighter Aboard Ship or LASH). Another development in this area is the Roll On-Roll Off system (RO-RO) by which a road vehicle and its load (which may be, but is not necessarily, a container) is driven on to a ferry vessel without being unloaded and is driven off again to continue its journey by road when the ferry arrives at its destination. There is a similar system in operation with train ferries.

All these methods lend themselves to the 'Through' or 'Combined' transport of goods. The exporter may deliver goods to a combined transport operator at an inland depot and make a single contract for their carriage to the buyer. The goods can then be stowed in a container of suitable type, possibly with other consignments from other exporters and be treated as a single unit until arrival at the eventual destination, all carriage arrangements being made by the combined transport operator.

While this system clearly has many practical advantages, it also presents many legal problems.[1] The present law on the carriage of goods, as has been seen, is based on the separation of the different modes of transport. The various international conventions are, in general, adapted to the peculiar features of the modes to which they apply and lay down different bases for and limitations of the liabilities of the carriers in the event of loss of or damage to the goods. Yet it may be impossible, if goods have throughout the transit been sealed in a container, to discover at what point any loss or damage occurred and hence under which convention liability should be determined.

There are also problems involving the documentation; a bill of lading will usually be a negotiable document of title; other documents, including

---

1   It presents other problems, of course, since it requires heavy capital investment and has its own expenses, but these are beyond the scope of this book.

those issued by a combined transport operator, are not necessarily in this category. There are problems in respect of contractual relationships: under a contract for the carriage of goods by sea the relationship of shipper and carrier is established and reasonably clear, but this is not necessarily the case as regards the contractual relationship between, sea, an exporter who has delivered goods to a combined transport operator and a road carrier who, under the arrangements made by the combined transport operator, is carrying the goods from the port of discharge to the buyer's warehouse. Finally, there is the problem of the application of modern methods to the established overseas sale contracts. Can, for instance, an fob seller perform his obligation under that contract by employing the services of a combined transport operator? Can a sea carrier stow any goods on deck if they are in a container and his ship is specially designed to take containers on deck? Can a sale contract involving combined transport be arranged, like a cif contract, to turn on the tender of documents by the seller?

There are, so far, more problems than solutions, not least because an established pattern of commerce, on which alone satisfactory legal solutions can be based, will obviously take time to emerge. Two factors, however, may be recognised. One is the need for an accepted international code on combined transport. The other is the development of sale contracts distinguished from the established ones so far considered in that they are based on the use of combined transport methods.

THE PROBLEMS OF COMBINED TRANSPORT

Documents

An exporter who delivers goods to a combined transport operator will receive a document acknowledging receipt of the goods. To a large extent the legal nature of this document will depend on the position of the operator who issues it.

If the operator is not a sea carrier or an agent (such as a loading broker) for a sea carrier, the document which he issues will not be a bill of lading, although it is frequently called a 'house' bill of lading. Consequently it will not be a document of title. This raises several problems. Such a document may not be good tender under a cif contract since it cannot, by mere transfer, pass the property in goods. Further, while the parties to a cif contract are of course free to stipulate that other documents may be substituted for a bill of lading, it will be recollected that the courts tend to take a strict view of this matter[2] and it is conceivable that in certain circumstances they might refuse to regard as a cif contract one which envisaged the tender of a document which gave no title to the buyer. Again, a document which is not capable of giving its holder rights of ownership to the goods to which it relates is obviously of less value as a security than is a document of title. Nevertheless, as a matter of practical commerce, banks do accept combined transport documents under documentary credit arrangements if the credit stipulates for this.

Even if the combined transport operator is himself a sea carrier or the agent for one, many problems remain. Such an operator can obviously issue a bill of lading but, particularly as many container depots are well inland, it can only be a 'received for shipment' bill of lading and not a 'shipped' one. It will thus be no evidence of the shipment of the goods, since 'shipment' will usually be taken to mean 'placed on board a ship' unless the parties have otherwise agreed.[3] Neither will it indicate the date of shipment. A shipped bill of lading is normally required for an fob contract[4] and for a cif contract although there is an increasing tendency for the contracts to provide for the tender of a received for shipment bill of lading.[5] It is true that the Hague–Visby Rules make provision for the conversion of a 'received for shipment' bill of lading into a shipped one by the carrier or his agent noting on it the ship on which the relevant goods have been shipped together with the date of shipment[6] but such notation appears to be rare in practice.

The goods handed by an exporter to a combined transport operator for carriage may be insufficient to form a full container load (FCL) in which case they will be referred to as a 'light' container load (LCL) and be stowed in a container with consignments from other exporters intended for the same destination. In this case, even if the combined transport operator is a sea carrier or the agent for a sea carrier he may not be able to issue a bill of lading for the particular consignment since the container and not parts of its contents will be 'the goods' throughout the transit. Any document issued in respect of such a consignment will clearly be of the nature of a delivery order and, as has been seen, the tender of such a document will

2   Page 78, above.
3   *Mowbray, Robinson & Co v Rosser* (1922) 91 LJKB 524, p 72 above.
4   *Yelo v SM Machado & Co Ltd* [1952] 1 Lloyd's Rep 183, p 63 above.
5   *Diamond Alkali Export Corpn v Bourgeois* [1921] 3 KB 443, p 78 above.
6   Carriage of Goods by Sea Act 1971, Sch, art III(7).

not necessarily comply with the requirements of a particular type of sale contract. It is only likely to do so if it takes the form of an order to a party in possession of the goods who can attorn to the consignee.[7] If the document issued by a combined transport operator is not a bill of lading, the question arises as to whether the Hague–Visby Rules will apply to that section of the transit carried out by a sea carrier. The position appears to be that the Rules would not apply automatically, since they are expressed to apply 'only to contracts of carriage covered by a bill of lading or any similar document of title ...'.[8] The Carriage of Goods by Sea Act 1971, section 1(6)(b) provides that the Rules shall have the force of law in relation to 'any receipt which is a non-negotiable document marked as such if the contract contained in or evidenced by it is a contract for the carriage of goods by sea which expressly provides that the Rules are to govern the contract as if the receipt were a bill of lading'. It would appear, therefore, that the parties can make provision for the application of the Hague–Visby Rules to the sea section of the carriage.

The combined transport document thus presents, by its very nature, various legal problems, many of which are due to the fact that it is not a document of title. Could it become one? There are two ways in which a document can achieve this status. First, by statute[9] and second, at common law. The statutory status is normally given only to extremely restricted classes of documents, such as those used in particular ports or trades and it seems unlikely that the status would be conferred in this manner on a combined transport document. The common law status is achieved when the courts recognise a mercantile custom to the effect that transfer of the particular document conveys title to the transferee. It was in this fashion that the bill of lading itself achieved the status of a document of title in *Lickbarrow v Mason*.[10]

It is not beyond the bounds of possibility, therefore, that a combined transport document should, in the foreseeable future, become a document of title in law if it comes to be regarded as one in commercial practice.

7   *Colin and Shields v W Weddel & Co* [1952] 2 All ER 337, [1952] 2 Lloyd's Rep 9, CA, p 28 above.
8   Carriage of Goods by Sea Act 1971, Sch, art I(b).
9   Eg Port of London (Consolidation) Act 1920, s 168.
10   (1787) 2 Term Rep 63. See also *Newson v Thornton* (1805) 6 East 17.

Contractual status

The relationship of the consignor of the goods to the various carriers involved in the transit will depend on two factors. One will be the actual terms of the contract made by the consignor and the combined transport operator; the other will be the nature of the arrangements made by the operator with the carriers or, if he himself is a carrier, the other carriers. If the combined transport operator undertakes on his own behalf all the arrangements for the carriage, then other carriers will be sub-contractors of the operator and will have no direct contractual relationship with the consignor. On the other hand if, as tends to be more common, the operator is contracting on the basis of existing arrangements between himself and various carriers to provide a combined transport service then he may well be acting as their agent in making the contract with the consignor, so that the latter will have a direct contractual relationship with the carriers, who will be parties to the contract between consignor and operator.

Liability

The various international conventions on the carriage of goods lay down different bases and extents of liability of the carrier, which will apply to different stages of combined transport. As has been seen, the basis of liability under the CIM and CMR Conventions is strict liability subject to the principle of *force majeur* and under the Hague–Visby Rules and the Warsaw Conventions is negligence. Moreover, the monetary limits of the carrier's liabilities are not only set at different levels but are calculated on different bases, either by gold value or Special Drawing Rights. In *Owners of Cargo lately aboard the River Guara v Nigerian National Shipping Line Ltd* [11] the problem was whether each container was to be treated as a unit or whether the items packed in the container should be considered for liability purposes under the 1922 Hague Rules. The court held that where a bill of lading listed a number of containers said to contain a specific number of separately packed items, then the reference point has to be the number of items packed in the containers. It can be seen from the judgment that the Hague Rules did not consider containerisation.

If the stage at which any loss of or damage to goods occurring is established then the relevant convention may apply, so that the consignor may, in respect of the same consignment, have to prove a different case and

11   [1998] 1 Lloyd's Rep 225, CA.

receive different compensation according to the point at which the loss or damage occurred. The period during which he may bring the action will also vary.

On the other hand, if the stage at which the loss or damage occurred is not established, how is liability to be decided? It is common to stipulate that in any such event the Hague–Visby Rules shall apply but it is not clear how valid this provision may be. There is, of course, nothing to prevent the parties expressly subjecting their contract to the Hague–Visby Rules in so far as it relates to the sea carriage. The problem would be likely to arise in a case where road transport was governed by the CMR Convention, since this Convention is expressed to apply to the entire transit including any incidental sea transit. Any clause applying the Hague–Visby Rules to the loss could therefore be void under the terms of the Convention.[12]

An associated problem is the uncertainty which the position noted above may lead to in respect of the extent to which goods despatched under a combined transport arrangement should be insured.

Apart from the varying liabilities of carriers under the different conventions, there is also the possibility of variations caused by the different contractual terms employed by carriers responsible for the different stages of a combined transport arrangement. It is common to stipulate in a combined transport contract that goods are to be carried on the terms and conditions normally employed by each individual carrier. (Such terms will, of course, only apply to the extent that any relevant convention permits.) It is possible to avoid this lack of uniformity by stipulating in the combined transport contract that the combined transport operator with whom the contract is made is to be responsible throughout, whichever carrier was actually carrying the goods when the loss or damage occurred.

Combined transport and established contracts

The application of combined transport techniques to the established forms of sale contracts obviously creates difficulties, some of which affect all such contracts, others only particular types.

In the first place, the seller will deliver the goods to a combined transport operator, usually at an inland depot. Can this, even if the operator is a sea

12   The Carriage of Goods by Road Act 1965, s 8(1) does provide for solving such problems by order in council but any such solution would affect English law only.

carrier or the agent for one, be equated to delivery to a carrier in the established contracts? Could a fob seller, for example, claim to have fulfilled his obligations by so doing? Presumably only if the normal incidents of the fob contract were modified. This is something that the parties are free to do but whether, having done so, they will be left with what the courts would regard as an fob contract is doubtful. No doubt at some stage the goods will pass over the rails of a ship and a bill of lading be issued by a sea carrier, but the original consignor will not receive it. The ship's rail has clearly lost all its significance as a transitional point in the performance of the contract.

The position may be somewhat different when the fob seller has undertaken to arrange for the carriage of the goods to the buyer, since in this case he may well be able to fulfil his obligations to a great extent by making a contract for combined transport. This still leaves problems, of course, since the freight payable to the combined transport operator, for which the seller will presumably invoice the buyer, will include the cost of the carriage of the goods to the port of shipment which would, under a normal fob contract, be for the seller's account. The problem of the provision of a bill of lading also remains as does the point of the passing of the property in the goods since, as has been said, the crossing of the ship's rail has lost its significance. The passing of property is usually important in connection with loss of or damage to the goods and if the goods are in a container it may be impossible to establish whether the loss or damage occurred before or after this point.

Similar problems obviously apply to the other contracts, particularly fas and cif contracts. The question therefore arises as to whether sale contracts could be developed which would parallel the established contracts while being based on combined transport. A contract on cif lines, for example, would appear to be practicable, if the combined transport document could be accepted as an equivalent of the bill of lading. There appears to be no reason why the consignor, having handed goods to the combined transport operator, should not tender the combined transport document, the invoice and the insurance policy or certificate[13] to the buyer against payment of the price. The risk would presumably pass to the buyer on delivery of the goods to the combined transport operator. There is no reason why the parties should not evince an intention that property was to pass to the

---

13 Combined transport techniques present fewer problems in respect of insurance, since it has long been usual to insure goods for the entire transit from seller to buyer.

buyer on transfer to him of the documents, subject to any right of disposal exercised by the seller.

The problems of containers

The problems so far considered have related to combined transport. While, as has been said, the development of containers and other methods of consolidating cargoes has accelerated the development of combined transport, the two developments may present different problems. (Indeed, it is not inevitable that a container should be carried by combined transport methods nor that unconsolidated goods should not be so carried.) Containers present their own problems.

The question of whether a container is a unit or package for the purposes of the limitation of the carrier's liability is dealt with by the Hague–Visby Rules.[14] Other questions remain. Must a container be seaworthy? How far would a carrier be liable if he provided a container unsuitable for a particular consignment? These maters, in the absence of international agreement, are for the contract between the parties. Another problem arises in connection with deck stowage. Many container vessels are designed to take a large proportion of their cargo on deck and vessels not primarily designed for the carriage of containers regularly carry them on deck. How far can this practice be equated with the carriage on deck of non-container goods? The uncertainty of the position and the basis of the solution were expressed by Roskill LJ in *J Evans & Son (Portsmouth) Ltd v Andrea Merzario Ltd*:[15]

> There was some discussion in this court – and the learned judge mentioned the point at the end of his judgment – whether the old law relating to deck cargo is still applicable to modern container traffic ... The learned judge said that he thought that old law did not apply to container traffic. It is not necessary to express any view whether the judge was right or wrong, though I am far from suggesting he was wrong. We do not have to decide that question in this case. The question may hereafter arise. When it does, no doubt evidence will be made available whether there is at the present time a custom or practice under which containers may be shipped on deck without the express permission from the cargo owners so to do. Whether or

14   Carriage of Goods by Sea Act 1971, Sch, art IV(5)(c).
15   [1976] 2 All ER 930 at 935, CA.

not that is so I do not know. I do not think we should express any view about that question in a case in which there is no evidence from shipowners what the current customary practice if any is.

Finally, as the above words clearly indicate, the problems just considered are legal problems which await legal solutions. Commercial development does not stand still because of this. Only the most arrogant – not to say ignorant – of lawyers could envisage the business world ceasing its operations and waiting with bated breath for the lawyers to arrive at legally satisfactory conclusions so that it could safely adopt combined transport methods in its transactions. In this matter the law must follow the practice.

COMBINED TRANSPORT AND DOCUMENTARY CREDITS

There have been problems associated with documentary credits financing the transport of goods by combined transport. The combined transport document covering the entire transit period is not statutorily recognised as a document of title. Also, the document is a 'received for shipment' bill rather than a 'shipped' bill which is the desired form for bankers. However, the 1993 edition of the ICC's Customs and Practice for Documentary Credits Rules now provide that, unless the credit stipulates an ocean bill of lading, a combined transport document is acceptable even in short or blank back form. The document may indicate a place of taking charge different from the port of loading and/or a place of final destination different from the port of discharge, and may relate to cargoes in containers and pallets. Even though the credit does require an ocean bill of lading, a combined transport document is acceptable if the document is issued and signed by a named carrier or his agent and contains a 'shipped' notation on a named ship. Under articles 23 and 26 UCP 500, the banks will accept a document which indicates merely that the goods have been taken in charge or received for shipment unless there is a contrary instruction.

COMBINED TRANSPORT REGULATION

The need for international agreement on combined transport has been recognised and a UN convention on International Multimodal Transport of Goods was adopted at Geneva in 1980. This convention is not yet in force but the International Chamber of Commerce has adopted Rules for Multimodal Transport Documents based on the UK draft. These rules, which apply only when specifically adopted by the parties to the carriage contract, relate to contracts for the carriage of goods by at least two different modes of transport.

Documents

The rules provide for the issue of a multimodal transport (MT) document which can be issued either in a negotiable form or in a non-negotiable form indicating a named consignee. The term 'document' includes electronic data interchange messages in so far as applicable law permits this.

The document is prima facie evidence of the fact that the MT operator has taken charge of goods as described unless there is a contrary indication in the document, such as 'shipper's weight, load and content', a phrase comparable to such expressions in a bill of lading as 'as declared by shipper but unknown to carrier'. Proof to the contrary is not admissible once the document has been transferred or an electronic data interchange message has been transmitted to and acknowledged by a consignee who has relied on and acted on the information in good faith.

Carrier's liability

The MT operator's responsibility for the goods extends from the time he has taken the goods in his charge until the time of delivery. He is, subject to certain specified defences, liable for loss of or damage to goods and, in some cases, delay in delivering them unless he can prove the absence of fault or neglect on the part of himself or his servants or agents or any other persons of whose services he makes use for the performance of the contract.

In respect of carriage by sea or inland waterways the carrier is not responsible for loss or damage caused by the events et out in art IV(2)(a) and (b) of the Hague–Visby Rules,[16] subject to the duty to use due diligence in respect of seaworthiness.

In the absence of evidence to the contrary goods may be assumed to have been lost if they have not been delivered within 90 days of the due delivery date.

Limitation of liability

The MT operator's liability is generally limited to 666.67 SDRs per package or unit or two SDRs per kilogram of gross weight, whichever is the higher,

16   See p 35.

unless the actual nature and value of the goods are declared and stated in the MT document. If the transport does not include carriage by sea or inland waterways the liability is 8.33 SDRs per kilogram of gross weight. A container or other consolidation unit is considered as a single package or unit unless the contents are separately enumerated.

The limitation may vary if loss or damage occurs on a stage where an international convention or mandatory national law imposes a different limitation.

The MT operator loses the benefit of the limitation if the loss or damage resulted from his personal act or omission done with intent to cause the loss, etc or recklessly and with knowledge that it would probably result.

Liability of consignor

The consignor has duties comparable to those of a shipper under the Hague–Visby Rules in respect of statements in the MT document and in respect of dangerous goods.

Limitation of action

Actions must be brought within nine months of the delivery of the goods or the date when they should have been delivered or the date at which they can be presumed lost.

SALE CONTRACTS BASED ON COMBINED TRANSPORT

In view of the difficulties inherent in making an established type of sale contract under a combined transport arrangement it is not surprising that new forms of contract have arisen which are based specifically on combined transport practices.

One such contact is the 'Delivered at Container Collection Depot' contract, naming the place where the depot is situated. Under this contract the seller is responsible for all charges up to the delivery of the goods to a combined transport operator at the named place. The goods are at the risk of the buyer from this time and he is responsible for all arrangements and costs thereafter. Subject to the contract, including any reservation by the seller of the right of disposal, the property passes to the buyer at this point.

The delivery of the goods to the operator at the container depot is obviously one logical point at which to divide the responsibilities of seller and buyer. The other is the arrival at the container depot at the buyer's end of the transit. A contract on these lines is frequently made and is often known as a contract 'Free Arrival Station'.[17] Such a contract has much in common with an Arrival or Ex-ship contract.

17   The unfortunate identity of initials of this and the 'Free Alongside Ship' contract should be noted.

Chapter 6

Insurance in the international sale transaction

THE INSURANCE OF GOODS IN TRANSIT

Since goods sent overseas, by whatever means, are subject to obvious risks of loss or damage, the contract of insurance usually plays a large part in any overseas sale transaction, particularly in the cif contract. The insuring of goods against the risks of carriage by sea is a very old practice and marine insurance is a highly developed branch of the law. In the United Kingdom the law on marine insurance is governed by the Marine Insurance Act 1906, a codifying Act, which sets out and gives statutory effect to the rules build up by the common law courts in centuries of litigation on policies of marine insurance. the Act is concerned with the insurance not only of goods but of ships, freight and other interests but this book is concerned with the Act only in so far as it relates to the insurance of goods, although in most cases the same principles of law will apply no matter what the subject matter of the insurance.

The insurance of goods carried by land and air has not achieved the extent or the standardisation which has developed in marine insurance. Insurance for goods to be carried by other than sea transport is still largely a matter of particular contracts rather than of contracts conforming to a universally accepted form. They tend, however, to be based on marine insurance contracts as far as circumstances permit. Indeed, it is quite common to issue marine policies to cover air carriage even though, in strict law, these cannot be recognised as true marine policies.[1] The contract of marine insurance is therefore the only insurance contract on goods that is essential to the study of international trade.

---

1   Marine Insurance Act 1906, s 3.

The insurable interest

An important feature of the contract of marine insurance is that, in common with other insurance contracts, it is a contract of indemnity, that is, one which has as its object the placing of the assured, as he is called in this field, in the position in which he would have been had the loss or damage not occurred. Several important legal consequences follow from this character, the most important of which is that, if the contract is to be valid, the assured must have some kind of legally recognised interest in the subject matter, so that he may in some way or another suffer loss or be involved in expense or become liable to a third party should the subject matter of the insurance be lost or damaged. If he has no such 'insurable interest' then he cannot suffer in this way and therefore cannot claim to be indemnified. In *Cepheus Shipping Corpn v Guardian Royal Exchange Assurance plc, The Capricorn* it was held that a speculative interest does not amount to an interest, unless agreed.[2]

The Marine Insurance Act 1906, section 5 states:

(1) Subject to the provisions of this Act, every person has an insurable interest who is interested in a marine adventure.

(2) In particular a person is interested in a marine adventure where he stands in any legal or equitable relation to the adventure or to any insurable property at risk therein, in consequence of which he may benefit by the safety or due arrival of insurable property, or may be prejudiced by its loss, or by damage thereto, or may incur liability in respect thereof.

The essence of an insurable interest, then, is that property in which the assured has some legal or equitable interest is at risk from marine perils. If the assured has no such interest in the subject matter, and no reasonable expectation of acquiring one, any insurance he effects on the subject matter will, under the Marine Insurance Act 1906, section 4, be void as a gaming or wagering contract. One difficulty that can arise as a result of this rule is that a genuine commercial interest may not be recognised by the law as an insurable interest. In these circumstances it is common for the assured to take out a policy which states 'Interest or no interest' or 'Issue of the policy to be proof of interest'. Such 'ppi' policies will be honoured by insurers provided that the interest, though not legally an insurable interest, is a genuine one and that there has been no deception

2   [1995] 1 Lloyd's Rep 622

on the part of the assured, but these policies, referred to as 'honour' policies, are nevertheless void under section 4 as gaming or wagering contracts.[3]

In *Cheshire & Co v Vaughan Bros*[4] warehousemen wished to insure anticipated profits on the storage of nitrates for which they had reserved space. They asked a broker to effect a ppi policy on the arrival of the nitrates since they had, of course, no insurable interest in them. The agent failed to disclose to the insurers the fact that the cargo of nitrates was liable to be diverted by government order to another port. The insurers avoided the contract on this ground and the warehousemen proceeded against the broker for the breach of his duty to effect the policy properly. It was held that they must fail. The broker's omission had in no way legally affected the warehousemen's position since, even if he had disclosed the risk, the policy effected would still have been legally void. Scrutton LJ referred to the 'unfortunate conflict between the statute law and the practice of business men', a conflict which, it is suggested, is as much due to the failure of the law to recognise genuine commercial interests as it is to any perverse inclination on the part of businessmen to make illegal contracts.

A person who has a reasonable expectation of acquiring an interest in a subject matter can make a valid contract of insurance to cover it, but will not be able to claim under the policy unless he actually has an interest at the time of the loss. Thus the buyer of goods may take out a policy on the goods he has contracted to buy but will not be able to claim in respect of any loss of or damage to them if the risk had not passed to him when the loss or damage occurred.

In *Anderson v Morice*[5] rice was sold and was insured by the buyer. When part of the cargo was on board the ship the rice was lost. The buyer was held to have had no interest at the time of the loss because the arrangement was such that the risk and the property did not pass to him until the cargo was completely loaded. On the other hand in *Colonial Insurance Co of New Zealand v Adelaide Marine Insurance Co*[6] the vessel on which wheat was being loaded was lost in a gale before loading was completed. The buyer of the wheat was held to have an insurable interest in such of it

3   For this reason they would not be regarded by a court as good tender under a cif contract. *Strass v Spillers and Bakers* [1911] 2 KB 759.
4   [1920] 3 KB 240, CA.
5   (1876) 1 App Cas 713, HL.
6   (1886) 12 App Cas 128.

as had already been loaded. The distinction between the cases was summarised in the judgment of the Privy Council in the second case.

> In putting the rice on board the *Sunbeam* [in *Anderson v Morice*] the sellers were not delivering it to Anderson, but were putting it on board a vessel, of which they were the charterers, for the purpose of completing the cargo which they had agreed to sell ... In the present case, in putting the wheat on board the *Duke of Sutherland*, the contractors were delivering it to the purchasers in pursuance of their contract to put it free on board.

A partial interest is insurable.[7] In *Inglis v Stock*[8] the Privy Council held that there could be an insurable interest in an unappropriated part of a bulk of sugar which was lost before becoming ascertained. A defeasible or contingent interest is also insurable, so that a buyer to whom the property in goods has passed has an insurable interest in them even though he retains a right to reject the goods as unsuitable and revest the property in the seller by so doing.[9] One point that remains unsettled in this area is whether an unpaid seller of goods, with a potential right to stop the goods *in transitu*, has an insurable interest in them after property has passed to the buyer.

The normal contractual terms in use now specifically provide that the assured must have an insurable interest, so that the requirement is a matter of contract as well as of law.

Assignment of interest and policy

The rights of the assured under a policy of marine insurance will normally be assignable by indorsing and delivering the policy to the assignee and it is in this way that the seller under a cif contract will transfer to the buyer the policy demanded by the contract. However, the transfer of property or risk in goods to a buyer, while it transfers the insurable interest, will not necessarily transfer the rights under any policy which the seller has taken out on the goods. In the first place there must be an express or implied agreement that the policy is to be transferred with the interest and the seller must have an interest when he assigns the policy. Difficulties do not normally arise in this respect in cif contracts since the agreement to assign

7   Marine Insurance Act 1906, s 8.
8   (1885) 10 App Cas 263, HL.
9   Marine Insurance Act 1906, s 7.

the insurance rights with the interest in the goods is clearly implied in the contract. This will not necessarily be the case under other contracts. In *North of England Oil-Cake Co v Archangel Insurance Co*[10] the bill of lading for goods was indorsed to the buyer but the seller retained the policy of insurance since he was not to be paid until the goods arrived. In February 1872 a lighter containing part of the cargo sank – a risk covered by the policy – and in June the policy was handed to the buyer and was formally assigned to him in October. It was held that the assignment was ineffective. There was no agreement, express or implied, that the policy should be assigned with the interest in the goods and when assignment actually took place the policy had ceased to be effective. As Cockburn CJ explained:[11]

> This is not like the common case of the sale of a floating cargo, where the seller parts with and the buyer takes at once the property and all risks. In such a case, the policy, according to the established practice, passes as part of the shipping documents, and on assignment the vendee can sue upon it in case of loss. And there is no hardship in this on the insurers, because they insured the safety of the cargo to the end of the voyage, and it is immaterial to them in whom the interest vests at the time of the loss; and there is great convenience in the practice, as it obviates the necessity of the vendee getting a fresh policy and facilitates the sale of cargoes at sea. But this is not an out and out sale; on the contrary, although the sale might at once transfer the property to the vendees, yet an essential term of the agreement was that payment was only to take place on the right delivery of the cargo, so that the interest, a substantial real interest, remained in the sellers. If the cargo had perished at sea, the sellers would not have got one shilling; therefore until delivery to the plaintiffs, the buyers, the interest in the policy remained in the sellers. But on delivery to the plaintiffs the sellers became entitled to payment and their interest in the policy ceased; and the policy was at an end. Consequently, although an actual assignment may be good after loss, in the present case the assignment was not in consequence of a previous agreement before the policy dropped, and therefore the sellers had no interest in the policy and nothing to assign.

10   (1875) LR 10 QB 249.
11   Ibid at 253.

Further, the policy must be intended, when it is taken out, to be capable of covering the assignee's interest. In *Yangtzse Insurance Association ltd v Lukmanjee*[12] logs sold under an Ex-ship contract were insured by the seller. The logs on arrival were put over the side and collected into rafts for floating ashore but were lost because of bad weather. The buyer claimed that the rights under the seller's insurance policy had been transferred to himself with the property in the goods but the Privy Council, distinguishing an Ex-ship contract from a cif contract, held that the policy taken out by the seller had been intended to cover his own interest only and could not be transferred to the buyer.

A policy may be assigned after a loss provided that the assignor had an interest at the time of the loss and there was a previous express or implied agreement to assign the policy. Thus, as has been seen,[13] the seller under a cif contract may validly tender the documents, including the policy of insurance, to the buyer after the goods have already been lost at sea.

Disclosure of material facts

The contract of marine insurance, like other contracts of insurance, is a contract of the utmost food faith (*uberrimae fidei*). In *Greenhill v Federal Insurance Co*[14] Scrutton LJ said:

> Now insurance is a contract of the utmost good faith, and it is of the gravest importance to commerce that that position should be observed. The underwriter knows nothing of the particular circumstances of the voyage to be insured. The assured knows a great deal, and it is the duty of the assured to inform the underwriter of everything that he is not taken as knowing, so the contracts may be entered into on an equal footing.

Thus, subject to certain exceptions,

> The assured must disclose to the insurer, before the contract is concluded, every material particular which is known to the assured, and the assured is deemed to know every circumstance which, in the ordinary course of business, ought to be known by him.[15]

---

12 [1918] AC 585.
13 Eg *Manbre Saccharine Co Ltd v Corn Products Co* [1919] 1 KB 198, p 77, above.
14 [1927] 1 KB 65 at 76.
15 Marine Insurance Act 1906, s 18(1).

The contract is normally 'concluded' when the 'slip' (the note of the terms of the insurance) is signed by the insurers. Thus information that reaches the assured after this but before the issue of the actual policy does not have to be disclosed.[16]

Non-disclosure of a material circumstance will entitle the insurer to avoid the contract.[17] The Marine Insurance Act 1906 defines a material circumstance as one which would influence the judgment of a prudent insurer in fixing the premium or deciding whether to take on the risk.[18] Apparently this does not mean that materiality (which is a question of fact) will only be tested objectively against the standards of a hypothetical 'prudent insurer'. In *Berger and Light Diffusers Pty Ltd v Pollock*[19] Kerr J said:

> It seems to me, as a matter of principle, that the Court's task in deciding whether or not the defendant insurer can avoid the policy for non-disclosure must be to determine as a question of fact whether, by applying the standard of the judgment of a prudent insurer, the insurer in question would have been influenced in fixing the premium or determining whether to take the risk if he had been informed of the undisclosed circumstances before entering into the contract. Otherwise one could in theory reach the absurd position where the Court might be satisfied that the insurer in question would not have been so influenced but that other prudent insurers would have been. It would then be a very odd result if the defendant insurer could nevertheless avoid the policy.

In that case steel injection moulds had been shipped and a claused bill of lading issued. The moulds had been bought cheaply by the assured, who had found them defective and shipped them to England for remedial treatment. The moulds, which were valued in the policy at £20,000, were irreparably damaged by water from a fractured pipe in the ship's hold and the assured claimed the full sum from the insurers, who sought to avoid

---

16   *Cory v Patton* (1872) LR 7 QB 304.

17   In *Manifest Shipping Co Ltd v Uni-Polaris Insurance Co Ltd, The Star Sea* [2001] UKHL 1, [2001] 1 Lloyd's Rep 389 it was held that the s 17 duty of the utmost good faith continued to apply after the conclusion of the insurance contract but once the parties were in litigation it was the procedural rules which governed the extent of the disclosure, though s 17 might influence the court in the exercise of its discretion.

18   Marine Insurance Act 1906, s 18(2).

19   [1973] 2 Lloyd's Rep 442 at 463.

the contract on the grounds of the non-disclosure of the history of the moulds, of the issue of a claused bill of lading and of the true value of the moulds, which was less than a third of the valuation. It was held that as a matter of fact these circumstances were not material in that the insurer could not show that knowledge of them would clearly have influenced his judgment.

There can clearly be an infinite number of kinds of information that should be disclosed as material. Examples are the fact that complaints had been made by customers about goods,[20] the true value of goods[21] and the fact that the vessel carrying the goods has sunk.[22]

Since the assured is deemed to know what he should know in the ordinary course of business, it is irrelevant that he is in fact ignorant of it, even if it has been deliberately withheld from him. In *Proudfoot v Montefiore*[1] the assured had employed an agent to buy goods in Smyrna. The agent shipped the goods and sent the documents to the assured. Four days later the ship sailed but stranded on the same day and became a total loss. The agent learned of this the following day but, instead of telegraphing to his principal, informed him by a letter posted on the next post day, which was two days after the agent had learned of the loss. Before receiving this letter the principal had insured the goods. It was held that in the ordinary course of business the agent should have telegraphed the information, in which case the principal would have been aware of it when he effected the insurance. The policy could therefore be avoided by the insurer for non-disclosure.

Where a policy is effected by an agent for the assured, as will usually be the case, the agent must disclose to the insurer any material circumstance known to him and he is deemed to know every material circumstance which, in the ordinary course of business, he should know or have been told. In addition, the agent must disclose every material fact which his principal, the assured, is bound to disclose unless the principal learned it too late to communicate it to his agent.[2] Where the policy effected by the agent is done in ignorance of a material fact known to the assured, then the contract cannot be avoided if the information has come too late to the

20   *Bird's Cigarette Manufacturing Co Ltd v Rouse* (1924) 19 Ll L Rep 301.
21   *Ionides v Pender* (1874) LR 9 QB 531.
22   *Proudfoot v Montefiore* (1867) LR 2 QB 511.
1   Ibid.
2   Marine Insurance Act 1906, s 19.

knowledge of the assured to be communicated. In *Pan Atlantic Insurance Co Ltd v Pine Top Insurance Co Ltd*[3], the court reviewed the authorities relevant to non-disclosure and said that in the event of non-disclosure the insurer was entitled to avoid the contract if the non-disclosure induced the making of the contract. In *Marc Rich & Co AG v Portman*[4] it was stated that even though the insured had been remiss in not actively seeking information, they had been induced into making the contract on the basis of non-disclosure. In *HIH Casualty and General Insurance Ltd v Chase Manhattan Bank*[5] it was held that while as a matter of public policy the parties cannot exclude by contract liability for one of the parties' fraudulent misrepresentation inducing that contract of insurance, it is possible for a contractual clause to exclude a party's liability for the fraudulent misrepresentation of its agent. Provided such clauses are clearly drafted, they will be put into effect.

Certain material circumstances need not, in the absence of enquiry by the insurer, be disclosed by the assured.[6] A circumstance which diminishes the risk need not be disclosed since the insurer is obviously not put at any disadvantage by the non-disclosure. Neither need a circumstance be disclosed if it is known, or must be presumed to be known, to the insurer. The insurer is deemed to know matters of common knowledge and to have a knowledge of such matters as an insurer should have in the ordinary course of business. But though an insurer may know, or be deemed to know, of a general situation it does not follow that a particular fact relating to that situation need not be disclosed. In *Bolivia Republic v Indemnity Mutual Marine Assurance Co*[7] supplies for Bolivian troops were insured for a river journey. One of the agents of the Government concerned with the effecting of the insurance was aware that a hostile expedition was being prepared to seize these supplies. This fact was not disclosed to the insurers, who sought to avoid the contract. It was held that they were entitled to do so. They were aware of the general nature of the disturbance in the district but could not be taken to know of the hostile expedition, which was clearly material information which should have been disclosed. Similarly, in *Harrower v Hutchinson*,[8] it was held that while insurers might be taken to know the general nature of the ports in a particular area they

3   [1994] 2 Lloyd's Rep 427, HL.
4   [1996] 1 Lloyd's Rep 430.
5   [2001] 1 All ER (Comm) 719.
6   Marine Insurance Act 1906, s 18(3).
7   [1909] 1 KB 785, 14 Com Cas 156.
8   (1870) LR 5 QB 584.

could not be taken to know that the assured might use an exposed bay only normally used for small vessels.

A circumstance need not be disclosed if the insurer waives knowledge of it. He will be deemed thus to waive disclosure if the facts are such as to put him on enquiry but he in fact makes no enquiry. In *Cantiere Meccanico Brindisino v Janson*[9] a floating dock was insured for towage from Avonmouth to Brindisi. The assured honestly believed that it did not require strengthening for the sea voyage and did not disclose to the insurer that this had not been done. Since the terms of the insurance laid down that the dock was to be accepted as being seaworthy[10] it was held that the insurer had been put on enquiry and since he had made none must be deemed to have waived disclosure of the facts relating to the seaworthiness of the dock.

Clearly there must be limits to the circumstances in which an insurer is deemed to have waived disclosure in this way. In *Greenhill v Federal Insurance Co*[11] a consignment of celluloid was insured for a voyage from Halifax to Nantes. The assured failed to disclose to the insurers that the cargo had already sustained considerable damage on its journey to Halifax for shipment. When the insurers sought to avoid the contract on the grounds of this non-disclosure the assured argued that they had waived the knowledge since they were aware that the goods were at Halifax and had made no enquiry as to how they had got there. Scrutton LJ said:[12]

> The argument as to waiver was put before us in a way which would, if sound, have entirely destroyed the obligation to disclose at all; because it was said: 'It is a possibility that this cargo which you are asked to insure may have suffered certain damage, and as there is a possibility, and you are told of this cargo, and you do not ask the question, you are bound by any possibility which might happen to the cargo.' That line of argument would entirely destroy the obligation to disclose at all, because, if you insure a ship, of course it is a possibility that anything may have happened to her. If you come to insure a cargo, it is a possibility that anything may have happened to it. I have always understood the proper line that an underwriter should take, except in matters that he is bound to know, is absolutely to abstain from asking any questions, and to leave the

9   [1912] 3 KB 452, CA.
10   On the 'Seaworthiness admitted' clause see p 148 below.
11   [1927] 1 KB 65, CA.
12   Ibid at 85.

assured to fulfil his duty of good faith, and make full disclosure of all material facts, without being asked. And it seems to me to be of great importance to the general duty of disclosure that that position of the underwriter should be maintained and not whittled away by alleged waiver.

A circumstance need not be disclosed if it is superfluous to do so by reason of any express or implied warranty in the contract. The rationale behind this rule is that if the assured does not disclose a fact which indicates that he is in breach of warranty the insurer is not prejudiced because he will in any case not be liable for any loss following the breach of the warranty.

Any act of dishonesty or fraud by the assured must have direct reference to the issue of materiality in order to enable the insurers to avoid the contract. This was considered in *K/S Merc-Scandia XXXXII v Underwriters of Lloyds Policy No 25T 105487 and Ocean Marine Insurance Co Ltd*[13] where the assured had used a forged document which they had thought would help their claim but the document was in fact of little assistance. The attempt to use a forged document was dishonest but the misrepresentation was immaterial in the Pan Atlantic sense and the insurers were not induced to do anything in relation to the claim.

Representations

The position in respect of positive representations by the assured is much the same as that in respect of disclosure. Material representations made before the contract is concluded must be substantially true; otherwise the insurer will be entitled to avoid the contract.[14] 'Representation' includes an expression of expectation or belief, which is deemed to be true if made in good faith. In *Ionides and Chapeaurouge v Pacific Fire and Marine Insurance Co*[15] a cargo of hides was insured and the insurer was informed that the vessel carrying it would be the Socrates, a new Norwegian vessel. This was an error. The vessel was in fact an old French vessel, the Socrate, and the mistake was due to the careless consultation of a shipping list. It was held that the insurer was entitled to avoid the contract on the grounds of the misrepresentation. Blackburn J said:[16]

13   [2000] 2 Lloyd's Rep 357.
14   Marine Insurance Act 1906, s 20.
15   (1871) LR 6 QB 674.
16   Ibid at 683.

And we think also that, if the representation was made, however honestly and innocently, that the ship was a new ship, when, in fact, she was an old one, the policy was vitiated thereby, for the age of the vessel must be material in considering the premium. It was argued that a representation, if only as to an expectation or belief, is substantially complied with if the assured really had honestly entertained that expectation on sufficient grounds, and that the representation that 'he thought' the ship was the Norwegian ship was literally true. We think this expression tantamount to an assertion that she was the Norwegian; but even if it were otherwise, the letter of advice would, but for the carelessness of those who read it, have made them aware that the ship was that of which the captain was Jean Card, and therefore the [assured] had not reasonable grounds for believing that she was the Norwegian ship.

Warranties

The term 'warranty' has two meanings in marine insurance. The first, referred to in the Act as a 'promissory warranty', is an undertaking by the assured that something will be done or not done or that some condition will be fulfilled, or it may be an affirmation that a particular state of affairs exists or not.[17] Thus the assured may warrant that a cargo is marked in a particular way.[18] In its second sense the word 'warranty' may be used to describe a term in the contract under which the insurer will not be liable for losses from certain causes, such as inherent vice. Such terms are now also referred to as 'general exclusions'.

If a warranty in the first, or promissory, sense is not exactly complied with by the assured, the insurer will be discharged from all liability in respect of losses occurring after the breach of warranty and it is immaterial that the breach was later remedied and the warranty complied with before the loss occurred.[19] The word 'warranty' is thus used here in a sense entirely different from that used in the Sale of Goods Act 1979 and is closer in meaning to the word 'condition' as used in that Act. Thus in *Overseas Commodities Ltd v Style*[20] tins of pork were insured under a policy which covered losses due, among other things, to inherent vice and hidden

---

17 Marine Insurance Act 1906, s 33.
18 *Overseas Commodities Ltd v Style* [1958] 1 Lloyd's Rep 546.
19 Marine Insurance Act 1906, s 34.
20 [1958] 1 Lloyd's Rep 546.

defects. The policy contained the clause, 'Warranted all tins marked by manufacturers with a code for verification of the date of manufacture'. Since some of the tins were not so marked the assured was in breach of the warranty and the insurer was discharged from liability.

The effect on the contract of insurance of a breach of warranty arose in *Bank of Nova Scotia v Hellenic Mutual War Risks Association (Bermuda) Ltd, The Good Luck*.[21] The insured vessel became a constructive total loss after being hit by a missile while it was, in breach of warranty, in a dangerous area. The defendant insurers had apparently been aware of such breaches but had taken no action. The plaintiff bank had lent money to the shipowners in the belief that the vessel was insured. Whether it was or not turned on the question of the effect of the breach of warranty on the contract of insurance. The House of Lords, reversing the decision of the Court of Appeal, held that the fulfilment of a warranty is a condition precedent to the liability of the insurer and that a breach discharges the insurer from liability so that the insurance in effect ceases to exist. The vessel was therefore not insured at the relevant time.

Warranties may be express or implied. An express warranty must be in writing in the policy (or in some document incorporated by reference to the policy). There are certain general implied warranties, such as the warranty that the adventure is legal and, under a voyage policy, that the ship will be seaworthy. Such warranties will not, of course, be implied if the contract expresses anything to the contrary. An insurer may, by his conduct, be deemed to have waived a breach of a warranty.[22]

The description of the goods

The rules on disclosure, representations and warranties have much relevance for the way in which goods to be insured are described in the contract of insurance. Thus any misdescription or failure to describe them may be a failure to disclose a material fact or a misrepresentation as to the goods or a breach of a warranty relating to the goods. Under the Marine Insurance Act, section 26 the subject matter insured must be designated with 'reasonable certainty' although the assured's interest need not be disclosed. The description may be brief and general but must clearly relate to the goods in question. In *Mackenzie v Whitworth*[23] Blackburn J said:

21 [1992] 1 AC 233, [1991] 2 Lloyd's Rep 191, HL.
22 *P Samuel & Co Ltd v Dumas* [1924] AC 431, HL.
23 (1875) 1 Ex D 36 at 40.

The insurance of goods in transit

A description of the subject matter of the insurance is required both from the nature of the contract and from the universal practice of insurers.[24] It is generally described very concisely as being so much 'on ship', 'on goods', on 'freight', on 'profits on goods', 'on advances on coolies', 'on emigrant money' and many other examples might be given. And if no property which answers the description in the policy be at risk, the policy will not attach, although the assured may have other property at risk of equal or greater value. The reason being that the assurers have not entered into a contract to indemnify the assured for any loss on that other property.

A policy on 'goods' will not cover deck cargo or live animals unless they are specifically insured as such but this is subject to usage.[1] This point arose in *British and Foreign Marine Insurance Co v Gaunt*[2] where wool, the subject of a contract fob Punta Arenas was, in accordance with the normal practice, brought out to the overseas vessel on the decks of smaller vessels and was damaged. The insurers contested their liability to pay on the grounds that the wool had not been specifically described in the policy as deck cargo and argued that the words 'In the absence of any usage to the contrary' meant not 'in the absence of trade usage' but 'in the absence of any usage in the insurance business'. The court rejected this argument.

> It was contended that the 'usage' contemplated by the Rule was a usage in the insurance business as to the description for the purposes of insurance. This cannot be so ... In as much as an insurer is bound to know the usages of trade, if a usage exists in the trade to carry goods of a particular kind on deck, he knows that such goods are likely to be so carried, and there is little reason for requiring a specific statement that such a method of carriage will or may be employed. The 'usage', therefore, must be a trade usage ... There was therefore no need to insure the wool specifically as deck cargo and the omission to do so does not afford any defence to the [insurers].[3]

The omission of a material element in the description of the goods may amount to a failure to disclose a material circumstance for which the insurer will be entitled to avoid the contracts. In *Wilson, Holgate & Co Ltd v*

24 This case was, of course, decided before the Marine Insurance Act 1906 codified the law. The description is now required by s 26 of the Act.
1 Marine Insurance Act 1906, Sch 1, r 17.
2 [1921] 2 AC 41, HL.
3 Ibid at 48, per Lord Birkenhead.

Lancashire and Cheshire Insurance Corpn Ltd[4] a cargo of palm oil was described in the policy as 'palm kernel oil', a different substance with different characteristics, and the fact that the oil was shipped in barrels that were old, frail and leaking was not disclosed. In this case, however, the goods had been correctly described in the slip and the policy misdescription was therefore irrelevant, while the non-disclosure of the state of the barrels was immaterial since it was proved that insurers did not normally concern themselves with the condition of barrels in which oil was shipped. Where an express warranty is concerned with any element of the description of the goods, the shipping of goods that do not conform to that description will be a breach of the warranty, as was the case in *Overseas Commodities Ltd v Style*.[5]

The duties of the assured in relation to disclosure, warranties and representations may be modified by express clauses in the contract of insurance. Thus a policy on goods will normally contain a 'Change of voyage' clause and a 'Seaworthiness admitted' clause. The first of these holds the subject matter to be covered in the event of 'any omission or error in the description of the interest ...' subject to the payment of a premium 'to be arranged'. A clause of this nature was discussed in *Hewitt Bros v Wilson*.[6] Machinery had been insured without disclosure that one machine was secondhand and the insurers sought to avoid liability on this ground, arguing that 'description of the interest' meant description of the insurable interest and not of the subject matter. The Court of Appeal rejected this interpretation. Lord Reading CJ said:[7]

> We must also bear in mind that when we are discussing here what would avoid the contract of insurance because of non-disclosure of material facts, the thing which it is not necessary to disclose is the insurable interest of the person insured. It is the one thing that he need not disclose ... But, of course, in a number of cases, and in this one, there is disclosure of the insurable interest, but if there had been none it would not have avoided the contract ... I agree with [the judge at first instance] that the phrase 'interest assured' means the subject matter insured.

It should be observed that in this case there was no allegation of dishonesty or intentional concealment on the part of the assured. All the

4   (1922) 13 Ll L Rep 486.
5   [1958] 1 Lloyd's Rep 546, p 144 above.
6   [1915] 2 KB 739, CA.
7   Ibid at 743.

members of the court agreed that had these elements been present the 'Change of voyage' clause would not have protected the assured. The assured cannot benefit from this clause if the misdescription cannot be corrected.

> It is plain, on authority, that this clause may be invoked even after loss and after the period covered by the policy is expired, but I know of no case ... in which, at the time when the assured seeks to invoke the clause, they have been and are unable to correct the misdescription.[8]

In a voyage policy there is an implied warranty that the ship carrying the goods shall be seaworthy. If insured goods are shipped in an unseaworthy ship there is a breach of this warranty and the insurer is discharged from liability. Since the shipper of goods has in practice little or no control over the seaworthiness of the vessel on which his goods are loaded, the 'Seaworthiness admitted' clause is used, its effect being that as between insurer and assured the unseaworthiness of the vessel will not affect the insurer's liability to pay for a loss. This clause will not, of course, affect any liability on the part of the shipowner to either assured or insurer.

Types of policy

Voyage and time policies

A policy may cover a subject matter for a particular voyage or voyages or for a period of time. Goods are almost invariably insured under voyage policies.[9] The ports of loading and discharge will normally be specified in the policy. If the goods are in fact shipped from another port or if the ship sails for a different discharge port from that named in the policy the risk does not attach, that is, the insurance never comes into effect.[10] If after the insurance has come into effect the destination of the ship is changed there is said to be a change of voyage and the insurer will be discharged from any liability in respect of any loss occurring after the intention to change was manifested, even though such loss occurs while the ship is still on the

---

8   *Overseas Commodities Ltd v Style* [1958] 1 Lloyd's Rep 546 at 559, per McNair J.

9   Some policies on goods will be expressed to operate for a period of time but the actual insurance covers the goods on particular voyages.

10 Marine Insurance Act 1906, ss 43, 44.

voyage contemplated by the policy.[11] If the vessel deviates 'without lawful excuse' the insurer is discharged from liability for any loss occurring after the deviation and it is immaterial that the vessel has regained its course before such a loss occurs.[12] Finally, the voyage must be prosecuted with 'reasonable despatch' or the insurer will be discharged from liability as from the time when the delay became unreasonable.

As in the case of unseaworthiness, the owner of insured goods has little or no control over the movement of the ship carrying them. Accordingly, contractual provision is usually made to prevent his being adversely affected by the variations noted above. Under the 'Transit' clause the insurance remains in force during 'delay beyond the control of the assured, any deviation, forced discharge, reshipment or transhipment and during any variation of the adventure arising from the exercise of a liberty granted to shipowners or charterers under the contract of affreightment'. Under the 'Change of voyage' clause the assured is held covered 'for a premium to be arranged' in the case of a change of voyage.

Unvalued and valued policies

A policy may or may not state an agreed value for the goods insured. If it does not, the value will be assessed in the event of loss or damage by reference to 'the prime cost of the property insured plus the expenses of and incidental to shipping and the charges of insurance upon the whole'.[13] The 'prime cost' will usually be the invoice value but this is not necessarily the case.[14] Unvalued policies on goods are rare for various reasons, one being that the insurable value does not necessarily take into account any profit on the goods carried. Goods are normally insured under valued policies, which specify an agreed value for the goods which, in the absence of fraud, is conclusive as between insurer and assured.[15]

A gross overvaluation may in itself be evidence of fraud, as in *Ionides v Pender*[16] where an overvalued cargo was lost in circumstances which

---

11   Ibid, s 45.
12   Ibid, ss 46, 47.
13   Ibid, s 16(3).
14   See eg, *Berger and Light Diffusers Pty Ltd v Pollock* [1973] 2 Lloyd's Rep 442.
15   Marine Insurance Act 1906, s 27. While the agreed value is not, under the Act, conclusive in determining whether there has been a constructive total loss or not, it is normal for the contract to provide that it shall be so conclusive.
16   (1874) LR 9 QB 531.

raised a suspicion that the ship had been scuttled. Such overvaluation may, as in that case, amount to a non-disclosure of the true value of the goods but overvaluation, even a very high overvaluation, will not by itself entitle an insurer to avoid the contract on this ground. On this point Kerr J in *Berger and Light Diffusers Pty Ltd v Pollock*[17] said:

> Overvaluation is only one illustration of the general principle that insurers are entitled to avoid policies on the ground of non-disclosure of material circumstances. It must therefore always be shown that the overvaluation was such that, if it had been disclosed, it would have entitled the insurer to avoid the contract because it would have affected his judgment as a prudent insurer in fixing the premium or determining whether or not to take the risk. This is not established by the mere fact that the Court subsequently, with knowledge of all the facts and the assistance of expert opinion, arrives at a much smaller value.

Floating policies

If an exporter is continually selling goods abroad it is obviously not convenient to take out a fresh policy on every occasion, particularly when goods of the same kind are being sent to the same areas. This inconvenience is removed by the use of a floating policy.[18] This is a single policy, stating the insurance in general terms, which will cover all consignments within its scope, usually for a limited period. The policy states an overall value and each time a consignment is sent which comes within the terms of the policy the assured declares this consignment and its value to the insurer and this value will be deducted from the balance of the original overall figure until this is exhausted, whereupon the policy will terminate. Unless the policy provides otherwise, all declarations must be made in the order of despatch or shipment and all consignments coming within the terms of the policy must be declared. The assured may thus not omit to declare consignments which are at little risk in an attempt to avoid depleting the balance on the policy.[19] The value of the goods must be honestly stated in the declaration but an omission or an erroneous declaration made in good faith may be remedied, even after loss or arrival, but must then, unless the

---

17   [1973] 2 Lloyd's Rep 442 at 465.
18   Marine Insurance Act 1906, s 29.
19   *Dunlop Bros & Co v Townend* [1919] 2 KB 127.

contract produces otherwise, be treated as an unvalued policy. Declarations under a floating policy must be made as soon as possible after shipment.[20]

When a floating policy is in use the seller under a cif contract obviously cannot tender the policy of insurance with the shipping documents and the contract must expressly stipulate for this to be replaced by a certificate of insurance.

A looser arrangement than the floating policy is an 'open cover'. This is an arrangement whereby the insurer agrees to issue policies, including floating policies, from time to time within the terms of the contract. Such an arrangement may be expressed to operate for a limited period of time or may be 'always open' in which case there is provision for termination by either party on giving due notice.

In situations where it is inconvenient to make declarations, as where many small consignments are despatched, a blanket policy may be used. This is a policy which, for a lump sum, covers all consignments within its terms for a stipulated time.

Loss and proximate cause

The policy will state the risks against the consequences of which the goods are insured. A loss must be 'proximately caused' by the materialisation of such a risk if the insurer is to be liable to pay.[1] In *Pink v Fleming*[2] a vessel was damaged in a collision and the insured cargo of oranges and lemons was discharged into lighters so that the vessel could be repaired. The fruit was damaged, partly by the handling and partly by deterioration due to the delay. The assured claimed that the loss was caused by the collision, a risk that was covered by the policy. In the Court of Appeal Lord Esher MR said:[3]

> This question can only arise where there is a succession of causes, which must have existed in order to produce the result. Where that is the case, according to the law of marine insurance, the last cause only must be looked to and the others rejected, although the result would not have been produced without them. Here there was a succession of causes. First, there was the collision. Without that no

20 *Union Insurance Society of Canton v Wills & Co* [1916] 1 AC 281.
1   Marine Insurance Act 1906, s 55(1).
2   (1890) 25 QBD 396, CA.
3   Ibid at 397.

doubt the loss would not have happened. But would such a loss have resulted from the collision alone? Is it the natural result of a collision that the ship should be taken to a port for repairs, and that, the cargo being of the kind that must be injured by handling, it should be injured in such a removal? A collision might happen without any of these consequences.

The proximate cause need not, however, be the immediate cause. In *Montoya v London Assurance Co*[4] hides forming part of a cargo were wetted by sea water during a storm. The hides fermented and became putrid and the fumes from them damaged a cargo of tobacco. The assured claimed that the damage to the tobacco was a loss by perils of the sea and succeeded. The damage to the hides was caused by this and the consequent damage to the tobacco followed inevitably.

Obviously the determination of the proximate cause of a loss, like all questions involving causation, is not easy and must be a question of fact in each case. Different elements of a loss may have to be attributed to different causes in the same situation. In *Ionides v Universal Marine Insurance Co*[5] 6,500 bags of coffee were insured under a policy which excluded liability for war risks. The ship carrying them went aground, largely because coastal lights had been extinguished as a hostile act during the American Civil War. About 1,120 bags were salvable but only 120 were in fact saved before Confederate forces intervened and prevented further salvage. The insurers claimed that the loss was caused entirely by war risks, for which they were not liable. The court held, however, that the proximate cause of the main loss was the stranding and that the hostilities which had led to the removal of the lights were not the proximate cause of this loss. The loss of 1,000 salvable bags through the intervention of the Confederate forces was, on the other hand, due to a war risk for which the insurers were not liable. The assured was therefore entitled to claim for the value of all the bags except this 1,000 and the 120 which were saved.

Subject to the terms of the contract, an insurer will not be liable for loss proximately caused by delay[6] (even though the delay is caused by a peril insured against), by wilful misconduct of the assured, by ordinary wear

---

4   (1851) 6 Exch 451. See also *Brownsville Holdings v Adamjee Insurance* [2000] 2 Lloyd's Rep 458.

5   (1863) 32 LJCP 170.

6   For an example of an insurer's being liable for consequences of delay by virtue of the contract terms see *The Pomeranian* [1895] P 349.

and tear and leakage and breakage, by inherent vice or nature of the subject matter or by vermin.[7]

Types of loss

A loss may be total or partial and, if total, may be an actual total loss or a constructive total loss.

Actual total loss

There is an actual total loss of goods when they are destroyed, or so damaged as to cease to be the thing insured, or where the assured is irretrievably deprived of them.[8] The question of whether damage has changed the nature of goods and how this is to be established was discussed in the Court of Appeal in *Asfar & Co v Blundell*.[9] A barge carrying dates had sunk in shallow water and been raised but the dates had become contaminated by sewage so as to be unfit for human consumption although they still had a value as a source of industrial alcohol. Lord Esher MR said:[10]

> There is a perfectly well known test which has for many years been applied to such cases as the present – that is whether, as a matter of business, the nature of the thing has been altered. The nature of a thing is not necessarily altered because the thing itself has been damaged; wheat or rice may be damaged but still remain the things dealt with as wheat or rice in business. But if the nature of the thing is altered, and it becomes for business purposes something else, so that it is not dealt with by business people as the thing which it originally was, the question for determination is whether the thing insured, the original article of commerce, has become a total loss. If it is so changed in its nature ... as to become an unmerchantable thing ... then there is a total loss.

On this basis there had therefore been a total loss of the dates.

On the other hand in *Francis v Boulton*[11] a barge sank while carrying rice valued at £450. The cargo was raised but the consignee refused to take

---

7   Marine Insurance Act 1906, s 55(2).
8   Ibid, s 57.
9   [1896] 1 QB 123, CA.
10   Ibid at 127.
11   (1895) 65 LJQB 153.

delivery of it. The rice was dried at a cost of £68 and was eventually sold for £111. It was held, distinguishing *Asfar & Co v Blundell*, above that the rice, though damaged, was still edible rice and its nature had not changed. There was therefore only a partial loss.

While the rule *de minimis non curat lex* might conceivably be applied in this area, so that the saving of a negligible proportion of the goods might not prevent a loss from being regarded as a total loss, it is clear that any such saving must have no real commercial significance. Some indication of the scope of the rule was given in *Boon and Cheah Steel Pipes Sdn Bhd v Asia Insurance Ltd*[12] where 668 steel pipes were insured and all but twelve were lost. Although this amounted to a loss of 98.2% of the cargo the court refused to regard it as a total loss. Raja Azlan Shah J said:[13]

> In my judgment, 12 pipes measuring a total of 360 feet, weighing 36 tons, costing $14,400 and insured at $16,000 affect far too high a proportion of the whole consignment of 668 pipes to be capable of being dismissed as a matter de minimis. It may well be that in the case of a single pipe or two out of the whole consignment, the rule would apply, but I fail to see how it is possible to hold that 12 pipes can be ignored or treated as trifling and brushed aside.

Constructive total loss

This is a concept peculiar to marine insurance. Goods may be still in existence but must be considered from a commercial point of view as being totally lost either because an actual loss appears inevitable or because it would only be possible to save them at a cost greater than their value after being saved.[14] In *Vacuum Oil Co v Union Insurance Society of Canton*[15] a vessel carrying the insured tins of petrol stranded. A large proportion of the tins was recovered but many tins were leaking. Some of the leaking tins were repaired and filled with the contents of other tins so that over half the original amount was saved. The assured claimed a constructive total loss on the grounds that it would be impossible to have such a cargo forwarded to its destination. The Court of Appeal accepted this argument. Atkin LJ said:[16]

12   [1975] 1 Lloyd's Rep 452 (High Ct of Malaysia).
13   Ibid at 460.
14   Marine Insurance Act 1906, s 60.
15   (1926) 25 Ll L Rep 546, CA.
16   Ibid at 552.

I am quite satisfied that it would have been perfectly impossible to get anybody, however optimistic the owner of a sailing vessel trading in the Mediterranean in these ports might be, to carry a cargo of leaking petroleum tins. The estimate made by the underwriters themselves was that about 900 tins might have leaked in the time it would have taken to do the voyage, and 900 tins represent between 3,500 and 4,000 gallons of petroleum, which during this time would have flowed and leaked into the hold of the unfortunate vessel which was supposed to be carrying them.

A constructive total loss must be caused by a peril covered by the policy. In *De Mattos v Saunders*[17] salt worth £1,900 was damaged when the ship carrying it stranded. The salt was saved by voluntary salvors and landed. One fifth of it was saleable, though not at a profit. This balance was seized and sold at the suit of the salvors in the Admiralty Court but the proceeds of the sale were absorbed in the costs. It was held that there was no constructive total loss. The assured could recover as a partial loss the damage caused by the stranding but the seizure was not a risk insured against. To prove a constructive total loss the assured must prove the extent of the damage to the goods, otherwise there is no basis for calculation of whether repair and forwarding will exceed the arrival value. That damage is likely to have occurred is not enough.[18]

There may be constructive total loss on goods, even though the goods remain intact, if the adventure itself is frustrated. In *British and Foreign Marine Insurance Co Ltd v Samuel Sanday & Co*[19] a British ship was carrying goods of British owners from the Argentine to Hamburg when the First World War broke out. The ship was ordered by the Admiralty to proceed to a British port. The owners of the goods warehoused them and claimed a constructive total loss. In the House of Lords, Lord Atkinson cited a statement by Lord Ellenborough[20] that:

> an insurance upon cargo for a particular voyage contemplates that the voyage shall be performed with that cargo, and any risk which renders the cargo permanently lost to the assured may be the cause of abandonment. In like manner a total loss of cargo may be affected

17 (1872) LR 7 CP 570.
18 *Boon and Cheah Steel Pipes Sdn Bhd v Asia Insurance Co Ltd* [1975] 1 Lloyd's Rep 452 at 454.
19 [1916] 1 AC 650, HL.
20 In *Anderson v Wallis* (1813) 2 M & S 240.

not merely by the destruction of that cargo but by the total permanent incapacity of the ship to perform the voyage.

On this basis their Lordships held that such frustration of the voyage for an indefinite time was a constructive total loss of the cargo.

When the assured decides to abandon the goods to the insurer as a constructive total loss, he must normally give notice of this abandonment to the insurer with reasonable diligence. If he fails to do so the loss must be treated as a partial loss only.[1] The assured must sue if the insurer refuses to accept the notice of abandonment. It is important to note that the course of action arises on the date of the casualty and not on the date of service of the notice of abandonment.[2]

For the purpose of calculating whether or not there is a constructive total loss the agreed valuation in the policy is not, by itself, conclusive as to the actual value of the goods but the parties may, and frequently do, stipulate that the agreed value shall be conclusive for this purpose.

It is usual to insert in a policy a 'Constructive total loss' clause which spells out the rule in order to make its application a matter of contractual stipulation in case a dispute should fall to be heard by a court of a jurisdiction not applying the rule as a matter of law.

Partial loss

Any loss which is not a total loss, actual or constructive, must be a partial loss.[3] Partial losses fall into three categories: general average losses, particular charges and particular average losses.

General average loss

The nature of general average was considered in chapter 2. If insured goods are sacrificed in a general average act or if the owner has to pay a contribution in respect of another's goods or the ship, this loss or expense will be recoverable under the policy as long as the risk which the sacrifice was intended to avert was a risk covered by the policy.

---

1   Marine Insurance Act 1906, s 62.
2   *The Kyriathi* [1993] 1 Lloyd's Rep 137.
3   Marine Insurance Act 1906, s 56(1).

Particular charges

These are expenses incurred to prevent loss of or damage to the goods insured from a peril insured against. They differ from general average expenses in that they are incurred to prevent a loss of the particular goods only as opposed to a loss threatening all the interests concerned in the adventure. Particular charges are recoverable only if the contract expressly provides for this, as it invariably does by the 'Sue and labour' or 'Duty of assured' clause. This clause amounts to a separate engagement by the insurer to pay these charges over and above the amount insured. Thus if goods were valued at and insured for £1,000 and £500 was expended in an attempt to save them from a loss which nevertheless occurred, the insurer would be liable to pay a total of £1,500 although the amount insured was only £1,000. He would not be compelled to pay more in respect of the particular charges than the amount insured.

An instance of the scope of the 'Sue and labour' clause occurred in *The Pomeranian*.[4] A ship damaged by heavy weather put into port for repairs which took two weeks to complete. The ship was carrying live cattle and extra fodder had to be bought to keep them alive during the extra time that they were on board. This expense was recoverable as a particular charge under the 'Sue and labour' clause.

The insurer will only be liable to pay for particular charges if they are incurred to prevent a loss from a peril insured against. In *F W Berk & Co Ltd v Style*[5] the insured cargo was packed in paper bags. When it was discharged into lighters for landing it was discovered that the bags were in bad condition and the cargo was re-bagged for landing. The insurer was not liable for the expense of this operation since the defective bags were the result of inherent vice of the cargo, which was not a risk covered by the policy.

To be the subject of particular charges damage must be real and not merely suspected. In *J Lysaught Ltd v Coleman*[6] galvanised iron sheets packed in wooden cases were subject to a rough passage and were unpacked at an intermediate port for examination. All the cases were opened and those with damaged contents were sold off; the rest were repacked to continue the voyage. The insurers were not liable for the expense incurred in unpacking and repacking the boxes of undamaged iron. 'The underwriters

4   [1895] P 349.
5   [1956] 1 QB 180, [1955] 2 Lloyd's Rep 382.
6   [1895] 1 QB 49, CA.

The insurance of goods in transit

do not guarantee that the goods when they arrive shall be free from suspicion of damage.'[7]

Particular charges may include legal expenses. In *Nishina Trading Co Ltd v Chiyoda Fire and Marine Insurance Co Ltd*[8] a shipowner in dispute with a charterer refused to put into a port to discharge cargo until hire had been paid. On the shipowner's instructions, the master sailed for another port, with the cargo still on board. On arrival there, the shipowner, with the collusion of the charterer, mortgaged the cargo and the cargo owners were compelled to take legal action to recover it. The action of the master was a 'taking at sea', which was covered by the policy, so that the legal expenses were necessary to prevent a loss as a consequence of this peril and hence were recoverable as particular charges under the 'Sue and labour' clause.

The clause in present day contracts not only permits the assured to take measures to avert or minimise losses or preserve rights but lays a positive duty on him to do so. The nature of this duty was considered in *Integrated Container Service Inc v British Traders Insurance Co Ltd*[9] The plaintiffs had insured containers with the defendants and then leased them to a firm which did not affect its own insurance and which went into liquidation. Since the plaintiffs' rights could not otherwise be preserved they incurred expenses to recover the containers and claimed against their insurers. The Court of Appeal held that the clause required the assured to take 'such measures as may be reasonable for the purpose of averting or minimising a loss'. The assured has merely to show that he acted reasonably; he does not have to show that if he had not acted then loss would 'very probably' have occurred. He must therefore show that he acted as a reasonable man intent on preserving his property and not wishing to incur a loss of that property. He does not have to act as an assured making a claim. The insurers were liable to pay all expenses incurred before the containers came back into the custody of the assured.

Particular average loss

This category comprises all partial losses which do not fall into either of the two other categories and thus covers, in fact, the vast majority of partial losses.

---

7   Ibid at 54, per Lopes J.
8   [1969] 2 QB 449, [1969] 2 All ER 776, CA.
9   [1984] 1 Lloyd's Rep 154, CA.

Salvage

Where goods are saved by voluntary salvors, they have a claim for salvage, a proportion of the value of the goods saved. A payment of this nature to salvors is a particular average loss. Where, however, goods are saved or rescued by a party *under a contract* with the owner of the goods or his representative, this is not a particular average loss but may be recoverable as particular charges or as general average expenditure, depending on the situation in which the contract to save the goods was made.[10]

Special contractual arrangements

The basic marine policy as contained in the Schedule to the Marine Insurance Act 1906 is in a form which has existed for centuries and is thus in form and content highly inappropriate for modern conditions. It was therefore supplemented by contractual terms, the 'cargo clauses' which were designed to modify and update it. The original 'cargo clauses', however, were continually added to and modified, often as a result of judicial decisions, until many of them became appallingly verbose and complex. This, and changes in commercial practice, led to their reorganisation in 1982 and while some of the changes were formal others effectively altered the nature and extent of the cover provided. The new form is known as a Lloyd's Marine Policy and the new cargo clauses are described as the Institution Cargo Clauses A, B and C respectively. The clauses have, of course, no legal status other than as standard contractual terms but their use is almost universal.

The clauses afford three different types of cover, with A giving the most complete and C the least cover. The type of insurance to be used in any particular sale transaction will usually be decided in the sale contract or be a matter of the usage of a particular trade. In *Oranje Ltd v Sargant & Sons*[11] a cif contract stipulated the type of cover to be effected by the seller. The seller in fact took out insurance offering less cover and was held liable to the buyer in respect of losses not covered by the policy effected and which would have been covered by the stipulated policy.

---

10   Marine Insurance Act 1906, s 65.
11   (1924) 20 Ll L Rep 329.

The period of cover

It is usual to employ a 'Transit' or 'Warehouse to warehouse' clause, so that the insurance covers the goods from the time of the commencement of the transit from the seller's or other warehouse until the goods reach their final destination at the buyer's place of business or other agreed point. This clause, in conjunction with the 'Termination of contract' clause, provides for the possibility of variation of the adventure with an overall time limit for cover of 60 days from the time when the goods are discharged from the overseas vessel. This marine cover for land or even air transit is permitted by virtue of the Marine Insurance Act 1906, section 2 as 'incidental' to a sea voyage.

The risks covered

The C cargo clauses cover the following causes of loss or damage.

(1)   Fire or explosion. There are normally no difficulties in recognising fire but the term 'explosion' may be less clear. In *Commonwealth Smelting Ltd v Guardian Royal Exchange Assurance Ltd*[12] part of a compressed air machine fractured and flew off, causing further damage. The air in the machine then blew the damaged pieces outwards. The Court of Appeal held that the damage was not caused by explosion but by the fracturing and flying off of material.

(2)   The vessel or craft being stranded, grounded, sunk or burnt.

(3)   The overturning or derailment of a land conveyance.

(4)   The collision or contact of a vessel, craft or conveyance with any external object other than water. The exception is, of course, intended to exclude 'heavy weather damage'.

(5)   The discharge of the cargo at a port of distress.

(6)   General average sacrifice.

(7)   Jettison.

(8)   General average and salvage charges.

(9)   A 'both to blame' collision clause. Where two vessels share the blame for a collision there will be an apportionment of damages which may result in expense falling on cargo owners.

The B cargo clauses cover the same causes as the C clauses and, in addition,

(10) Earthquake, volcanic eruption or lightning.

12   [1986] 1 Lloyd's Rep 121, CA.

(11) The entry of sea, lake or river water into vessel, container or storage place.

(12) Washing overboard (as opposed to deliberate jettison) or dropping.

(13) The total loss of any package lost overboard during loading onto or unloading from any vessel or craft.

The A cargo clauses cover all risks apart from the specific exclusions common to all three sets, although the A clauses cover deliberate damage or destruction by wrongful acts and also piracy, which the B and C clauses exclude.

The main exclusions of the insurer's liability, which apply to all three sets, are of

(1) Loss or damage attributable to wilful misconduct of the assured.

(2) Ordinary leakage, loss of weight or wear and tear.

(3) Defects in packing.

(4) Inherent vice or nature of the cargo. Inherent vice was considered on p 38. In *T M Noten BV v Harding*[13] the question arose as to whether damage to a cargo of gloves was the result of inherent vice or of fault on the part of the carrier. There was evidence that the damage was caused by some external source after loading whereas inherent vice must be present in the goods at the commencement of the carriage if the exclusion is to apply.

(5) Delay.

(6) Insolvency or financial default of carriers etc.

(7) Nuclear weapons of all kinds. This exclusion is separate from the normal war exclusions because such weapons create a risk of loss or damage far beyond any war zone.

(8) Unseaworthiness if the assured or his servants are privy to it. If they are not, the insurers waive their rights under the warranty of seaworthiness implied in the contract by the Marine Insurance Act 1906.[14]

(9) Arrest, restraint and detention. This exclusion covers risks of the kind referred to in art IV(2)(g) of the Hague-Visby Rules (see p 37) and includes acts by persons seizing or attempting to seize power. Piracy is excluded under this head by the B and C clauses.

The following risks, though excluded by the A, B and C clauses, can be covered on special terms.

13 [1990] 2 Lloyd's Rep 283, CA.
14 See *Manifest Shipping & Co Ltd v Uni Polaris Insurance Co Ltd, The Star Sea* [1997] 1 Lloyd's Rep 360, CA.

(1) War risks.
(2) Labour disputes, riots, civil commotions and terrorists.

Subrogation and double insurance

Since the contract of marine insurance is a contract of indemnity, the assured is not entitled to profit by it. If he were to be permitted to receive payment for a loss from the insurer and then recover damages for the loss from the party responsible he would obviously receive more than an indemnity. Accordingly an insurer who has paid out on a loss is subrogated to all the rights of the assured in respect of that loss. Thus in *Dickenson v Jardine*[15] most of an insured cargo of tea was jettisoned in an attempt to refloat the carrying ship which had gone aground. It was held that the assured could claim payment for this loss from the insurer without first making any claim for contribution from the other interests concerned in the adventure. On paying the assured's claim the insurer stood in the position of the assured as regards the general average contributions and could claim them on his own behalf.

If the assured does receive compensation from another source he is bound to hand this over to an insurer who has paid for that loss, but the insurer himself is not entitled to demand more than the indemnity he has paid. In *Yorkshire Insurance Co Ltd v Nisbet Shipping Co Ltd*[16] an insurer paid for a loss. Some time later the Privy Council finally found for the assured against a Canadian defendant responsible for the loss. Damages were assessed in Canadian dollars and, because of a devaluation of the pound sterling, represented a grater sum in sterling than the amount that the insurer has paid to the assured. It was held that the insurer was not entitled to receive the excess.

Since the assured is entitled to an indemnity only, he is not entitled to recover more by taking out different policies with different insurers to cover the same risks on the same adventure for the same period. This is known as 'double insurance'. The assured is entitled only to the value of the goods or the amount of the loss and if there are two different insurers then each will be bound to pay a part of this in proportion to the amounts for which they have insured the goods. An insurer who in these circumstances pays more than his rateable proportion will be entitled to

15   (1868) LR 3 CP 639.
16   [1962] 2 QB 330, [1961] 2 All ER 487.

claim the excess from any other insurers.[17] An assured who receives, through double insurance, a sum greater than the agreed indemnity is deemed to hold the balance in trust for the insurers.[18]

Underinsurance

If goods are insured for part of their value only the assured is deemed to be his own insurer for the amount uninsured and thus to be liable for a rateable proportion of any loss. Thus an assured who insured for £600 goods valued at £1,000 would be entitled to receive from the insurer only 60% of any loss.[19]

INSURANCE BY THE ECGD

The seller of goods overseas can insure against most losses he is likely to suffer as a result of loss or damage occurring to the actual goods, but this kind of loss is not the only risk to which the transaction is subject. There is the risk that the buyer may become insolvent or refuse, without valid reason, to pay for the goods. There is also the possibility that, willing though the buyer may be to accept and pay for the goods, his own government may, for various reasons, prevent him from doing so. These risks, which may be broadly classified as commercial and political risks, cannot usually be covered by an ordinary commercial insurance policy.

Since these risks are likely to deter exporters it has been government policy to encourage trade by providing cover against such risks as not being of the kind 'normally insured with commercial insurers'. The service, originally established after the First World War, has been administered largely by the Export Credits Guarantee Department under the Department of Trade and Industry. Recent changes in governmental philosophy have led to the view that the scheme amounts to subsidising exporters and there have been alterations in the system. Much of the business of short term guarantees has been sold to a Dutch group Nederlandsche Creditetuerzekering Maatschappij (NCM) and other smaller providers of insurance, although the ECGD continues at present to re-insure the risks. Short-term cover provides protection for sales on credit terms up to 180

17 But not if one insurer is merely an insurer of 'increased value'. *Boag v Standard Marine Insurance Co ltd* [1937] 2 KB 113, [1937] 1 All ER 714, CA.
18 Marine Insurance Act 1906, ss 32, 80.
19 Ibid, s 81.

days. The risks covered usually include the insolvency of the buyer, failure of the buyer to pay within six months upon receipt of goods, or failure to take delivery of the goods. Another change has been the introduction of the 'portfolio' system by which levels of risk to be insured are considered country by country. The continuance of the scheme in its present form is therefore a questionable matter. However, the ECGD still offers cover including support for export finance at favourable fixed interest rates; insurance for non-payment on sale contracts; guarantees of payment to banks providing export finance, usually where medium-term credit has been extended to the buyer.

The usual guarantee is in the form of an insurance policy issued to a seller, or to a confirming house through which he is selling, but it may also take the form of a guarantee given by the ECGD directly to a bank or other institution which is providing finance to the seller for the transaction. The first type is in most respects similar to a normal insurance policy and the ordinary rules of insurance will apply to the arrangement. Thus in *Re Miller, Gibb & Co Ltd*[20] a selling company failed to receive payment from the buyer because of Brazilian exchange control regulations. The ECGD therefore paid the sellers the 90% of the price which was covered by the policy. The full price of the goods was later released but by that time a liquidator had been appointed for the selling company. The ECGD claimed 90% of the sum and it was held that they were entitled to receive it. As the Export Credit Guarantee was a contract of insurance the ordinary rules of insurance applied and the ECGD was thus subrogated to the selling company's rights in so far as the latter had been indemnified for the loss. The Department was entitled to the 90% of the price in its own right and did not have to prove as a creditor in the winding up.

Similarly, as under a normal commercial policy, the ECGD is not entitled under the rules on subrogation to receive more than the indemnity it has paid.[21] In *L Lucas Ltd v Export Credits Guarantee Department*[22] payment by the buyer of the price of goods, which was stipulated in US dollars, was delayed by exchange control restrictions in the United Arab Republic. The ECGD paid the sellers. The buyer eventually remitted the price and part of it was paid after a devaluation of the pound sterling so that the sterling equivalent was higher than the original payment would have been. The

20 [1957] 2 All ER 266, [1957] 1 Lloyd's Rep 258.
21 See eg, *Yorkshire Insurance Co Ltd v Nisbet Shipping Co Ltd* [1962] 2 QB 330, [1961] 2 All ER 487.
22 [1974] 2 All ER 889, [1974] 1 WLR 909, HL.

ECGD claimed a proportion of his excess. The House of Lords held that the ECGD had no claim to this since they were only subrogated to the sellers' rights to the extent to which they had indemnified the sellers. Lord Simon put the point succinctly:[1] 'The contract ... is a contract of indemnity. There is nothing either in the public scheme out of which it arises or in the terms of the agreement itself which suggests in any way a profit-sharing venture.'

Comprehensive short term guarantees

This guarantee covers the seller's export contracts made either on cash terms or on credit terms involving periods not normally exceeding six months, although transactions involving longer periods of credit can be covered. The arrangement is comprehensive in that it covers all the seller's export contracts. The seller makes periodical declarations of shipments that he has made and the total premium due is calculated on the basis of these declarations.

Limits are placed on the amount of credit which may be allowed by the seller to a particular buyer. These limits will depend on various factors, such as the seller's overall cover limit, whether the buyer has done business with the seller previously and, if so, the amount of credit allowed on such occasions, and on recommendations from banks and credit agencies and on information on the ECGD's own records.

The risks covered by this arrangement are those of the buyer's failure to pay for the goods he has accepted or of his failure to accept and pay for the goods. The policy does not cover the case where the buyer validly refuses to accept goods because the seller is in breach of the contract of sale. In such a case, no payments will be made to the seller (or even have the loss ascertained) until either the buyer retracts his assertion of the seller's breach of contract or until the seller establishes, through an action brought against the buyer, that he himself is not in breach of the contract of sale.

In addition the policy covers risks of a political nature, such as the inability of the buyer to pay the price, or to pay it on time, because of restrictions on import, such as the refusal of an import licence or restrictions on payment such as those imposed by exchange regulations or moratoria. Also covered are non-payment or non-acceptance caused by war, hostilities or revolution

1   Ibid at 889.

in the buyer's country or war between the buyer's country and the United Kingdom. The risks of this nature covered are, however, those which may occur, not those which must. The seller will not, for example, be covered against the failure of the buyer to obtain an import licence if that licence was required at the time when the contract of sale was made, or if buyer and seller have failed to comply with any requirement in existence when the contract was made. The amount of the cover will normally be 90% of the contract price, but will be less where the buyer rejects the goods and may be more where the loss is due to certain political causes. The cover will not, of course, be in any event more than the relevant percentage of the credit limit approved by the NCM for the particular buyer.

The usual policy includes 'pre-shipment' risks, such as an anticipatory repudiation of the contract by the buyer or the imposition of an export licence requirement by the United Kingdom Government. It is possible, for a lower premium, to obtain cover only against losses occurring after the goods have been shipped. Such a policy will normally be effected by a seller who can readily make alternative arrangements for the disposal of the goods should a pre-shipment risk materialise.

Specific policies, as opposed to comprehensive policies, can be issued. These are normally in connection with large scale sales, as of ships or plant, or with construction contracts. Under a specific policy the seller may be covered when the credit term under the sale contract is five years or even longer.

Assignment and direct guarantees

A seller who has ECGD or NCM cover is in a better position than one who has not in obtaining financing for export transactions from banks or other lending bodies. Such a body may require that the seller assigns to it the benefit of the ECGD guarantee, in which case arrangements are made for the ECGD to pay directly to the financing body any money due in respect of a loss on the particular transaction or transactions. From the point of view of the financing body there are two disadvantages in this arrangement. One is that the ECGD will, as insurer, be able to plead against the body any defence which it would have had against the assigning seller. If, for example, the seller had made a material misrepresentation to the ECGD in respect of a shipment the ECGD could avoid the policy in respect of that shipment even though the benefit of it had been assigned to an innocent party. A further disadvantage is that the financing body cannot receive payment in respect of a loss from which the seller himself would not have been protected, such as a loss through the seller's own failure to comply with export or import regulations which were in force when the sale contract was made.

Because of these disadvantages it is preferable, from the point of view of the financing body, to obtain a direct guarantee from the ECGD, which guarantees payment to the body in the event of the buyer's failing to pay, no matter what the grounds of this failure. Thus the financing body will have fuller protection than the seller, who would only be entitled to payment if the buyer's failure to pay is caused by one or more of the specified reasons. When it issues a direct guarantee of this type the ECGD will obtain a recourse agreement from the seller under which the ECGD may claim from the seller any sum paid to the financing body in respect of a failure of the buyer for which the seller himself would not have been entitled to payment under the policy. The direct guarantee, unlike the ordinary policy, is not a contract of insurance. Like the ordinary policy, however, it may be specific or comprehensive, that is, it may cover one transaction or the whole range of the seller's transactions.

Chapter 7
Payment in international sales

As indicated in chapter 1 the seller under an overseas sale contract is likely to require a method of payment more certain than those on which he is prepared to rely in sales in his own country. This is not necessarily the case; where a seller has confidence in the honesty and the solvency of an overseas buyer he may employ simple, direct and hence cheaper methods. But to expand or maintain his markets a seller must be prepared to deal with parties with whom he has not dealt before and in dealing with whom there must always be an element of risk which he can reduce by establishing a method of payment which does not depend solely on the solvency or integrity of his buyer. In all these methods a large part may be played by the negotiable instrument known as a bill of exchange.

BILLS OF EXCHANGE

The bill of exchange, sometimes referred to as a 'draft', is a very old established method of transferring money and is now governed by the Bills of Exchange Act 1882, section 3(1) of which defines it as 'an unconditional order in writing, addressed by one person to another, signed by the person giving it, requiring the person to whom it is addressed to pay on demand or at a fixed or determinable future time a sum certain in money to or to the order of a specified person or to bearer'.

A cheque is one form of bill of exchange but a special one in that it is always addressed to a banker and payable on demand, whereas other bills of exchange may be drawn on any person and may be payable, for example, 'three months after date' or 'ten days after sight'. When the person to whom the bill is addressed 'accepts' the bill by writing the word 'Accepted' on its face and signing it, he thereby undertakes to pay the bill in accordance with its terms and becomes liable on it as 'acceptor'.

The bill of exchange is a negotiable instrument, that is, it can be transferred by indorsement and delivery, or, if it is a bearer bill, by simple delivery; a holder of it may sue on it in his own name; no notice of assignment need be given to the acceptor and, most important, a holder in due course of the bill takes it free from equities, that is, unaffected by any third party rights or claims in respect of it. (It is in this last respect that a bill of exchange differs from a bill of lading.) Any holder who indorses the bill to another party becomes liable on it as a party to the bill. Should the bill be presented for payment to the acceptor at the proper time and be dishonoured, the holder will have rights of action against the acceptor, the drawer and all other prior parties to the bill. To be a holder in due course of a bill of exchange a person must take a bill which is complete and regular on the face of it, before it is overdue, in good faith and without notice, at the time of negotiation, of any defect in the title of the transferor. The simplicity of transfer of the bill of exchange and the security obtained by a holder in due course, who can indorse the bill for cash or for the credit of an account, make it invaluable in international trade transactions.

DIRECT PAYMENT

Where the seller is confident of the integrity and, more important, the solvency of his buyer, he may arrange for a direct payment. This may be done in various ways. The buyer may simply send the price to the seller by what is known as telegraphic transfer or mail transfer, whereby the buyer's bank communicates with a bank in the seller's country (a correspondent bank) instructing it to pay the seller. Another form of direct payment is by use of a banker's draft. The buyer obtains from his bank an order, drawn on a bank in the seller's country and naming the seller as payee. A banker's draft is usually a negotiable instrument and subject to all the rules relating to negotiable instruments although it may be expressly made not negotiable.

Another method, though one less used than formerly, is for the seller to send to the buyer the documents relating to the goods together with a bill of exchange drawn by the seller on the buyer. The buyer accepts the bill of exchange and returns it to the seller. The advantage of this method is that the buyer, although he does not yet have the goods, can deal with them by means of the bill of lading or other document of title to the goods and will not be required to pay for the goods until the bill of exchange becomes due. Conversely, the seller has the bill of exchange which he can discount to his bank and thus receives value for the goods. Both parties are thus freed from the disadvantage of having goods or capital tied up while the goods are in transit. The method has one marked disadvantage, however. Under the Sale of Goods Act 1979, section 19(3) there is an implication of law in this situation that the seller has reserved the right of disposal of the goods until such time as the buyer accepts and returns the bill of exchange. But this reservation of the right of disposal may give very little protection to the seller. The buyer who thus gains possession of the bill of lading but does not accept the bill of exchange will have no property in the goods but he is nevertheless a buyer in possession of the documents of title to goods under a sale agreement and under the Sale of Goods Act 1979, section 25 will be able to give a good title to any person who takes the bill of lading in good faith and in the ordinary course of business. This situation occurred in *Cahn and Mayer v Pockett's Bristol Channel Steam Packet Co Ltd*.[1] Ten tons of copper were sold cif Rotterdam, payment to be made by acceptance of a bill of exchange at 30 days from the date of the bill of lading. The seller sent the bill of lading to the buyer with the bill of exchange for acceptance. The buyer was insolvent when the documents reached him. He handed the bill of lading to his bankers, who handed it to a sub-buyer who paid cash to the bankers. The bankers credited the buyer's account with the amount. When he learned of the insolvency the seller purported to stop the goods *in transitu*. The court held that the buyer, although he had not accepted the bill of exchange, was in possession of a document of title to the goods and had transferred it in the ordinary course of business to the sub-buyer, who had taken it in good faith. The sellers' claim to the goods therefore failed.

COLLECTION

Under this arrangement, the seller instructs his bank to make arrangements, normally through a bank in the buyer's country, to collect payment from the buyer on a bill of exchange drawn on him by the seller. The bill of exchange may be sent to the bank accompanied by the documents relating to the goods, which the bank will hand to the buyer when he pays on the bill of exchange. This is known as a documentary remittance. If the bill of exchange is sent without the documents attached it is known as a clean remittance.

1   [1899] 1 QB 643, CA.

The International Chamber of Commerce has devised the 'Uniform Rules for Collections (1995 Revision)' which regulate the rights and responsibilities of banks and their customers in collection arrangements. These Rules have no legal force unless they are specifically adopted by the parties in their contracts but they are very widely used.

Under the normal arrangement, the seller's bank (the remitting bank) will be an agent of the seller for the collection of the price and the collecting bank in the buyer's country will be an agent of the remitting bank. There will thus be no privity of contract between the seller and the collecting bank. In *Calico Printers' Association Ltd v Barclays Bank Ltd*[2] the seller shipped goods to Beirut and sent the documents and a sight bill to an English bank for collection, coupled with a request that if the documents were not taken up the bank should endeavour to store and insure the goods. The English bank sent the documents and the bill of exchange to a collecting bank in Beirut. Because of the laxity of commercial practice there, there was a delay by the buyer in taking up the documents and before he did so the goods were destroyed by fire while they were uninsured. The sellers failed to recover in an action for breach of contract against the Syrian bank by reason, among other things, of the absence of privity. Wright J said,[3] 'English law has in general applied the rule that even where the subagent is properly employed there is no privity between him and the principal'.

If the remitting bank simply collects for the seller it will, as has been said, be his agent. The bank may also, however, discount the bill of exchange for the seller, that is, credit his account with the amount of the bill, with deductions for commission and charges. In this case the bank will become a holder of the bill of exchange and thus a party to it, with rights in it quite independently of the bank's position as the seller's agent.

> I am unable to accept the contention that a banker cannot at one and the same time be an agent for collection of a cheque and a holder of that cheque for value ... I readily accept that if a bank holds a cheque merely, and I emphasise the word 'merely', as his customer's agent for collection he cannot be a holder for value and still less a holder in due course; but that is an entirely different proposition.[4]

2   (1930) 38 Ll L Rep 105.
3   Ibid at 109.
4   *Barclays Bank Ltd v Astley Industrial Trust Ltd* [1970] 2 QB 527 at 538, [1970] 1 All ER 719 at 727, per Milmo J.

The point arose in *Barclays Bank Ltd v Aschaffenburger Zellstoffwerke AG*[5] where a seller indorsed in blank to his bank bills of exchange which had been accepted by the buyers. The buyers refused to pay all the money due on the bills and, in an action by the bank, pleaded that they had a set-off against the sellers and therefore against their agents, the bank. It was held, however, that the bank, as holder in due course of the bills, was not affected by the set-off against the indorser (the sellers) even though the set-off was against a principal for whom the bank was an agent. The status of the bank as agent for collection and its status as holder in due course of the bills were independent. On the other hand the court was prepared to accept that there might be circumstances in which a bank, even though it was a holder in due course of a bill of exchange, might be so as trustee for the seller for whom it was collecting on it, in which case set-off would be available against it.

As an agent for the seller, the remitting bank must comply strictly with the seller's instructions and will be liable to him as principal for the consequences of any failure to do so. The collecting bank will be in a similar position with respect to its principal, the remitting bank. In practice, though, banks will exclude various liabilities by express terms in the contracts they make with their customers and with other banks.[6] A remitting bank will have a free choice as to the collecting bank which it is to employ and will not be liable to the seller for any default by the collecting bank. Other liabilities of bankers excluded by the Rules are those in respect of the regularity of the form of bills of exchange or other documents, in respect of the loss of, or omission or error in, any documents transmitted or of the consequences of strikes, lockouts or other causes beyond the bank's control.

DOCUMENTARY CREDITS

General

Documentary credits, or bankers' commercial credits as they are sometimes called, represent the most secure method by which a seller may obtain the price of goods he has contracted to sell. In essence, the credit is established under the terms of the sale contract; the buyer instructs his bank (the issuing bank) to open a credit in the seller's name, normally through a bank in the seller's country (the correspondent bank); this bank notifies

5   [1967] 1 Lloyd's Rep 387, CA.
6   Eg *Calico Printers' Association Ltd v Barclays Bank Ltd* (1931) 39 Ll L Rep 51, CA.

the seller of the opening of the credit, on which the seller may draw only on presentation of the correct shipping documents to the bank. The machinery and the reasons for its use were described, in what has become a classic statement, by Scrutton LJ in *Guaranty Trust Co of New York v Hannay & Co*:[7]

> The enormous volume of sales of produce by a vendor in one country to a purchaser in another has led to the creation of an equally great financial system intervening between vendor and purchaser, and designed to enable commercial transactions to be carried out with the greatest money convenience to both parties. The vendor, to help the finance of his business, desires to get his purchase price as soon as possible after he has despatched the goods to his purchaser; with this object he draws a bill of exchange for the price, attaches to the draft the documents of carriage and insurance of the goods sold and sometimes an invoice for the price, and discounts the bill – that is, sells the bill with documents attached to an exchange house. The vendor thus gets his money before the purchaser would, in the ordinary course, pay; the exchange house duly presents the bill for acceptance, and has, until the bill is accepted, the security of a pledge of the documents attached and the goods they represent. The buyer on the other hand may not desire to pay the price till he has resold the goods. If the draft is drawn on him, the vendor or exchange house may not wish to part with the documents of title until the acceptance given by the purchaser is met at maturity. But if the purchaser can arrange that a bank of high standing shall accept the draft, the exchange house may be willing to part with the documents on receiving the acceptance of the bank. The exchange house will then have the promise of the bank to pay, which, if in the form of a bill of exchange, is negotiable and can be discounted at once. The bank will have the documents of title as security for its liability on the acceptance, and the purchaser can make arrangements to sell and deliver the goods.

The value of this system thus lies in the security that it affords to all the parties concerned. The seller has the payment of his price assured, provided he tenders the correct documents, by a reputable bank, usually one in his own country. The correspondent bank will receive the documents before it allows the seller to draw for the price and will thus be able to hold them as security pending payment by the issuing bank. The issuing bank, in

7   [1918] 2 KB 623 at 659, CA.

turn, will have the documents as security for payment by its own customer, the buyer. In fact this may be of small service to the bank in cases where the buyer cannot pay the bank without reselling the actual goods, since the bank will have to release the documents to him so that he can obtain the goods to resell them. The bank will obtain a letter of trust from the buyer but this may not be as effective as would be the security of the documents themselves.

Nearly all arrangements for documentary credits will be made subject to the terms of the International Chamber of Commerce's 'Uniform Customs and Practice for Documentary Credits' (1993 Revision). These define a documentary credit as:

> any arrangement, however named or described, whereby a bank (the issuing bank) acting at the request and in accordance with the instructions of a customer (the Applicant) or on its own behalf
> (i) is to make payment to or to the order of a third party (the Beneficiary) or is to accept and pay bills of exchange (drafts) drawn by the beneficiary, or
> (ii) authorises another bank to effect such payment, or to accept and pay such bills of exchange (drafts) against stipulated documents, provided that the terms and conditions of the credit are complied with, or
> (iii) authorises another bank to negotiate.

Types of documentary credits

Documentary credits are of various types. The particular type to be employed in a transaction will be usually laid down in the contract of sale under which the credit is arranged.

Revocable and irrevocable credits

A revocable credit is one which the buyer has established but which he may later cancel or modify in so far as the seller has not already drawn on it. This type of credit clearly does not give the security that a seller normally looks for. In *Cape Asbestos Co Ltd v Lloyds Bank Ltd*[8] payment was arranged to be made by a revocable credit. This credit was revoked by the buyer, but the bank gave no notice of this revocation to the seller, who

8   [1921] WN 274.

shipped a further instalment of goods to the buyer under the belief that the credit was still in operation. It was the usual practice of the bank as a matter of courtesy to give notice that a credit had been revoked but it had failed to do so on this occasion. It was held that the bank was under no legal duty to inform the beneficiary of the revocation of the credit. Such a duty might arise by a term of the contract but since any arrangement is likely to be made under the Uniform Customs, which lay down that the bank is not bound to give this notice, it is not easy to see how in practice the bank could be required to do so.

An irrevocable credit is one which is expressly stated to be irrevocable. Thus it cannot be cancelled or modified provided that the seller presents the correct documents to the bank in the contract period. This arrangement obviously gives considerable security to a seller but may have disadvantages for the buyer, since he is committed to the credit. In *Discount Records Ltd v Barclays Bank Ltd*[9] an irrevocable credit was opened in favour of the sellers. The goods shipped were not in accordance with the terms of the contract of sale and the buyer sought to cancel the credit and to obtain an injunction to prevent the banks from paying under it on the grounds that the sellers had been fraudulent and that the buyer was thus entitled to release from his legal obligations. The court refused to grant the injunction on the grounds that fraud was merely alleged and not proved and in these circumstances it would not be proper to allow an irrevocable credit to be effectively revoked. Megarry J said:[10]

> I would be slow to interfere with bankers' irrevocable credits, and not least in the sphere of international banking, unless a sufficiently good cause is shown; for interventions by the Court that are too ready or too frequent might gravely impair the reliance which, quite properly, is placed on such credits.

The possibility remains, therefore, that a court might, in a sufficiently serious case, allow a buyer to avoid payment on an irrevocable credit. Colour is lent to this view by the American case (distinguished in the *Discount Records* case) of *Sztejn v J Henry Schroder Banking Corpn*[11] in which it was said, 'Where the seller's fraud has been called to the bank's attention before the drafts and documents have been presented for

---

9   [1975] 1 All ER 1071, [1975] 1 Lloyd's Rep 444.
10   Ibid at 1075 and 448, respectively.
11   31 NYS 2d 631 (1941).

payment, the principle of the independence of the bank's obligation under the letter of credit should not be extended to protect the unscrupulous seller.' The question is clearly one of policy: the balancing of the undesirability of assisting fraud against the necessity for maintaining the stability of established commercial institutions.

The irrevocability of the credit will not, of course, deprive a buyer of any actions he may have against a seller in respect of breaches of the contract of sale.

Confirmed and unconfirmed credits

This distinction is now well recognised as being a different one from that just discussed, though it should be noted that the terms were sometimes confused in dicta in cases decided before the modern system of documentary credits was fully established. A credit is confirmed when the correspondent bank, in addition to notifying the seller of the opening of the credit in his favour, adds its own confirmation of the credit. A seller will, whenever possible, stipulate for a confirmed credit in the contract of sale since this will give him rights against a bank in his own jurisdiction. An unconfirmed credit is one under which the correspondent bank merely advises the seller of the opening of the credit but does not itself undertake any obligation under it. A correspondent bank will naturally not confirm a revocable credit.

Other types of documentary credits

Many variations exist, some confined to the particular parts of the world or to particular trades. Two of the most important are the back-to-back and the revolving credits.

Revolving credits

A revolving credit is employed when buyer and seller deal regularly with one another or have arranged to deal over a period. In such a situation it is inconvenient to set up a separate documentary credit for every transaction. Accordingly a credit is established with a maximum limit for drawings by the seller. As the seller presents documents and draws on the credit the buyer replenishes it.

Back-to-back credits

A seller, unless he is a manufacturer, will in most cases have to buy the goods he intends to sell. He may, therefore, require his buyer to set up a credit in his favour and then use this credit to support a second credit which he opens in favour of his own supplier. This arrangement, which may, of course, extend to a whole string of buyers and sellers[12] is known as a 'back-to-back' credit. The second or further credits will naturally differ from the first in respect of the price and the periods for which the credit is valid. Difficulties can occur in respect of this form of credit if different forms of sale contract are involved; if, for example, a seller buys on fas terms to sell on cif terms. Moreover, a banker who issues the second (or further) credit must clearly be able to comply with the terms of the first credit since otherwise the original buyer, who opened it, will be able to reject the documents.

'Red Clause' credits

Various other forms exist, one of the more important of which is the 'Red Clause' credit. The essential feature of this type of credit is that in order to pay his supplier the seller is allowed to draw on the credit before shipment of the goods. This type clearly depends to a large extent on the integrity of the seller, but as Scrutton LJ said in a case on this type of credit,[13] 'To understand business one must realise that it proceeds on the basis of confidence, not of fraud, and that it usually goes right. The Courts see the cases where it goes wrong.'

The relationship of the parties

The buyer, who arranges for the credit to be opened, will have a contractual relationship with the issuing banker, his agent. The issuing bank will then appoint a correspondent bank as its own agent[14] and there will normally be no privity of contract between the buyer and the correspondent bank.[15]

---

12 As in *Ian Stach Ltd v Baker Bosley Ltd* [1958] 2 QB 130, [1958] 1 All ER 542.
13 *South African Reserve Bank v Samuel & Co* (1931) 40 Ll L Rep 291 at 292, CA.
14 *Equitable Trust Co of New York v Dawson Partners Ltd* (1926) 27 Ll L Rep 49 at 52, 53, 57, HL.
15 *Calico Printers' Association Ltd v Barclays Bank Ltd* (1930) 38 Ll L Rep 105, p 172, above.

If, however, a correspondent bank fails to comply with the issuing bank's instructions the buyer will, of course, be able to reject the documents.

The theoretical basis of the contractual relationship between the seller and either of the banks is not altogether clear.[16] The bank is recognised as being under a contractual obligation, either directly or through a correspondent, to pay the seller who tenders valid documents but it is the buyer who provides the consideration for the contract which obliges the bank to do this. The seller, therefore, appears to be in the position of a beneficiary under a contact to which he is not a party and which he would not normally, under the doctrine of privity of contract, be able to enforce. Various attempts have been made to rationalise the situation and to find a legal basis for the bank's obligation to pay the seller.[17] It is clear, however, that the important feature of the bank's liability to the seller is not its theoretical legal basis but the fact that it is recognised in practice by buyers, sellers, banks and courts. In *Hamzeh Malas & Sons v British Imex Industries Ltd* Jenkins LJ said:[18]

> it seems to be plain enough that the opening of a confirmed letter of credit constitutes a bargain between the banker and the vendor of the goods which imposes on the banker an absolute obligation to pay[19] irrespective of any dispute there may be between the parties as to whether the goods are up to contract or not. An elaborate commercial system has been built up on the footing that bankers' confirmed credits are of that character, and in my judgment it would be wrong for this court in the present case to interfere with that established practice.

The opening of the credit

When the sale contract provides for the opening of a documentary credit by the buyer, his obligation to do so may take one of two forms. It may be

16   See L Zhou 'Legal Position Between Advising Bank 7th and Confirming Bank: Contrast and Comparison', JIBL.

17   For a review see Gutteridge and Megrah *The Law of Bankers' Commercial Credits* (7th edn, 2002), 17(7), 225–228.

18   [1958] 2 QB 127 at 129, CA. Article 37(c) now contains the rule that the goods must be fully described in the invoice in accordance with the credit instructions but in the other documents they may be described in general terms.

19   Perhaps not absolute, in view of the possibility of non-payment if fraud by the seller were clearly established. See *Discount Records Ltd v Barclays Bank Ltd* [1975] 1 All ER 1071, [1975] 1 Lloyd's Rep 444, p 176, above.

a condition precedent to the contract of sale or a condition of the contract of sale. The situation was explained by Denning LJ in *Trans Trust SPRL v Danubian Trading Co Ltd*[20]

> What is the legal position of such a stipulation?: Sometimes it is a condition precedent to the formation of a contract, that is, it is a condition which must be fulfilled before any contract is concluded at all. In those cases the stipulation 'subject to the opening of a credit' is rather like a stipulation 'subject to contract'. If no credit is provided, there is no contract between the parties. In other cases a contract is concluded and the stipulation for a credit is a condition which is an essential term of the contract. In those cases the provision of the credit is a condition precedent, not to the formation of the contract, but to the obligation of the seller to deliver the goods. If the buyer fails to provide the credit, the seller can treat himself as discharged from any further performance of the contract and can sue the buyer for damages for not providing the credit.

In that case, the seller had required the credit in order to obtain the goods from his own supplier. If no credit was forthcoming the transaction could not be carried out and the buyer was aware of this fact. In these circumstances the opening of the credit was held to be a condition precedent to the existence of a contract of sale.

The credit opened by the buyer must be of the agreed type or the seller will be able to repudiate the contract. If, however, he accepts the credit as opened he may be deemed to have waived his right to repudiate. In *Panoutsos v Raymond Hadley Corpn of New York*[21] goods were sold on the basis that each shipment was to be regarded as a separate contract. The sale contract demanded a confirmed credit but the credit opened was revocable and therefore not confirmed. The sellers made some shipments under the contract, then refused to make further shipments on the grounds of the incorrect credit. It was held that he sellers, while they would have been entitled to repudiate when advised of the credit, had, by making shipments, waived this right to the extent that they would have to give reasonable notice of an intention to stop shipments on the grounds of the incorrect credit.

---

20   [1952] 2 QB 297 at 304, [1952] 1 All ER 970 at 976, CA.
21   [1917] 2 KB 473, CA.

Time of opening

It is important not only that a credit of the right type is opened but that it is opened in good time. A credit is not 'opened' merely by the buyer's instructing the issuing bank to open it. The seller must be informed of the opening by the correspondent bank.[1] If the contract stipulates a time for the opening of the credit the buyer must comply with this stipulation. Such a time may be a specific date or the occurrence of an event (such as the receipt of a provisional invoice). It is more common, however, to stipulate that a credit is to be opened 'immediately'. 'Immediately' was stated by Porter J in *Garcia v Page & Co Ltd*[2] to mean 'in such time as is needed by a person of reasonable diligence to get that credit established'. In *A E Lindsay & Co Ltd v Cook*[3] a credit was to be opened 'immediately'. The date for shipment of the goods was to be 28 September but the seller was not advised of the opening of the credit until 6 October. Applying the law as stated in *Trans Trust SPRL v Danubian Trading Co Ltd*[4] it was held that the opening of the credit on time was a condition precedent to the seller's duty to ship the goods.

A seller may by his conduct be deemed to have acquiesced in the late opening of the credit. In *Garcia v Page & Co Ltd*[5] the contract of sale made on 27 May 1935 stipulated that a documentary credit was to be opened immediately and that shipment of the goods was to be made during the first half of the following September. There was a delay in providing the credit and on 22 August the sellers threatened to repudiate the contract if the credit was not opened by 24 August. A credit was opened with a bank in Spain on 24 August but on 27 August the sellers rejected this credit as not complying with the contract terms and purported to repudiate the contract. A satisfactory credit was opened on 3 September, that is, three days after the shipment period had begun. It was held that while the opening of the credit was clearly a condition precedent to the seller's duty to perform his part of the contract, the sellers in this case were aware of the delay but had apparently acquiesced in it until 22 August. The case was therefore remitted to the arbitrators to decide whether the seller's conduct

1   *Bunge Corpn v Vegetable Vitamin Foods (Pte) Ltd* [1985] 1 Lloyd's Rep 613.
2   (1936) 55 Ll L Rep 391 at 392.
3   [1953] 1 Lloyd's Rep 328.
4   [1952] 2 QB 297, [1952] 1 All ER 970, CA, p 180, above.
5   (1936) 55 Ll L Rep 391. See also *Baltimex Baltic Import and Export Co Ltd v Metallo Chemical Refining Co Ltd* [1955] 2 Lloyd's Rep 438.

amounted to a grant to the buyers of a further reasonable time in which to open the credit.

The date on which the goods are to be shipped is clearly of importance in relation to the time of opening of the credit, particularly if the parties have not specified a time for the opening. Until he is advised that the credit has been opened the seller cannot be assured that the buyer is in earnest and that he, the seller, will in fact get his money when he delivers the goods Thus when a sale contract provides for a period of time during which shipment is to be made, the credit must, subject to any express stipulation to the contrary, be opened before the shipment period begins. In *Pavia & Co SpA v Thurmann-Nielsen*[6] Denning LJ said:[7]

> In a contract which provides for payment by confirmed credit, when must the buyer open the credit? In the absence of express stipulation, I think the credit must be available to the seller at the beginning of the shipment period. The reason is because the seller is entitled, before he ships the goods, to be assured that, on shipment, he will get paid. The seller is not bound to tell the buyer the precise date when he is going to ship; and whenever he does ship the goods, he must be able to draw on the credit. He may ship on the very first day of the shipment period. If, therefore, the buyer is to fulfil his obligations he must make the credit available to the seller at the very first date when the goods may be lawfully shipped in compliance with the contract.

Similarly, when the contract provided for the buyer to furnish the credit 'ten days prior to estimated load date' it was held that the seller was entitled to receive the credit ten days before the commencement of the stipulated shipping period.[8]

The time of opening is even more critical when there is a 'string' of sale contracts, as in *Ian Stach Ltd v Baker Bosley Ltd*[9] Goods were sold fob Benelux port August/September shipment. Payment by irrevocable letter of credit divisible and transferable. The buyer had resold the goods and was relying on the opening of a credit by his sub-buyer to finance his own opening of a credit in favour of the seller who needed this to finance a credit in favour of his own supplier. Diplock J said:[10]

6   [1952] 2 QB 84, [1952] 1 All ER 492, CA.
7   Ibid at 88 and 495 respectively.
8   *Sohio Supply Co v Gatoil (USA) Inc* [1989] 1 Lloyd's Rep 588, CA.
9   [1958] 2 QB 130.
10 Ibid at 143.

It seems to me that, particularly in a trade of this kind, where, as is known to all parties participating, there may well be a string of contracts all of which are financed by, and can only be financed by, the credit opened by the ultimate user which goes down the string getting less and less until it comes to the actual supplier, the business sense of the arrangement requires that by the time the shipping period starts each of the sellers should receive the assurance from the banker that if he performs his part of the contract he will receive payment. It seems to me that in a case of this kind, and in the case of an ordinary fob contract financed by a confirmed banker's credit, the prima facie rule is that the credit must be opened ... by the earliest shipping date.

While the timely opening of the credit is recognised as a condition which the buyer must meet if the seller is not to be entitled to repudiate the contract it does not follow, as will be seen, that the buyer has thereby discharged all his obligations in respect of the payment of the price.[11]

The tender of documents

The buyer will send to the issuing bank instructions as to the documents which the seller is to present to the bank (or to the correspondent bank) in order to be allowed to draw on the credit. It is a term of the contract between the buyer and his bank that the bank will allow the seller to draw only if the documents are in strict accordance with these instructions and a bank which accepts documents which do not comply will be liable to the buyer. Furthermore, it will be a term of the contract between bank and seller that the seller presents the correct documents.[12] In *Moralice (London) Ltd v E D and F Man*[13] McNair J said:

When a cif contract provides that payment shall be by means of presentation of documents against an irrevocable credit, that necessarily involve not only in the contract between the confirming bank and the seller, but in the contract between the buyer and the seller, that the documents must be such as will strictly comply with the terms of the letter of credit.

11 See p 189, below.
12 For a discussion see Bennett 'Strict Compliance Under the UCP 500' [1997] LCMLQ 7.
13 [1954] 2 Lloyd's Rep 526 at 533.

Documentary credits

In that case the contract was for the sale of 5,000 bags but the bill of lading tendered to the bank indicated that there were three bags short. The bank was held to be entitled to reject the documents. The *de minimis* rule is not applicable to documentary credits.

The reasons for this rule of strict compliance, as it is called, are not hard to discover. The first reason is the position in which a bank would find itself if it allowed the seller to draw on tender of documents which the buyer would not accept. This was made clear by Lord Sumner in *Equitable Trust Co of New York v Dawson Partners Ltd*:[14]

> It is both common ground and common sense that in such a transaction the accepting bank can only claim indemnity [from the buyer] if the conditions on which it is authorised to accept are in the matter of the accompanying documents strictly observed. There is no room for documents which are almost the same, or which will do just as well. Business could not proceed securely on any other lines. The bank's branch abroad, which knows nothing officially of the details of the transaction thus financed, cannot take upon itself to decide what will do well enough and what will not. If it does as it is told, it is safe; if it departs from the conditions laid down, it acts at its own risk. The documents tendered were not exactly the documents which the [bank] had promised to take up and prima facie they were right in refusing to take them.

The second reason for the bank's insistence on the strict compliance of the tender with its instructions lies in the bank's position in relation to the sale contract. The bank is not a dealer in goods; it cannot be expected to know trade terms and practices or to know why the buyer has stipulated for a particular item and what importance he might attach to that item. The point arose in *J H Rayner & Co Ltd v Hambro's Bank Ltd*[15] where the sale was of 'Coromandel groundnuts'. The buyer's application for the opening of the credit required documents indicating these goods. The documents presented by the seller to the bank included an invoice for 'Coromandel groundnuts' but a bill of lading indicating the shipment of 'machine shelled groundnut kernels'. At first instance Atkinson J admitted evidence to show that trade practice regarded the terms as identical in meaning and concluded that the bank should have accepted the documents. The Court of Appeal reversed this ruling. Mackinnon LJ said:[16]

14   (1927) 27 Ll L Rep 49 at 52, HL.
15   [1943] KB 37, 74 Ll L Rep 10, CA.
16   Ibid at 41 and 13 respectively.

it is quite impossible to suggest that a banker is to be affected with knowledge of the customs and customary terms of every one of the thousands of trades for whose dealings he may issue letters of credit ... It would be quite impossible for business to be carried on, and for bankers to be in any way protected in such matters, if it were said that they must be affected by a knowledge of all the details of the way in which particular trades carry on their business.

The position of banks in this respect is clearly recognised in the Uniform Customs and Practice for Documentary Credits. General provision Article 3(a) states, 'Credits, by their nature, are separate transactions from the sales or other contracts on which they may be based and banks are in no way concerned with or bound by such contracts.' Article 4 states, 'In credit operations all parties concerned deal with documents and not with goods, services and/or other performances to which the documents may relate.'

While the principal documents likely to be tendered to a bank under a documentary credit arrangement (the invoice, bill of lading and insurance policy) are usually standard form documents, the contract may call for the presentation of other documents in respect of which it may be less easy to decide whether they comply with the requirements laid down by the buyer. In *Bank Melli Iran v Barclays Bank (Dominion, Colonial and Overseas) Ltd*[17] the buyer of trucks required from the seller a certificate from a 'US government undertaking confirming that the trucks are new'. The document actually tendered by the seller was unsatisfactory in two respects. In the first place it did not identify the trucks to which it referred as those which were the subject of the contract and, in the second place, it certified not that the trucks were 'new' but that they were 'new, good' trucks. It is indicative of the strict attitude of the courts in this area that this difference in wording was held to render the document unsatisfactory on the grounds that 'new' and 'new, good' might have different meanings in trade usage. (The correspondent bank was, however, relieved from the consequences of its acceptance of this document because the conduct of the issuing bank was held to have been such as to ratify the acceptance.)

The doctrine of strict compliance does not necessarily demand that every document in the set presented should state every detail required. It may be sufficient that all necessary information is clearly presented by the documents taken as a whole. In *Midland Bank Ltd v Seymour*[18] the contract

17   [1951] 2 Lloyd's Rep 367.
18   [1955] 2 Lloyd's Rep 147.

demanded documents relating to 'Hongkong duck feathers – 85% clean' and '12 bales each weighing about 190 lbs'. Of the documents tendered to the bank, the invoice described the goods fully in the above terms and stated the shipping mark but the bill of lading, while it stated the shipping mark, noted the cargo as '12 bales Hongkong duck feathers'. The buyer purported to reject these documents. Devlin J said:[19]

> The set of documents must contain all the particulars, and, of course, they must be consistent between themselves, otherwise they would not be a good set of shipping documents. But here you have a set of documents '[each of] which not only is consistent with itself, but also incorporates the particulars that are given in the other' – the shipping mark on the bill of lading leading to the invoice which bears the same shipping mark and which would be tendered at the same time, which sets out the full description of the goods.

The duty of the bank accepting documents is to:

> examine documents with reasonable care to ascertain that they appear on their face to be in accordance with the terms and conditions of the credit ... The bank is under no duty to take further steps to investigate the genuineness of a signature which, on the face of it, purports to be the signature of the person named or described in the credit.

This was stated by Lord Diplock giving the judgment of the Privy Council in *Gian Singh & Co Ltd v Banque de l'Indochine*.[20] In that case the credit required the tender of a certificate signed by a named person to be identified by a passport number. The certificate was tendered, apparently signed by the named person and a passport, bearing the correct number and the apparent signature of the named person, was presented for the bank's inspection. The bank accepted the documents. Both the certificate and the passport were forgeries. The buyer sued the bank but failed to obtain a judgment that he had been wrongly debited with the sum paid to the beneficiary. Obviously a bank can hardly be required to submit every document tendered to it to exhaustive examination. As Lord Diplock said,[21] 'In business transactions financed by documentary credits banks must be able to act promptly on presentation of the documents. In the ordinary case visual inspection of the documents presented is all that is called for.'

19   Ibid at 153.
20   [1974] 2 All ER 754 at 757, PC.
21   Ibid at 758.

Moreover a bank may not withhold acceptance of documents for an indefinite time while it is examining them but must accept or reject them within a reasonable time.[1]

A sale contract will often express some tolerance to be allowed to the seller in respect of the quantity of goods or other matters; it may, for example, refer to the quantity as 'about 1,000 tons'. The exact tolerance may be specified, as, for example, '1,000 tons plus or minus 2%'. The insertion of such a tolerance in the contract reduces the chances of delay in payment which might otherwise occur since, as has been seen, the *de minimis* rule cannot be held to apply to documentary credits.[2] The Uniform Customs and Practice for Documentary Credits allow for a tolerance of plus or minus 5% as regards the quantity of the goods which will apply unless the credit stipulates for an exact amount or specifies quantity in terms of a 'number of packing units or individual items', provided that the total amount of the price to be drawn does not exceed the total amount of the credit. If the credit employs some such term as 'about' or 'circa', this will be assumed to allow for a tolerance of plus or minus 10% in the amount of the credit, the quantity of the goods or the unit price.[3]

Since the bank may wish to hold the documents as a security against payment to itself, it is concerned that the documents with which it has to deal should, as far as possible, in fact give it security. In consequence the bank has an interest in the type of document presented. For this reason the Uniform Customs and Practice for Documentary Credits 500 lists individual articles which distinguish between various types of transport documentation. The individual articles 23–30 set out the circumstances under which the banks may accept different types of transport documentation. Under the new provisions, any transport document issued by a freight forwarder are acceptable unless otherwise stated provided the freight forwarder executes them as a carrier or as a multimodal transport operator or as agent acting on their behalf. Where goods are being carried by sea, the new provisions (as did the former UCP 400 rules) will not accept a transport document which states that the goods are or will be loaded on deck unless specifically authorised. However, a transport document which states that the goods may be carried on deck, or which

1   *Bankers Trust Co v State Bank of India* [1991] 1 Lloyd's Rep 587.
2   See eg, *Moralice (London) Ltd v E D and F Man* [1954] 2 Lloyd's Rep 526 at 533, p 183, above.
3   Art 39.
4   Art 31(i).

does not indicate where the goods will be carried, is acceptable.[4] Claused bills of lading are also not acceptable unless specifically authorised. The banks will accept combined transport documents if the credit provides for these and in this case will not demand evidence of the shipment of the goods on a sea-going vessel. Insurance documents must be as specified and must be issued by insurers or their agents. Cover notes issued by brokers are not acceptable unless allowed for by the credit. Insurance documents should indicate coverage of the cif value of the goods and make clear the type and extent of the cover afforded by the insurance.

As a general rule the buyer is entitled to receive the original documents. Unless otherwise stipulated in the credit, article 20(b) states that a document produced by reprographic, automated or computerised systems or a carbon copy may be treated as an original if it is marked as original and where necessary appears to be signed. In *Glencore International AG v Bank of China*[5] the issuing bank rejected documents as a certificate issued by the beneficiary was not marked 'original'. The document originated from a word-processing system and printer and then photocopied. One of the photocopies was signed by the beneficiary with an original signature in blue ink. It was held that the original signature was not sufficient to render the document an original for the purposes of article 20(b) if the document was not otherwise original. However, in *Kredietbank Antwerp v Midland Bank plc*[6] the Court of Appeal held that where the document is clearly an original, article 20(b) does not import the requirement that it should be stamped or marked 'original'.

Electronic documents

The new electronic supplement to the Uniform Customs and Practice on Documentary Credits came into force in April 2002. The supplement, termed eUCP, contains 12 articles which, if incorporated into a credit, will rule when there are electronic or part electronic presentations of documents. The eUCP is expected to revolutionise the way documentary credits are used and herald the beginning of a virtually paperless-based trade documentation. BOLERO has adopted the new eUCP rules.

---

5   [1996] 1 Lloyd's Rep 135, CA.
6   [1999] 1 All ER (Comm) 801.

Indemnities by sellers

The effects of the rule of strict compliance are mitigated in practice by the use of an indemnity. A bank which would be entitled to reject documents because of a discrepancy which appears to be a minor one may nevertheless accept them in return for an indemnity from the seller against the consequences to the bank of the acceptance. This practice prevents the delay and inconvenience occasioned by the necessity for the bank or the seller obtaining the buyer's consent to the acceptance of the documents.

'Short-circuiting'

When a contract of sale has established a documentary credit as the mode of payment, the seller has a duty to present the documents to the bank and is not entitled to short-circuit the documentary credit procedure by presenting the documents directly to the buyer and demanding payment from him. In *Soproma SpA v Marine and Animal By-Products Corpn*[7] the documents tendered by the seller to the bank were in several respects unsatisfactory. The bills of lading were indorsed to the correspondent bank instead of being indorsed in blank; they were also marked 'freight collect' instead of 'freight paid' as required. A certificate of analysis which should have indicated 'minimum 70% protein' in fact stated '67% protein'. These documents were rejected. The sellers then obtained documents which did conform to the requirements of the credit but by the time they had done so the term of the credit had expired. They therefore tendered the documents directly to the buyers and demanded payment. It was held that they were not entitled to do this. Payment by documentary credit had been agreed on by all parties as a term of the contract of sale. The sellers having made an invalid tender had failed to comply with the terms of the credit. The direct presentation to the buyer was irrelevant and ineffective.

Establishment of a credit as payment

As has been seen, the buyer must, when payment is to be made by documentary credit, open a credit of the correct type and open it in good time if he is to discharge his obligations under the contract of sale. Does he thereby discharge all his duties in respect of payment? In *Soproma SpA v Marine and Animal By-products Corpn*[8] McNair J said:

7   [1966] 1 Lloyd's Rep 367.
8   Ibid at 386.

Documentary credits

Under this form of contract ... the buyer performs his obligation as to payment if he provides for the sellers a reliable and solvent paymaster from whom he can obtain payment – if necessary by suit although it may well be that if the banker fails to pay by reason of his insolvency the buyer would be liable; but in such a case ... the basis of the liability must in principle be his failure to provide a proper letter of credit which involves (inter alia) that the [bank] is financially solvent.

Whatever the basis of the buyer's liability in this respect, it would appear that, unless the contract expresses or clearly implies the contrary, the opening of the documentary credit by the buyer will operate not as payment but as conditional payment. This was stated by Lord Denning MR in *W J Alan & Co v El Nasr Export and Import Co.*[9] In the same case Stephenson LJ said:[10]

If the confirming bank has defaulted, the sellers might not have been prevented by having agreed to the letter of credit and to payment of the price by the bank from looking to the buyers either for the price agreed in the contract or for damages for breach of their contractual promise to pay the letter of credit. For the buyer promised to pay by letter of credit, not to provide by letter of credit a source which did not pay.

Whether the opening of the credit by the buyer is intended by the parties to operate as a conditional or as an absolute payment is a question which can be decided only by reference to the particular contract. In *E D and F Man Ltd v Nigerian Sweets and Confectionery Ltd*[11] the bank accepted documents from the sellers and agreed to accept the sellers' drafts. The documents were sent by the bank to the buyers, who remitted the amount of the credit to the bank. The bank became insolvent before paying the sellers' drafts. Ackner J held that on the basis of the contract the buyers were still liable to pay the sellers. 'It seems to be clear ... that the sellers did not stipulate for the credit to be issued by [the bank] in such circumstances that it was to be inferred that they looked to that particular bank to the exclusion of the [buyers].'

9   [1972] 2 QB 189 at 212, CA.
10 Ibid at 220.
11 [1977] 2 Lloyd's Rep 50.

Expiry

The Uniform Customs and Practice for Documentary Credits require that a date for the expiry of the credit is expressly stipulated, even though a final date for shipment is expressed.[12] Any later extension of the expiry date is not deemed to extend the latest date for shipment and documents presented before the expiry date showing shipment after the last date for shipment will not be accepted.[13]

Assignment and transfer of credits

A documentary credit, by its very nature, is not negotiable in the sense that a bill of exchange is negotiable, and the seller beneficiary cannot transfer it to another party by delivery or indorsement. There appears to be no reason why a beneficiary should not assign his rights to the proceeds of a documentary credit under the ordinary rules as to assignment of choses in action, but this is a different matter from the assignment of the actual credit. Credits may expressly be made transferable. Article 48 of the Uniform Customs and Practice on Documentary Credits states:

> (a) A transferable Credit is a Credit under which the Beneficiary (First Beneficiary) may request the bank authorised to pay, incur a deferred payment undertaking, accept or negotiate (the 'Transferring Bank') or in the case of a freely negotiable Credit, the Bank specifically authorised in the Credit as a Transferring Bank, to make the Credit available in whole or in part to one or more other Beneficiary(ies) (Second Beneficiary(ies)).

A transferable credit may be transferred once only. Fractions of a transferable credit may be transferred provided that the credit allows partial shipments.[14]

A credit may be transferred only if it is expressed by the issuing bank to be transferable and the issuing bank will, of course, only do this on the buyer's express instructions. The correspondent bank will not be entitled to transfer a credit if the buyer has not stipulated for this, since he may not wish the credit to be transferable if he wishes to deal only with a particular seller, because, for example, of his reputation for quality or technical skill.

12   Art 42(a). See *Bayerische Vereinsbank AG v National Bank of Pakistan* [1997] 1 Lloyd's Rep 59.
13   Art 43(a).
14   Art 48(g).

In *Bank Negara Indonesia 1946 v Lariza (Singapore) Pte Ltd*[15] the Privy Council held that the designation of a credit as 'transferable' in a contract of sale did not oblige an issuing bank to transfer it except as expressly agreed, nor did it constitute consent by the bank for any subsequent request for transfer. Not surprisingly this decision has been criticised as introducing uncertainty into documentary credit transactions.[16]

The transfer is effected by the seller, after receiving the credit advice from the bank, requesting the bank to transfer the credit to a named second beneficiary, who will in most cases be the seller's own supplier. The price and the period of validity of the credit as transferred will usually differ from those established by the credit originally, since the seller will be paying less to his supplier than he himself receives from the buyer and may expect an earlier delivery. If the seller wishes to keep his source of supply concealed from his buyer (in order to prevent the buyer dealing directly with the supplier in future transactions) he will arrange for his own invoice to be substituted for the supplier's in the documents transferred to the seller.

The legal nature of the transfer is not altogether clear. One school of thought, prevalent in the United States, holds that there is a novation, that is, that a new contract springs up between the bank and the second beneficiary and that the first beneficiary drops out. The other view is that the transfer operates as an equitable assignment so that the original beneficiary may still be under liability in respect of the transaction.[17] There is very little English authority on the point.

The use of a back-to-back credit[18] may have much the same practical effect as a transfer and may similarly be used to prevent the ultimate buyer discovering the source of the goods. In this case the seller will send the documentary credit letter to his own bank (ie not the issuing or corresponding bank) and ask it to open a credit in favour of his supplier on the strength of the original credit. In this case the seller will always substitute his own invoice for that of his supplier. The seller's bank will obtain the shipping documents from the supplier, substitute the seller's

---

15   [1988] AC 583, [1988] 2 WLR 374.
16   See eg, Schmitthoff: 'The Transferable Credit' (1988) JBL 49.
17   For a review see Smith: 'Transmitting the Benefit of a Letter of Credit' (1991) JBL 447.
18   Page 178 above.

invoice for the supplier's and tender the documents to the correspondent or issuing bank for payment. The seller's bank is thus dependent for the invoice on its own customer and not on the supplier who presents the original documents.

Chapter 8
Disputes in international transactions

THE CONFLICT OF LAWS

The problem of conflict

It is inevitable in the field of international trade that problems should arise concerning the applicability of the laws of different countries. If one imagines, for example, the by no means unlikely situation of a contract between an English firm and a German firm being made in France for the sale of goods to be shipped in the Argentine on a Dutch ship for carriage to a Danish port it is not difficult to appreciate the nature and scope of the problem of deciding which laws is to apply.

As far as English law is concerned there will be two questions to decide. The first is whether an English court has jurisdiction to hear a case. In the absence of an express term to the contrary in the contract, an English court will usually assume jurisdiction if the contract was made in England.[1] Once the court has decided that it has jurisdiction to hear the case, the second question will be which law is to apply, or, as it is called, which law is 'the proper law of the contract'. If this is decided to be English law the case will proceed as any English case. If not, the relevant rules of the applicable foreign law will have to be proved as a matter of fact by expert witnesses.[2] It does not follow that only one system of law may be considered. Matters relating to the form and validity of the contract may fall to be decided by one system of law and matters relating to its

---

1   *Entores Ltd v Miles Far East Corpn* [1955] 2 QB 327, [1955[2 All ER 493, CA.
2   *Castrique v Imrie* (1870) LR 4 HL 414.

performance by another.[3] In *Libyan Arab Foreign Bank v Manufacturers Hanover Trust Co (No 2)*[4] a transaction involved two contracts, the proper law of one of which was held by the commercial court to be English law while the proper law of the other was the law of New York. The court assumed that this distinction would still apply even though the transaction had been in the form of a single contract.

The proper law of the contract

The essential method of ascertaining the proper law of a contract was described by Lord Wright in *Mount Albert Borough Council v Australasian Temperance and General Mutual Life Assurance Society Ltd*:[5]

> The proper law of the contract means that law which the English or other court is to apply in determining the obligations under the contract. English law in deciding these matters has refused to treat as conclusive, rigid or arbitrary criteria such as *lex loci contractus* or *lex loci solutionis*, and has treated the matter as depending on the terms of the contract, the situation of the parties, and generally on all surrounding facts. It may be that parties have in terms in their agreement expressed what law they intend to govern, and in that case prima facie their intention will be effectuated by the court, but in most cases they do not do so. The parties may not have thought of the matter at all. Then the court has to impute an intention or to determine for the parties what is the proper law which ... they ... would have intended if they had thought about the question when they made the contract. No doubt there are certain prima facie rules to which a court in deciding on any particular contract may turn for assistance but they are not conclusive.

There are thus two possible situations to be considered. One is that the parties have specified the law to be applied to their contract – or possibly clearly implied it; the other is that they have not done so, in which case their intentions on the point must be deduced by the court.

---

3   See eg, *AV Pound & Co Ltd v MW Hardy & Co Inc* [1956] AC 588, [1956] 1 All ER 639, HL.
4   [1989] 1 Lloyd's Rep 608.
5   [1938] AC 224 at 240.

The parties' choice of law

Under English law, parties are free to stipulate in their contract the system of law which is to be applied to it. Such 'choice of law' clauses are frequently employed in standard form sale contracts employed in various trades. The courts will normally enforce a choice of law clause provided, as Lord Wright stated in the leading case of *Vita Food Products Inc v Unus Shipping Co Ltd*[6] 'that the intention expressed is bona fide and legal, and provided there is no reason for avoiding the choice on the grounds of public policy'. Parties frequently choose laws that have, or appear to have, no connection with the particular contract, for various reasons, one of which was stated by Lord Diplock in *Compagnie d'Armement Maritime SA v Cie Tunisienne de Navigation SA.*[7]

> In international transactions, particularly on commodity markets where the same shipment of goods may be brought and sold many times before delivery of the actual goods to the last buyer, it is a great commercial convenience that all contracts relating to such sales should be subject to the same proper law irrespective of the place of shipment or discharge, the residence or nationality of the parties or the place where the contract was made.

The choice on such a ground of an otherwise irrelevant law would clearly be valid but such a choice would almost certainly not be effective if it were made deliberately to avoid some provision of the law that would normally apply to the contract. Even if the choice is of a relevant law an English court may disregard it if its effect is to avoid a mandatory provision of English law. In *The Hollandia*[8] machinery was shipped in Leith on a Dutch vessel to Amsterdam for the first stage of its carriage to the Dutch West Indies. The bill of lading incorporated a term that the law of The Netherlands had not acceded to the Hague–Visby Rules and still applied the earlier Hague Rules, under which the maximum liability of the carrier was considerably lower than in the new rules. The House of Lords held that the Hague–Visby Rules were binding in English law, that art III(8) of the Rules prohibited reduction by contract of the carrier's liability[9] and that, since the effect of the choice of law clause would be to reduce that liability by means of a contractual term, the clause was invalid and should be ignored.

6   [1939] AC 277 at 290.
7   [1971] AC 572 at 609, [1970] 3 All ER 71 at 96.
8   [1983] 1 AC 565, [1982] 3 All ER 1141.
9   See p 39.

When the parties have expressed a valid choice of law in their contract there will be a very heavy burden on a party claiming that it should not apply. In *The Kislovodsk*[10] a cargo owner brought an action in England against a Russian carrier in respect of damage to a cargo of coffee carried from Mombasa to Rotterdam. The Russian undertaking, which was based in Leningrad, applied for a stay of proceedings on the grounds that the contract of carriage stipulated that disputes should be decided there. The stay was granted. 'The Court should be very slow to refuse a stay if the claim is just the sort of claim which could be expected when the agreement was made. The [cargo owners] must show strong grounds for not giving effect to the foreign jurisdiction clause.'[11] The inconvenience occasioned to the cargo owners by the necessity of proceeding in a foreign court was not such 'strong grounds'.

On the other hand in *Carvalho v Hull, Blyth (Angola) Ltd*[12] a contract made in 1973 provided that a named district court in Angola should be 'the sole Court competent to adjudicate to the exclusion of all others'. At that time Angola was part of the Portuguese legal system but became independent before the action was brought. The defendants, in Angola, applied for a stay of action on the basis of the jurisdiction clause. The Court of Appeal refused to grant the stay on two grounds. In the first place there were reasons connected with the plaintiff's personal position that made it 'just and proper' for the court to exercise its discretion to refuse a stay. In the second place, because of political and constitutional changes in Angola, the existing district court could not be regarded as being in any real sense the same court as that specified in the contract.

The intention to choose a particular law may be implied by the contract. If the parties appoint an arbitration body in a particular country there is a clear implication that they intend the courts of that country to have jurisdiction over any dispute arising from the contract. There may be a further implication that they also intend the law of that country to be the proper law of their contract. Many cases[13] have been decided in accordance with English law solely on the basis of a clause providing for arbitration in London. But such a clause will by no means be decisive. In *Compagnie d'Armement Maritime SA v Cie Tunisienne de Navigation SA*[14] where the

10   [1980] 1 Lloyd's Rep 183 and see *The Waylink* [1988] 1 Lloyd's Rep 475, CA.
11   Ibid at 184, per Sheen J.
12   [1979] 3 All ER 280, [1979] 1 WLR 1228, CA.
13   Including the famous *Suisse Atlantique Société d'Armement Maritime SA v Rotterdamsche Kolen Centrale NV* [1967] 1 AC 361, [1966] 2 All ER 61, HL.
14   [1971] AC 572, [1970] 3 All ER 71.

situation was similar but where there was a dispute concerning the proper law, Lord Reid said:[15]

> Of course the fact that the parties have agreed that arbitration should take place in England is an important factor and in many cases it may be the deciding factor. But it would in my view be highly anomalous if our law required the mere fact that arbitration is to take place in England to be decisive as to the proper law of the contract.

Inferring the proper law

Where the parties have not expressed or clearly implied their intention as to which law should be applied to their contract, that intention will have to be inferred by the court from the contract and from all the circumstances connected with it. The overall principle is that the proper law of the contract in this situation is 'the system of law by reference to which the contract was made or that with which the transaction had its closest and most real connection'.[16] In *Offshore International SA v Banco Central SA*[17] a Spanish company contracted to build an oil drilling rig for a company registered in Panama. A deposit of $3 million was paid to the constructors and its repayment in the event of cancellation was to be by an irrevocable letter of credit issued by a Spanish bank through a correspondent bank in New York. The letter of credit did not contain any express term as to the law which was to apply to it. A dispute arose on whether the law of New York or that of Spain was the proper law of the contract. Ackner J held that the law of the country of the issuing bank did not automatically apply. The payment, in American dollars, was to be made through a New York bank against documents to be presented in New York. The law of New York thus had the closest and most real connection with the contract.

While the principle is clear, it is obviously not always easy to put into practice. In *The Assunzione*[18] the Court of Appeal was faced with the task of determining the law proper to a contract for carrying wheat from Belgium to Italy on an Italian ship chartered by French charterers, a contract made in France, following negotiations between brokers in France and Italy, on a standard form English contract. The closest and most real connection

15   Ibid at 584 and 75 respectively.
16   *Bonython v Commonwealth of Australia* [1951] AC 201 at 219.
17   [1976] 3 All ER 749.
18   [1954] P 150, CA.

was held, in the event, to be with Italian law, largely because the performance by both parties was to take place in Italy.

In fact the place of performance will often be the deciding factor, as in *Benaim & Co v Debono*[19] where a contract was made in Malta to sell fish fob Gibraltar, payment against documents through a bank in Gibraltar. The fact that shipment and the passing of the property in the goods was to take place in Gibraltar was held to make the law of that place the proper law of the contract. In *Amin Rasheed Shipping Corpn v Kuwait Insurance Co*,[20] the House of Lords, considering the proper law of an insurance contract, took into account that the policy was a renewal of one originally issued by an English company through English brokers and English re-insurance brokers, that claims were payable in London and that at the relevant time there was no marine insurance law in Kuwait applicable to the contract.

Other factors which may sway the decision are the language and nature of the contractual documents, including their terminology; the currency in which payment is to be made; the places of business of the parties and their nationalities and the flag of any ship involved. There is also a presumption that the parties have chosen a system of law under which their contract would be valid but the extent of its application is doubtful.[1]

Foreign illegality

Although English law is the proper law of a contract and that contract is valid under English law considered by itself, it may be illegal on public policy grounds because it involves the breach of a foreign law. Foreign revenue and penal laws are not generally enforceable in this country at the suit of a foreign government: as Lord Denning has said,[2] 'These Courts do not sit to collect taxes for another country or to inflict punishments for it.' But a party to a civil action may plead the foreign illegality of a contract even if the illegality is in respect of a law of a penal or revenue nature.

In *Foster v Driscoll*[3] several persons combined to sell and ship whisky intended to be sold in the United States at a time when the import and sale

19　[1924] AC 514.
20　[1984] AC 50, [1983] 2 All ER 884, HL.
1　See eg, *Sayers v International Drilling Co NV* [1971] 3 All ER 163, [1971] 1 WLR 1176, CA.
2　In *Regazzoni v K C Sethia (1944) Ltd* [1956] 2 QB 490 at 515.
3　[1929] 1 KB 470, CA.

of alcoholic drinks was illegal in that country. It was held that a party in beach of this contract could plead as a defence the illegality involved in the breach of United States law. In *Regazzoni v K C Sethia (1944) Ltd*[4] jute was sold by an Indian seller cif European port. To the knowledge of both buyer and seller the goods were to be delivered at Genoa with the intention of shipping them to South Africa. The sale of jute to South Africa had, for political reasons, been made illegal by the Indian Government. The seller could plead the illegality as an excuse for failing to deliver the goods.

The illegality may be fortuitous and not necessarily a deliberate breach as in the cases so far mentioned. In *Ralli Bros v Cia Naviera Sota y Aznar*[5] an English firm chartered a Spanish ship from a Spanish firm to carry jute from Calcutta to Barcelona at a freight of £50 per ton. Part of this freight was payable on delivery of the jute in Barcelona. By the time this became payable the Spanish authorities had imposed an upper limit on freight rates and the contract freight was above this limit. The Court of Appeal held that the payment of this freight was illegal under Spanish law and although the proper law of the contract was English law the payment could not be enforced against the charterers. Scrutton LJ set out the basis of the rule on foreign illegality:[6]

> I should prefer to state the ground of my decision ... on the ground that where a contract requires an act to be done in a foreign country, it is, in the absence of very special circumstances, an implied term of the continuing validity of such a provision that the act to be done in the foreign country shall not be illegal by the law of that country. This country should not in my opinion assist or sanction the breach of the laws of some other independent states.

The nature of the 'very special circumstances' in which a foreign illegality might not vitiate a contract was indicated by Lord Reid in *Regazzoni v K C Sethia (1944) Ltd*[7] when he said, 'It may be there are exceptions. I can imagine a foreign law involving persecution of such a character that we would regard an agreement to break it as meritorious.'

If a contract can be performed legally it will not necessarily be illegal merely because the most convenient way of performing it would involve a

4   [1958] AC 301, [1957] 3 All ER 286.
5   [1920] 2 KB 287.
6   Ibid at 304.
7   [1958] AC 301 at 325.

foreign illegality. In *Toprak Mahsulleri Ofisi v Finagrain Cie Commerciale, Agricole et Financière SA*[8] a Turkish organisation contracted to buy US wheat c and f, payment by irrevocable documentary credit. The Turkish financial authorities, concerned to conserve foreign exchange, asked the buyers to arrange for the contract to be changed to fob terms and declined, unless this were done, to provide the official consent without which the opening of the documentary credit in Turkey would be illegal. The buyers when sued for failure to provide the credit, pleaded that they were excused by the illegality involved in opening it without the official consent. It was held, however, that there was no stipulation in the contact of sale that the credit had to be opened in Turkey and therefore no necessary illegality in performance.

PROCEEDINGS AND JURISDICTION

At common law civil procedure is now largely governed by the Civil Procedure Rules (CPR) 1998 and its amendments and practice directives.

Defendants outside the jurisdiction

At common law a person can only be made a party to an action and a writ (now called a claim form following the CPR 1998) served on him if he is within the jurisdiction of the court or if, though outside it, he has submitted to it. A party is deemed to have submitted to the jurisdiction of the court if he voluntarily appears in the action, though not if he appears only in order to contest the jurisdiction.[9] A defendant outside the jurisdiction will be held to have submitted to the jurisdiction if he is party to a contract on which the action is based and which contains a clause giving the court jurisdiction.

Further situations in which a writ may be served on a party outside the jurisdiction are set out in the Civil Procedure Rules 6 20(I) – (3A). Briefly, these can be listed as follows:
(a) when the defendant is domiciled or ordinarily resident in the jurisdiction;
(b) when the party on whom it is desired to serve the writ is a necessary or proper party to an action brought against another party who is within the jurisdiction;

8   [1979] 2 Lloyd's Rep 98.
9   *Re Dulles Settlement (No 2)* [1951] Ch 842, CA.

(c) when an injunction is sought ordering the defendant to do or refrain from doing some act within the jurisdiction, as long as the injunction is the substantial relief sought;

(d) when the action concerns a contract which was made within the jurisdiction (including one made by an agent within the jurisdiction);

(e) where the action concerns a breach of a contract which occurred within the jurisdiction; and

(f) where a tort has been committed within the jurisdiction.

The factors to be taken into account by a court considering an application for leave to serve a writ on a party outside the jurisdiction were outlined by the House of Lords in *Spiliada Maritime Corpn v Cansulex Ltd.*[10] The plaintiffs commenced an action in an English court and obtained leave ex parte to serve a writ on the defendants in Vancouver on the grounds that the action was to recover damages for breach of a contract governed by English law. The defendants asked for the ex parte order to be discharged on the ground that the case had not been shown to be a proper one for services out of the jurisdiction. The House of Lords said that courts should grant a stay if there was a competent court which was a more appropriate forum than the English court, bearing in mind the interests of all parties.[11] The fact that the defendant may undergo difficulties if the case were heard in an English court is not by itself a sufficient reason for granting a stay. A court should have regard to factors indicating that the most real and substantial connection was with another forum. The convenience of the parties, expense, availability of witnesses and the residences or places of business of the parties are such factors. A court should refuse a stay if it decides, after consideration of these factors, that there is no other suitable forum. However, although a defendant may have established, on the basis of these factors, a valid argument for a stay, the court may nevertheless refuse it on other grounds, for example, that the plaintiff would not obtain justice in the foreign jurisdiction. In *Lubbe v Cape plc*[12] the House of Lords would not grant a stay on the grounds that no legal aid was available to the claimants in South Africa unlike in England; there was no real possibility of a contingency fee arrangement available to the claimants in South Africa; and that the South African system did not have procedures for dealing with group actions.

10 [1987] AC 460, [1986] 3 All ER 843, HL.
11 It was evolved in *Mareva Cia Naviera SA v International Bulkcarriers SA* [1975] 2 Lloyd's Rep 509, CA.
12 [2000] 1 WLR 1545, HL.

Proceedings and jurisdiction

The freezing injunction

If a defendant outside the jurisdiction has assets within the jurisdiction it may be possible to apply for an injunction to restrain him from removing those assets from the jurisdiction. Such an injunction, formerly known as a 'Mareva' injunction, is now called a freezing injunction under the Civil Procedure Rules 1998. A freezing injunction may be made any time, including the time before the action is actually commenced and the time after judgment has been made. However, there are constraints imposed on the granting of a freezing injunction before a claim form is lodged. The matter must be urgent or it is otherwise necessary to do so in the interests of justice. If the injunction is granted the courts may require proceedings to be brought as soon as is practicable.

The Siskina[13] established the principle that at common law a Mareva injunction could not be granted if the English court had no jurisdiction over the substantive claim. However, where the EU Council Regulation on Jurisdiction and the Recognition and Enforcement of Judgments in Civil and Commercial Matters 2000 applies, article 31 will apply. This permits application to be made to the courts of a member state for a freezing order even if the courts of another member state have jurisdiction over the substantive matter.

The injunction is particularly useful in that it provides a fund from which a plaintiff who obtains judgment in this country may recover damages without the need to enforce the judgment in a foreign jurisdiction. The injunction establishes a right *in personam* merely and not a right *in rem*. Thus it cannot be used to defeat a secured creditor.[14]

European rules on jurisdiction

Under the Contracts (Applicable Law) Act 1990, giving effect to a European Community Convention on jurisdiction, a person or body domiciled in a member state of the Community must be sued in the courts of that member state where the convention so requires. Some jurisdictions may not be enforced against parties domiciled in other member states, one being the

---

13 *The Siskina* [1977] 3 All ER 803 at 821.
14 *Cretanor Maritime Co Ltd v Irish Marine Management Ltd* [1978] 3 All ER 164, CA.

jurisdiction of English courts over persons actually present in the jurisdiction.[15] This subject is dealt with in more detail in chapter 9.

Sovereign immunity

At common law any foreign sovereign, an expression which includes a foreign government, has always been immune from suit in the English courts although this immunity could be waived. This rule, which derives from international law, was until 1978 applied absolutely by the courts. With the growth of commercial activities by states and state bodies the rule became somewhat absurd and led to inconvenience and injustice. This growth of state activity and its effect on international law was summarised by Lord Denning MR in *Trendtex Trading Corpn Ltd v Central Bank of Nigeria*[16] where the defendant bank claimed sovereign immunity when sued on the non-payment of a documentary credit.

> In the last 50 years there has been a complete transformation in the functions of a sovereign state. Nearly every country now engages in commercial activities. It has departments of state – or creates its own legal entities – which go into the market places of the world. They charter ships. They buy commodities. They issue letters of credit. This transformation has changed the rules of international law relating to sovereign immunity. Many countries have now departed from the rule of absolute immunity. So many have departed from it that it can no longer be considered a rule of international law. It has been replaced by a doctrine of restrictive immunity. This doctrine gives immunity to acts of a governmental nature ... but no immunity to acts of a commercial nature.

This view received statutory recognition in the State Immunity Act 1978, which applied to all foreign states. This Act restated the general principle of sovereign immunity but created numerous exceptions, the general effect of which is that a state or a state organisation cannot claim immunity in respect of its ordinary commercial transactions which do not relate directly to the exercise of the state's sovereign authority.

15   As in *Maharanee of Baroda v Wildenstein* [1972] 2 QB 283, [1972] 2 All ER 689, CA, where the defendant was served with the writ while visiting this country to attend Ascot.

16   [1977] QB 529 at 555, [1977] 1 All ER 881 at 890.

Proceedings and jurisdiction

It must be stressed that this Act does not extend the jurisdiction of the English courts; it merely permits their previous jurisdiction to be exercised in circumstances where, before the Act, it would have been ineffective.

The Protection of Trading Interests Act 1980

Whether an action against a defendant based in the United Kingdom may be commenced in a foreign court will, of course, be a matter for the law of the foreign country. Some mention should be made, however, of an area in which the legislature has had to intervene to protect British interests in this respect. The Protection of Trading Interests Act 1980 as amended[17] is designed to counter the effect of judgments and legislation in the United States, one of which was the imposition on British firms of multiple – and hence penal – damages for breaches of United States anti-monopoly legislation.

This Act gives the Secretary of State general powers to counter any measures taken under the laws of another state which might damage the United Kingdom's trading interests. In particular, the Secretary of State may prohibit compliance with any demand by a foreign authority for disclosure of documents or information; multiple damages will not be enforceable in the United Kingdom and parties carrying on business in the United Kingdom may sue in the courts of this country for any amount by which multiple damages paid exceed any loss actually suffered.

ARBITRATION

Arbitration and litigation

Parties to international sale agreements and associated transactions frequently arrange that any dispute arising shall be submitted to arbitration. The advantages of arbitration are that it is usually – but by no means always – quicker and cheaper than litigation. The parties can entrust the resolution of their dispute to a person or persons of their own choice who will be familiar with the workings of their trade. Moreover, an arbitrator's decision can be final although cases may also go to a court on appeal.

---

17   By Magistrates Courts Act 1980, Schs 7 and 9 and the Civil Jurisdiction and Judgments Act 1982, s 38. The Shipping and Trading Interests (Protection) Act 1995 also provides protection for British shippers and shipping conferences.

Disputes on matters of fact, such as the quality of goods, can be expeditiously resolved by arbitration while those involving purely legal questions may well be more quickly and cheaply dealt with by the commercial court.[18] Where questions of mixed law and fact are involved it is possible to appoint a judge of the commercial court as sole arbitrator. This removes the possibility of subsequent judicial review by the court on a question of law and avoids the need to separate questions of law from those of fact.

The Arbitration Act 1996

The Arbitration Act 1996 came into force on 31 January 1997, being applicable to all arbitrations commencing on or after that date. Prior to this Act, the relevant law was to be found in the Arbitration Acts 1950, 1975 and 1979. The Arbitration Act has consolidated most of the earlier legislation and the prime reason for the 1996 Act was because arbitration law was to be found scattered across three statutes and extensive case law. The 1996 Act has rationalised the legislation. Part II of the Arbitration Act 1950 (enforcement of certain foreign awards) continues to apply under the 1996 Act. Part II gives effect to international measures, notably the Geneva Protocol of 1923 on arbitration clauses and the Geneva Convention on the Execution of Foreign Arbitral Awards 1927, contained in Schedules 1 and 2. Under section 101 of the 1996 Act, a New York Convention award is now also recognised as enforceable. The New York Convention provides for the enforcement of international arbitration agreements and the enforcement of foreign arbitration awards.

A new feature of the 1996 Act is that of the 'seat of arbitration'. This relates to the juridical seat of the arbitration as distinct from the actual physical location of the arbitration proceedings. Normally, the two will be located in the same place but, for example, where different parts of the proceedings are held in different countries, the juridical seat may be situated elsewhere. The parties to the agreement may specify the seat in the arbitration agreement or delegate to another person or tribunal agreed and authorised by them. If the arbitration agreement is silent, section 3 says that the seat may be determined objectively, having regard to the parties' agreement and all the relevant circumstances. Where the seat of arbitration is in England, Wales or Northern Ireland, the 1996 Act will apply. In the

18 *Compagnie d'Armement Maritime SA v Cie Tunisienne de Navigation SA* [1971] AC 572 at 600.

recent case of *Dubai Islamic Bank PJSC v Paymentech Merchant Services Inc*[19] all the preparatory work of the appeals body was made in California, therefore, California held the closest connection with the transaction. The seat was not in England and Wales and the English court had no power to review the award.

Under the 1996 Act extensive powers over the conduct of the arbitration proceedings are given to the parties. For example, the parties are permitted to determine such matters as:

(1)   the size and composition of the arbitration tribunal;[20]
(2)   the procedure to be adopted; [21]
(3)   the availability of the High Court on a point of law. [22]

Appointment of arbitrators

The parties may appoint a single arbitrator. A reference in any agreement to arbitration is taken to mean a single arbitrator unless the agreement states the contrary. The agreement may designate a person or body who is to appoint the arbitrator and if he (or it) does not do so, or if the parties themselves cannot agree on an arbitrator, the court has power to appoint.

In some cases parties each appoint an arbitrator. If so, and if the arbitrators fail to agree, the arbitrators must forthwith appoint an umpire to decide the issue. Where each party is to appoint an arbitrator and only one party does so the appointed arbitrator may decide the issue alone. If three arbitrators are appointed any award by two of them will be binding even if the third arbitrator was appointed by the first two, though this will not apply where the third appointment was expressed to be that of an umpire. Section 15 (2) of the Act provides that where there is an agreement that the number of arbitrators shall be two or any other even number then the appointment of an additional arbitrator as chairman of the tribunal will be required.

Where the parties themselves prescribe the mode of appointment they are opting for an 'ad hoc' arbitration, ie one in which the arbitrator decides on procedures, subject only to general legal rules and to the limits set for him by the parties. If, on the other hand, they opt for an institutional arbitrator,

---

19   [2001] 1 Lloyd's Rep 65.
20   Sections 15–18.
21   Sections 38–41.
22   Sections 69, 87(1).

ie one appointed by a named body, then the method of his appointment and the procedures he adopts will be governed by the rules laid down by the relevant institution. An institution in this context may be a trade association or a general body such as UNCITRAL, the ICC Court of Arbitration or the London Court of Arbitration. A substantial advantage of institutional arbitration is that an institution will usually offer administrative assistance for the arbitration.

Arbitration agreements

Arbitration is a valid way of settling a dispute only if the parties have agreed to it. They may do this in advance by inserting in their original contract an arbitration clause which will come into effect if a dispute arises. Alternatively, they may enter into a separate arbitration agreement after the original contract has been concluded. This will, of course, normally be done only if a dispute actually arises. Such an agreement will decide the jurisdiction of the arbitrator who may not exceed the powers conferred on him by the parties.

The Arbitration Act 1996 restates much of the previous legislation but is intended to strengthen arbitration in England, Wales and Northern Ireland. It aims to increase the attraction of London as an international arbitration centre. Some of the changes by the Arbitration Act 1996 are, for example, giving the arbitrator power to limit the amount of costs recoverable and providing for the immunity of the arbitrator. Also, by section 29(1) an arbitrator will not be liable for anything done or omitted in the discharge of his or her functions as an arbitrator unless he or she has acted in bad faith.

The Arbitration Act 1996 defines an arbitration agreement as a 'written agreement to submit present or future differences to arbitration whether they are contractual or not.' The clause must be in writing and the document or documents in which the clause is expressed must be accepted or acted upon by the parties. In *Excomm Ltd v Bamaodah, The St Raphael*[1] it was stated that it was unnecessary for the arbitration agreement to be contained in the same document as the original contract as long as it was in writing. Oral agreements to arbitrate are not covered by the Acts and although they are valid at common law they have obvious disadvantages in respect of their possible uncertainty or ambiguity. An arbitration agreement can be concluded electronically. If there is prolonged inactivity by both parties

1   [1985] 1 Lloyd's Rep 403, CA.

to the arbitration agreement a court may assume that the parties have agreed to abandon the arbitration or that one of the parties has repudiated the agreement and the other has accepted the repudiation.[2]

Arbitrators' powers

An arbitrator cannot go beyond the powers which the parties confer on him by their agreement. Neither can he decide on the validity of the arbitration clause itself, since he derives his own power from this clause. The court may therefore have to be asked to decide such questions as whether the dispute is covered by the clause or what the question is for the arbitrator to decide.

Subject to the above, the arbitrator has wide powers and the process is similar to that of the court. He may examine witnesses on oath, make final and interim awards, including awards on costs, may order specific performance in most cases and make any adjustments under the Law Reform (Frustrated Contracts) Act 1943. The Arbitration Act 1996 also gives him power to make interlocutory orders.

An arbitrator cannot, however, make a reference to the European Court of Justice since he is not a national 'court or tribunal' deriving its authority from a member state.[3] Where a reference is necessary an appeal must be brought under the Arbitration Act 1996 so that the court may make this reference.[4]

English arbitration and appeals

English arbitration, centred on London, has achieved a wide reputation for efficiency and fairness which has resulted in many parties agreeing that their disputes shall be settled by arbitration there, even when there is otherwise no connection between their contract and English law. Foreign parties frequently take objection, however, to the right, under English law, of appeal to the courts from the decisions of arbitrators on points of law, since in many countries an arbitration decision is final and appeals naturally involve time and expense. The 1996 Act has been designed to prevent

2   *Gebr Van Weelde Scheepvaarartkantor BV v Cia Naviera Sea Orient SA, The Agrabele* [1987] 2 Lloyd's Rep 223.
3   *Bulk Coil (Zug) AG v Sun International Ltd (No 2)* [1986] 2 All ER 744, [1986] 2 CMLR 732.
4   Arbitration Act 1996, s 69(2) and (8).

numerous appeals by limiting the opportunities for appeal to the High Court.

Exclusion of appeal

The ability to exclude the right of appeal has been changed by the 1996 Act to place greater importance on the decision of arbitration awards. Prior to the 1996 Act leave to appeal guidelines were found in the case of *The Nema*[5], a House of Lords decision, interpreting the previous legislation. Reference to *The Nema* is still relevant until further case law on this area assists.

In *The Nema* the House of Lords took the view that, even though questions of law were involved, a distinction needed to be drawn between awards relating to one-off contracts, in which the wording was unlikely to be repeated, and those involving standard terms, the construction and interpretation of which would be beneficial to the commercial world. Lord Diplock, however, did feel that even with one-off contracts the decision of an arbitrator should be preferred to that of the House of Lords, because of the arbitrator's specialist knowledge. Lord Diplock set out the following factors which the court should take into consideration in deciding how to exercise its discretion. What the judge should normally ask himself in this type of arbitration, particularly where the events relied on are one-off events, is not whether he agrees with the decision reached by the arbitrator; but rather does it appear on a perusal of the award either that the arbitrator misdirected himself in law or that his decision was such that no reasonable arbitrator could reach.

If the arbitrator is dealing with the construction of standard terms and this would assist the clarity and certainty of English commercial law, then leave to appeal may be allowed but the court would still have to be satisfied that a strong prima facie case had been made out that the arbitrator's construction was wrong.

Parties are allowed to challenge an arbitration award on grounds other than a point of law, for example on grounds of lack of substantive jurisdiction,[6] or serious irregularity affecting the tribunal, the proceedings

---

5   [1982] AC 724, [1981] 2 All ER 1030, HL. The rules were explained in *Antaios Cia Naviera SA v Salen Rederierna AB* [1985] AC 191, [1984] 3 All ER 229.

6   S 67

or the award.[7] The right of the parties to exclude appeal to the courts will depend on two factors: the nature of the arbitration and the stage at which the agreement to exclude appeal was made. For the purpose of the first point, arbitrations are classified as 'domestic' or 'non-domestic'. The Arbitration Act 1996, section 85(2) states that an arbitration is domestic if neither party to it is a national of or normally resident in another country or if no corporation involved is incorporated in or controlled from another country. Other arbitrations are non-domestic.

In the case of domestic arbitrations an agreement to exclude appeal will be effective only if it is made after the arbitration has begun. (One purpose behind this rule is to prevent a party in a strong bargaining position from refusing to contract at all unless appeal from arbitration is excluded.)

Non-domestic arbitrations, which will include the vast majority of those concerned with disputes in international sale transactions, can be divided into 'special category' arbitrations and others. The special categories are arbitrations involving questions or claims within the admiralty jurisdiction of the High Court, disputes on contracts or insurance and disputes on commodity contracts. In these arbitrations appeals may be excluded if either the agreement to do so is made after the arbitration has begun or if the arbitration is concerned with a contract expressed to be governed by a foreign law.

In other categories of non-domestic arbitration an agreement to exclude appeal will be valid whenever made.

Appeals from arbitration

If not excluded, an appeal may be made to the High Court by consent of the parties or by leave of the court, with a possibility, also by leave of the court, of a further appeal to the Court of Appeal.[8] Appeals are by way of judicial review on questions of law arising out of the award but judicial review procedure can be applied only if the award states reasons in detail, since a court cannot otherwise form an opinion on the question of law. Under the Arbitration Act 1996 (previously covered by Arbitration Act

---

7   S 68
8   Where the parties agree to dispense with reasons this will be deemed to be an exclusion of the right to appeal.

1979) an arbitrator must state reasons unless it is an agreed award, or the parties have agreed to dispense with reasons. Donaldson LJ has said:[9]

> All that is necessary under the Act of 1979 (now the 1996 Act) is that the arbitrators should give a 'reasoned award', ie the arbitrators should set out what, in their view of the evidence, did or did not happen, and should explain succinctly why in the light of what happened they had reached their decision and what that decision was. They are not expected to analyse the law and the authorities.

If the arbitrator gives no reasons for his award or reasons which the court considers insufficient, the court may require the arbitrator to state his reasons in sufficient detail to enable it to consider any question of law in the award which may arise on appeal. If the parties have agreed to dispense with reasons this will be deemed as an exclusion of the right to appeal.

ICC Court of Arbitration

There is as yet no official internationally accepted system of commercial arbitration and, as so often in the field of international trade, much work is done by non-governmental bodies. A good example of arbitration facilities provided by such bodies is the Court of Arbitration of the International Chamber of Commerce.

The parties opt in their contract for any dispute to be finally settled under the Chamber's Rules of Conciliation and Arbitration. In the event of a dispute the parties may opt for conciliation, in which case a Conciliation Committee of three members is appointed by the President of the Chamber. The dispute will go to arbitration if conciliation procedure fails or if no request for conciliation was made. In these cases the Court of Arbitration is appointed from a specific list of experienced arbitrators. The arbitrator appointed will not be a national of the country of any party to the dispute. The arbitrator draws up terms of reference before proceedings begin and submits a draft of his decision to the Court of Arbitration. Parties make a shared advance payment to cover costs. The arbitrator's decision is final, a fact recognised by the English courts.[10]

9   In *Westzucker GmbH v Bunge GmbH* [1981] 2 Lloyd's Rep 130, [1981] Com LR 179, CA.
10 *Marine Contractors Inc v Shell Petroleum Development Co of Nigeria* [1984] 2 Lloyd's Rep 77, CA.

Arbitration

ENFORCEMENT OF FOREIGN JUDGMENTS AND AWARDS

Judgments

At common law the judgment of a foreign court cannot be directly enforced in this country. Enforcement is possible under various statutes, of which the most important is the Foreign Judgments (Reciprocal Enforcement) Act 1933, under which the judgments of particular foreign countries, specified by order in council, can be enforced by registration in the United Kingdom. Such a judgment will not be registered if an English court decides that the foreign court had no jurisdiction to make the judgment.[11]

As opposed to enforcing the judgment directly, the plaintiff may bring an action in the English courts, using the foreign judgment as the basis of his claim. The judgment of the English court will, of course, be directly enforceable. A common – and convenient – procedure is to apply for summary judgment and use the foreign judgment as evidence that the defendant has no real defence. Again, the English court must be satisfied that the foreign court had jurisdiction to decide the case.

A foreign judgment will not be directly enforced or succeed as the basis of an action in the English courts if it can be shown to be contrary to English public policy or to be tainted by fraud.

Arbitration awards

At common law a foreign arbitration award may be enforced by bringing an action in the English courts provided that the arbitration was valid in accordance with its proper law and that the award itself is valid and final by that law. Awards may be enforced directly if they come within the Arbitration Act 1996, which gives effect to the New York Convention on the Recognition and Enforcement of Foreign Arbitral Awards 1958. Awards of Commonwealth arbitration bodies may be enforced under the Administration of Justice Act 1920 or the Foreign Judgments (Reciprocal Enforcement) Act 1933.

11   See Chapter 9 for discussion of enforcement of judgments obtained from another EU country.

Chapter 9
European Community law and international sales

In recent years EC law has had considerable impact on international sales, particularly in two areas. One is the area of commercial disputes between parties domiciled within member states; the other is that concerned with the free movement of goods within the Community, which has created a need for new procedures and documentation for all member states to recognise. These have removed difficulties arising from differing national procedures within the EC but there is as yet no uniform system for dealing with the movement of goods between member and non-member states.

DISPUTES

The Rome Convention

This Convention, the European Community Convention on the Law Applicable to Contractual Obligations, was adopted by the Council of the EC in Rome in 1980 and was introduced into the UK in 1991 by the Contracts (Applicable Law) Act 1990. It regulates the situation when there is a conflict of law issue between parties in different member states or between a party in a member sate and one in a non-member state.

The Convention provides that the proper law of the contract shall be the law intended by the parties. If the parties do not provide for the applicable law then the law most closely connected with the contract will be applied. (This is, of course, the same approach as that adopted by the English courts but differences in the Convention's approach may lead to a result different from that at which an English court would arrive.)

Although there is a freedom of choice the parties cannot contract out of the mandatory rules of law of a particular country if all other factors existing at the time of choice are connected with that country only. There are differences between general English law and the Convention in respect of the 'closest connection'. Under article 4(2) there is a rebuttable presumption that the law will be the law of the 'characteristic performance'. The presumption is that the contract is most closely connected with that country where the party who is to effect the performance which is characteristic of the contract has, at the time of the conclusion of the contract, his permanent residence or, in the case of a company or association, its central administration.

Since characteristic performance is held to take place where the party who has to carry out the performance has his place of business, it will be the seller under an international sale contract who effects the characteristic performance by delivering the goods. In the case of contracts of carriage, however, there will, under article 4(2), be a presumption that the proper law is either that of the country in which the carrier has his main office and in which he has loaded or discharged the goods or the country in which both carrier and cargo owner have their main offices. If neither of these situations exists the general presumption of 'closest connection' will apply.

The Contracts (Applicable Law) Act 1990 does not apply article 7 of the Convention. This article provides that when applying the law of a foreign country the judge may apply the rules of another foreign country with which the matter has a close connection if, under the law of the latter country, those rules must be applied whatever the law applicable to the contract. For example, an Australian court hearing a case involving a contract in which the parties have opted for US law could, if the contract had a close connection with France, apply the EC rules on competition which a French court would have to apply. This extension of the definition of the closest connection could, in effect, mean that the extra-territorial effect of mandatory rules of a third country could be considered. This was considered too controversial a procedure to be incorporated into the 1990 Act.

Jurisdiction and enforcement of judgments within the EC

The Brussels Convention on Jurisdiction and Enforcement of Judgments in Civil and Commercial Matters 1968[1] was brought into effect in the UK

1　The civil law system applying in continental countries is based on codes and the Commercial Code is usually separate from the general Civil Code. This distinction between 'commercial' and 'civil' is not made in English law.

by the Civil Jurisdiction and Judgments Act 1982. This convention attempted to reduce the multiplicity of jurisdictions in which a plaintiff may choose to bring proceedings (often called 'forum shopping') and to ensure that judgments covered by the convention were enforceable in all member states of the EC. It applied to all civil and commercial matters except revenue, customs and such administrative matters as social security etc. In 1998 the EU revised the Convention and this has resulted in the publication of the Regulation on Jurisdiction and the Recognition and Enforcement of Judgments in Civil and Commercial Matters 2000. The Regulation applies to legal proceedings instituted and documents formally drawn up or registered as authentic instruments after the date it came into force. A Council Regulation was issued under the Treaty of Amsterdam 1999, to speed up the implementation. However, Denmark remains outside the new regime by virtue of exercising their opt-out. Therefore, the Brussels Convention will remain in force in relations between Denmark and other member states of the EU. To clarify the situation after 1 March 2002 in relation to the United Kingdom: when the issue of jurisdiction in civil and commercial matters is being considered where the defendant is domiciled in an EU country, other than Denmark, the new Council Regulation will apply; where the defendant is domiciled in Denmark, the Brussels Convention will apply; where the defendant is domiciled in an EFTA country which is not an EU member state, the Lugano Convention will apply; where the defendant is domiciled in any other country, common law rules will apply.

The domicile of a party is an important factor in determining which court has jurisdiction. Domicile means the country or jurisdiction in which an individual is resident and the circumstances of his residence must show he has a substantial connection with that country. In the case of an association or corporation its 'seat' is relevant. 'Seat' means the place where the company is incorporated or formed under the law of a country and the place where it has its registered office or other official address or where its central management and control are exercised. This is formally recognised under article 60(1) of the Regulation.

Under article 17 of the convention a clause in a contract conferring jurisdiction on a particular court of a contracting state (sometimes called 'an express prorogation' clause) is effective if the agreement conferring jurisdiction is in writing or evidenced in writing or, in international trade or commerce, is in a form which accords with the practices or customs in that trade of which the parties are or ought to be aware. The clause may in some circumstances apply even after the expiry of the agreement in which it is contained. In *Iveco Fiat SpA v Van Hool SA*[2] a written agreement between an Italian and a Dutch company included a clause providing that the District Court of Turin should have exclusive jurisdiction. The agreement also specified that it should be renewed in writing but that after expiry it would be the legal basis for the future relationship between the parties. The European Court of Justice held that article 17 of the convention applied and that the Turin court had exclusive jurisdiction even after the agreement had expired. Exclusive jurisdiction clauses are, of course, used where parties wish disputes to go to courts rather than to arbitration.

The convention permits the exclusive jurisdiction clause to be waived by the party for whose benefit it was inserted. However, the fact that the stipulated forum is that of only one of the parties does not necessarily indicate that the clause was inserted merely for his benefit.[3]

Regulation of the courts' jurisdiction

When there is no express or implied choice of law the Regulation (and the Brussels and Lugano Conventions) applies a general rule on jurisdiction under article 2. The effect of this is that within the EC only one court will have jurisdiction in any civil or commercial matter and that court will be the court of domicile of the defendant. In *Kloeckner & Co AG v Gatoil Overseas Inc*[4] a German seller sued an Italian buyer in a German court for payment of the purchase price. The buyer then brought proceedings in an Italian court for annulment of the contract. It was held by the European Court of Justice that the disputes involved the same subject matter, namely the enforceability of the contract, and as the German court was competent to try the case the buyer's action could not be pursued in the Italian court. In *Société Group Josi Reinsurance Co SA v Universal General Insurance Co*,[5] the fact that the claimant was domiciled in Canada, which was not a contracting state, was held to be immaterial for the purposes of article 2. Therefore it is the defendants' domicile which is important. Where the original court in which an action is brought is competent to deal with the dispute, proceedings cannot be commenced in a second court of a different contracting state.

---

2   Case 313/85 [1986] ECR 3337, [1988] 1 CMLR 57.
3   *Anterist v Crédit Lyonnais:* Case 22/85 [1986] ECR 1951, [1987] 1 CMLR 333.
4   [1990] 1 Lloyd's Rep 177.
5   [2000] 3 WLR 1625

Article 5 of the Regulation (as did the Brussels Convention) provides for an alternative in some situations to the forum of the defendant. 'Forum shopping' has thus not been totally extinguished. In matters relating to a contract, for example, the courts for the place of performance of the obligation have jurisdiction. In *Medway Packaging Ltd v Meurer Maaschinen GmbH & Co KG*[6] it was held that the place of performance under article 5 of the Brussels Convention is the place of performance of the contractual obligation on which the action is founded. Thus in *Union Transport Group plc v Continental Lines SA*[7] a firm of shipowner's brokers domiciled in Belgium was bound under a contract to provide a ship under charter. The first stage of their obligations was to nominate the ship to be provided. They failed to do this. The House of Lords held that the performance which determined jurisdiction was not the actual provision of the ship but the nomination, which was to have been made in London. The English courts therefore had jurisdiction under article 5. It is important to note that defining what comes within the scope of the word 'contract' may be difficult. In *Agnew v Lanförsäkring ølagens AB*,[8] the House of Lords held that the breach of the duty of good faith pleaded as regards a reinsurance contract was a matter of the Lugano Convention (which is identical to the corresponding provision under the Brussels Convention). Also, it would appear that claims centred on pre-contractual statements might also be covered within article 5(1)[9].

Article 5 also covers actions in tort, in which the relevant court will be that of the jurisdiction in which the harmful event occurred. The place where the harmful event occurred is both the place where the wrongful event occurred and where the plaintiff sustained damage or harm. Where several harmful events occurred in several different states, each of those states has jurisdiction (*Shevill v Press Alliance SA*)[10]. The convention also provides for 'additional' and 'exclusive' jurisdictions. The former provides for additional fora in matters concerning insurance and consumer transactions and the latter provides for exclusive jurisdiction in, for example, matters concerning patents, trade marks, designs and proceedings concerning the enforcement of foreign judgments.

6   [1990] 1 Lloyd's Rep 383.
7   [1992] 1 All ER 161, [1992] 1 WLR 15, HL. See also Case 266/85 *Shenavai v Kreischer* [1987] ECR 239.
8   [1997] 4 All ER 937.
9   See Case C–334/00 *Fonderie Officine Meccaniche Tacconu SpA – HWS Henirich Wagner Sinto Machinenfabrik GmbH* [2000] OJ C302/41.
10   [1995] 2 WLR 499.

Unless there are exceptional circumstances a judgment given in one contracting state must be recognised in other contracting states and the substance of the judgment cannot be made the subject of renewed proceedings. In the UK the procedure for enforcing a judgment given in another contracting state is to have it registered for enforcement in the relevant part of the UK. The Convention does not apply to proceedings or issues in proceedings in contracting states concerning the recognition and enforcement of judgements given in non-contracting states.[11]

The judgments and orders of the European Court of Justice and the decisions of other organs of the EC and orders of the Community institutions are directly enforceable in the UK, subject to certain conditions. The Secretary of State appends an order of enforcement and this is registered by the High Court. The effect of this is that the relevant judgments or orders are enforceable in the UK as if they were judgments or orders of the court in which they were registered.

THE FREE MOVEMENT OF GOODS

Articles 9–37 of the Treaty of Rome 1957 provide for the free movement of goods within the EC. This means that there is a free circulation of Community goods from one member state to another and that their transport is not affected by internal tariffs, certificates of origin etc.

The Community itself is protected from imports from other countries by a common external tariff, usually referred to as the Common Customs Tariff. In accordance with the EC treaty the UK has enacted the Customs and Excise Duties (General Reliefs) Act 1979 which states that goods may be relieved from customs duty if it is necessary or expedient to comply with the Community regulations.

Community goods are those which wholly originate within the Community and also those which come from a non-Community country and have been put into free circulation in the Community.

Documentation for Community Transit

The Community Transit Documents cover the movement of goods between member states. These Documents have to be certified by the customs

11   *Owens Bank v Bracco (No 2)* [1994] 1 All ER 336.

authorities of the exporting member state since their purpose is to prove to the customs authorities of the importing country that the goods are entitled to 'free circulation status'. The basis of the documentation is the Single Administrative Document (SAD). This Document has simplified the customs procedure in the UK, since it has replaced previous different customs declarations for import, export and transit.

The Community Transit Document notes the status of the goods, eg a T1 declaration is given for goods which:

(1) are, or which include, goods originating in a non-Community state but which may have been imported into a member state, or which

(2) are not subject to full import formalities or payment of customs duties, or which

(3) on importation were subject to import formalities but the duties and/ or charges have been or are being repaid in whole or part, or which

(4) are entitled to be treated as Community goods and are or will be subject to customs export formalities for Common Agricultural Policies (CAP) export refunds on export from the Community or come under the European Coal and Steel Community and are therefore not in free circulation in the Community.

A T2 declaration is required for Community goods and there are other declarations for goods in free circulation in Spain and Portugal.

A Community status document may be sent with the goods, although it is more convenient than necessary.

Community Transit

The Community Transit method for the transport of goods eases movement of goods between member states by removing the problems caused by differing national transit procedures. The SAD is not only used as a transit document but is also evidence that the goods are Community goods so that the beneficial intra-Community rates of import charge will be levied or that they are not.

The steps involved in the Community Transit movement start with the authentication of the documents at the office of departure. The goods will also have been cleared at the office. The goods are then under the Community Transit Customs control until transport terminates when the goods and documents are presented at the office of destination within the time schedule for the completion of the movement of the goods. If the goods or seals are damaged during transit then the nearest customs authority must be informed.

In most cases when goods are exported under this procedure a guarantee must be obtained to cover duty and similar charges which may become payable on the goods as a result of any irregularity during the transit. The guarantee is usually in writing and given by a person or organisation other than the exporter.

EC preferential tariff treatment

Some non-members of the EC provide preferential tariff treatment for exports from EC countries. To obtain this the exporter must comply with the 'origin rules' of the non-member country granting the preference. These origin rules obviously vary from country to country but in general the exporter must supply a prescribed certificate of origin endorsed by the customs authority of the exporting country. This must be supplied to the customs authorities of the importing country within a specified period after endorsement in the exporting country, otherwise the full non-preferential duties will be required.

Appendix 1
Specimen form of bill of lading

This form is based on the one reproduced in the second edition of this work, and reproduced there with the kind permission of Witherby & Co Ltd.

CODE NAME   CONGENBILL   EDITION 1978

Shipper

BILL OF LADING

TO BE USED WITH CHARTER-PARTIES

Consignee

Notify address

Vessel	Port of loading

Port of discharge

Shipper's description of goods   Gross weight

Specimen

(of which   on deck at Shipper's risk, the Carrier not being responsible for loss or damage howsoever arising)

Freight payable as per CHARTER-PARTY dated

SHIPPED at the Port of Loading in apparent good order and condition on board the Vessel for carriage to the Port of Discharge or so near thereto as she may safely get the goods specified above.

FREIGHT ADVANCE
Received on account of freight

Weight, measure, quality, condition, contents and value unknown.

IN WITNESS whereof the Master or Agent of the said Vessel has signed the number of Bills of Lading indicated below all of this tenor and date any one of which being accomplished the others shall be void

Time used for loading   days   hours

FOR CONDITIONS OF CARRIAGE SEE OVERLEAF

Freight payable at	Place and date of issue
Number of original Ba/L	Signature

C.15 Printed and bound by
Witherby & Company Limited, 32/36 Aylesbury Street
London EC1R 0ET
by authority of The Baltic and International
Maritime Council (BIMCO) Copenhagen

BILL OF LADING

TO BE USED WITH CHARTER-PARTIES
CODE NAME   CONGENBILL
EDITION 1978
ADOPTED BY
THE BALTIC AND INTERNATIONAL
MARITIME CONFERENCE (BIMCO)

Conditions of Carriage.

(1) All terms and conditions, liberties and exceptions of the Charter Party, dated as overleaf, are herewith incorporated. The Carrier shall in no case be responsible for loss of or damage to cargo arisen prior to loading and after discharging.

(2) General Paramount Clause.

The Hague Rules contained in the International Convention for the Unification of certain rules relating to Bills of Lading, dated Brussels the 25th August 1924 as enacted in the country of shipment shall apply to this contract. When no such enactment is in force in the country of shipment, the corresponding legislation of the country of destination shall apply, but in respect of shipment to which no such enactments are compulsorily applicable, the terms of the said Convention shall apply.

Trades where Hague-Visby Rules apply

In trades where the International Brussels Convention 1924 as amended by the Protocol signed at Brussels on February 23rd 1968 – the Hague-Visby Rules – apply compulsorily, the provisions of the respective legislation shall be considered incorporated in the Bill of Lading. The Carrier takes all reservations possible under such applicable legislation, relating to the period before loading and after discharging and while the goods are in the charge of another Carrier and to deck cargo and live animals.

(3) General Average.

General Average shall be adjusted, stated and settled according to York-Antwerp Rules 1974, in London unless another place is agreed in the Charter.

Cargo's contribution to General Average shall be paid to the Carrier even when such average is the result of a fault, neglect or error of the Master, Pilot or Crew. The Charterers, Shippers and Consignees expressly renounce the Netherlands Commercial Code, Art. 700, and the Belgian Commercial Code, Part II, Art. 148.

(4) New Jason Clause.

In the event of accident, danger, damage or disaster before or after the commencement of the voyage, resulting form any cause whatsoever, whether due to negligence or not, for which, or, for the consequence of which, the Carrier is not responsible, by statute, contract or otherwise, the goods, Shippers, Consignees or owners of the goods shall contribute with the Carrier in general average to the payment of any sacrifices, losses or expenses of a general average nature that may be made or incurred and shall pay salvage and special charges incurred in respect of the goods.

If a salving ship is owned or operated by the Carrier, salvage shall be paid for as fully as if the said salving ship or ships belonged to strangers. Such deposit as the Carrier or his agents may deem sufficient to cover the estimated contribution of the goods and any salvage and special charges thereon shall, if required, be made by the goods, Shippers, Consignees or owners of the goods to the Carrier before delivery.

(5) Both-to-Blame Collision Clause.

If the Vessel comes into collision with another ship as a result of the negligence of the other ship and any act, neglect or default of the Master, Mariner, Pilot or the servants of the Carrier in the navigation or in the management of the Vessel, the owners of the cargo carried hereunder will indemnify the Carrier against all loss or liability to the other or non-carrying ship or her Owners in so far as such loss or liability represents loss of, or damage to, or any claim whatsoever of the owners of said cargo, paid or payable by the other or non-carrying ship or her Owners to the owners of said cargo and set-off, recouped or recovered by the other or non-carrying ship or her Owners as part of their claim against the carrying Vessel or Carrier. The foregoing provisions shall also apply where the Owners, operators or those in charge of any ship or ships or objects other than, or in addition to, the colliding ships or object are at fault in respect of a collision or contact.

For particulars of cargo, freight,
destination etc., see overleaf.

Appendix 2
Carriage of Goods by Sea Act 1992

BE IT ENACTED by the Queen's most Excellent Majesty, by and with the advice and consent of the Lords Spiritual and Temporal, and Commons, in this present Parliament assembled, and by the authority of the same, as follows:—

1.—(1) This Act applied to the following documents, that is to say—

(a) any bill of lading;

(b) any sea way bill; and

(c) any ship's delivery order.

(2) References in this Act to a bill of lading—

(a) do not include references to a document which is incapable of transfer either by indorsement or, as a bearer bill, by delivery without indorsement; but

(b) subject to that, do include references to a received for shipment bill of lading.

(3) References in this Act to a sea waybill are references to any document which is not a bill of lading but—

(a) is such a receipt for goods as contains or evidences a contract for the carriage of goods by sea; and

(b) identifies the person to whom delivery of the goods is to be made by the carrier in accordance with that contract.

(4) References in this Act to a ship's delivery order are references to any document which is neither a bill of lading nor a sea waybill but contains an undertaking which—

(a) is given under or for the purposes of a contract for the carriage by sea of the goods to which the document relates, or of goods which include those goods; and

(b) is an undertaking by the carrier to a person identified in the document to deliver the goods to which the document relates to that person.

(5) The Secretary of State may by regulations make provision for the application of this Act to cases where a telecommunication system or any other information technology is used for effecting transactions corresponding to—

(a) the issue of a document to which this Act applies;
(b) the indorsement, delivery or other transfer of such a document; or
(c) the doing of anything else in relation to such a document.

(6) Regulations under subsection (5) above may—

(a) make such modifications of the following provisions of this Act as the Secretary of State considers appropriate in connection with the application of this Act to any case mentioned in that subsection; and
(b) contain supplemental, incidental, consequential and transitional provision;

and the power to make regulations under that subsection shall be exercisable by statutory instrument subject to annulment in pursuance of a resolution of either House of Parliament.

2.—(1) Subject to the following provisions of this section, a person who becomes—

(a) the lawful holder of a bill of lading;
(b) the person who (without being an original party to the contract of carriage) is the person to whom delivery of the goods to which a sea waybill relates is to be made by the carrier in accordance with that contract; or
(c) the person to whom delivery of the goods to which a ship's delivery order relates is to be made in accordance with the undertaking contained in the order,

shall (by virtue of becoming the holder of the bill or, as the case may be, the person to whom delivery is to be made) have transferred to and vested in him all rights of suit under the contract of carriage as if he had been a party to that contract.

(2) Where, when a person becomes the lawful holder of a bill of lading, possession of the bill no longer gives a right (as against the carrier) to possession of the goods to which the bill relates, that person shall not have any rights transferred to him by virtue of subsection (1) above unless he becomes the holder of the bill—

(a) by virtue of a transaction effected in pursuance of any contractual or other arrangements made before the time when such a right to possession ceased to attach to possession of the bill; or

(b) as a result of the rejection to that person by another person of goods or documents delivered to the other person in pursuance of any such arrangements.

(3) The rights vested in any person by virtue of the operation of subsection (1) above in relation to a ship's delivery order—

(a) shall be so vested subject to the terms of the order; and

(b) where the goods to which the order relates form a part only of the goods to which the contract of carriage relates, shall be confined to rights in respect of the goods to which the order relates.

(4) Where, in the case of any document to which this Act applies—

(a) a person with any interest or right in or in relation to goods to which the document relates sustains loss or damage in consequence of a breach of the contract of carriage; but

(b) subsection (1) above operates in relation to that document so that rights of suit in respect of that breach are vested in another person,

the other person shall be entitled to exercise those rights for the benefit of the person who sustained the loss or damage to the same extent as they could have been exercised if they had been vested in the person for whose benefit they are exercised.

(5) Where rights are transferred by virtue of the operation of subsection (1) above in relation to any document, the transfer for which that subsection provides shall extinguish any entitlement to those rights which derives—

(a) where that document is a bill of lading, from a person's having been an original party to the contract of carriage;

or

(b) in the case of any document to which this Act applies, from the previous operation of that subsection in relation to that document;

but the operation of that subsection shall be without prejudice to any rights which derive from a person's having been an original party to the contract contained in, or evidenced by, a sea waybill and, in relation to ship's delivery order, shall be without prejudice to any rights deriving otherwise than from the previous operation of that subsection in relation to that order.

3.—(1) Where subsection (1) or section 2 of this Act operates in relation to any document to which this Act applies and the person in whom rights are vested by virtue of that subsection—

(a) takes or demands delivery from the carrier of any of the goods to which the document relates;

(b) makes a claim under the contract of carriage against the carrier in respect of any of those goods; or

(c) is a person who, at a time before those rights were vested in him, took or demanded delivery from the carrier of any of those goods,

that person shall (by virtue of taking or demanding delivery or making the claim or, in a case falling within paragraph (c) above, of having the rights vested in him) become subject to the same liabilities under that contract as if he had been a party to that contract.

(2) Where the goods to which a ship's order relates form a part only of the goods to which the contract of carriage relates, the liabilities to which any person is subject by virtue of the operation of this section in relation to that order shall exclude liabilities in respect of any goods to which the order does not relate.

(3) This section, so far as it imposes liabilities under any contract on any person, shall be without prejudice to the liabilities under the contract of any person as an original party to the contract.

4. A bill of lading which—

(a) represents goods to have been shipped on board a vessel or to have been received for shipment on board a vessel;

and

(b) has been signed by the master of the vessel or by a person who was not the master but had the express, implied or apparent authority of the carrier to sign bills of lading,

shall, in favour of a person who has become the lawful holder of the bill, be conclusive evidence against the carrier of the shipment of the goods or, as the case may be, of their receipt for shipment.

5.—(1) In this Act—

'bill of lading', 'sea waybill' and 'ship's delivery order' shall be construed in accordance with section 1 above;

'the contract of carriage'—

(a) in relation to a bill of lading or sea waybill, means the contract contained in or evidenced by that bill or waybill;

and

(b) in relation to a ship's delivery order, means the contract under or for the purposes of which the undertaking contained in the order is given;

'holder', in relation to a bill of lading, shall be construed in accordance with subsection (2) below;

'information technology' includes any computer or other technology by means of which information or other matter may be recorded or communicated without being reduced to documentary form; and

'telecommunication system' has the same meaning as in the Telecommunications Act 1984.

(2) References in this Act to the holder of a bill of lading are references to any of the following persons, that is to say—

(a) a person with possession of the bill who, by virtue of being the person identified in the bill, is the consignee of the goods to which the bill relates;

(b) a person with possession of the bill as a result of the completion, by delivery of the bill, of any indorsement of the bill or, in the case of a bearer bill, of any other transfer of the bill;

(c) a person with possession of the bill as a result of any transaction by virtue of which he would have become a holder falling within paragraph (a) or (b) above had not the transaction been effected at a time when possession of the bill no longer gave a right (as against the carrier) to possession of the goods to which the bill relates;

and a person shall be regarded for the purposes of this Act as having become the lawful holder of a bill of lading wherever he has become the holder of the bill in good faith.

(3) References in this Act to a person's being identified in a document include references to his being identified by a description which allows for the identity of the person in question to be varied, in accordance with the terms of the document, after its issue; and the reference in section 1(3)(b) of this Act to a document's identifying a person shall be construed accordingly.

(4) Without prejudice to sections 2(2) and 4 above, nothing in this Act shall preclude its operation in relation to a case where the goods to which a document relates—

(a) cease to exist after the issue of the document; or

(b) cannot be identified (whether because they are mixed with other goods or for any other reason);

and references in this Act to the goods to which a document relates shall be construed accordingly.

(5) The preceding provisions of this Act shall have effect without prejudice to the application, in relation to any case, of the rules (the Hague–Visby Rules) which for the time being have the force of law by virtue of section 1 of the Carriage of Goods by Sea Act 1971.

6.—(1) This Act may be cited as the Carriage of Goods by Sea Act 1992.

(2) The Bills of Lading Act 1855 is hereby repealed.

(3) This Act shall come into force at the end of the period of two months beginning with the day on which it is passed; but nothing in this Act shall have effect in relation to any document issued before the coming into force of this Act.

(4) This Act extends to Northern Ireland.

Appendix 3
Carriage of Goods by Sea Act 1971 and the Hague–Visby Rules

CARRIAGE OF GOODS BY SEA ACT 1971

(1971 c 19)

BE IT ENACTED by the Queen's most Excellent Majesty, by and with the advice and consent of the Lords Spiritual and Temporal, and Commons, in this present Parliament assembled, and by the authority of the same, as follows:—

1. Application of Hague Rules as amended.—(1) In this Act, 'the Rules' means the International Convention for the unification of certain rules of law relating to bills of lading signed at Brussels on 25th August 1924, as amended by the protocol signed at Brussels on 23rd February 1968 [and by the Protocol signed at Brussels on 21st December 1979].

(2) The provisions of the Rules, as set out in the Schedule to this Act, shall have the force of law.

(3) Without prejudice to subsection (2) above, the said provisions shall have effect (and have the force of law) in relation to and in connection with the carriage of goods by sea in ships where the port of shipment is a port in the United Kingdom, whether or not the carriage is between ports in two different States within the meaning of Article X of the Rules.

(4) Subject to subsection (6) below, nothing in this section shall be taken as applying anything in the Rules to any contract for the carriage of goods by sea, unless the contract expressly or by implication provides for the issue of a bill of lading or any similar document of title.

(5) The Secretary of State may from time to time by order made by statutory

instrument specify the respective amounts which for the purposes of paragraph 5 of Article IV of the Rules and of Article IV bis of the Rules are to be taken as equivalent to the sums expressed in francs which are mentioned in sub-paragraph (a) of that paragraph.

(6) Without prejudice to Article X(c) of the Rules, the Rules shall have the force of law in relation to—

(a) any bill of lading if the contract contained in or evidenced by it expressly provides that the Rules shall govern the contract, and

(b) any receipt which is a non-negotiable document marked as such if the contract contained in or evidenced by it is a contract for the carriage of goods by sea which expressly provides that the Rules are to govern the contract as if the receipt were a bill of lading,

but subject, were paragraph (b) applies, to any necessary modifications and in particular with the omission in Article III of the Rules of the second sentence of paragraph 4 and of paragraph 7.

(7) If and so far as the contract contained in or evidenced by a bill of lading or receipt within paragraph (a) or (b) of subsection (6) above applies to deck cargo or live animals, the Rules as given the force of law by that subsection shall have effect as if Article I(c) did not exclude deck cargo and live animals.

In this subsection 'deck cargo' means cargo which by the contract of carriage is stated as being carried on deck and is so carried.

2. Contracting States, etc—(1) If Her Majesty by Order in Council certifies to the following effect, that is to say, that for the purposes of the Rules—

(a) a State specified in the Order is a contracting State, or is a contracting State in respect of any place or territory so specified; or

(b) any place or territory specified in the Order forms part of a State so specified (whether a contracting State or not),

the Order shall, except so far as it has been superseded by a subsequent Order, be conclusive evidence of the matters so certified.

(2) An Order in Council under this section may be varied or revoked by a subsequent Order in Council.

3. Absolute warranty of seaworthiness not to be implied in contracts to which Rules apply.—There shall not be implied in any contract for the carriage of goods by sea to which the Rules apply by virtue of this Act any absolute undertaking by the carrier of the goods to provide a seaworthy ship.

4. Application of Act to British possessions, etc—(1) Her Majesty may by Order in Council direct that this Act shall extend, subject to such exceptions, adaptations and modifications as may be specified in the Order, to all or any of the following territories, that is—

(a)   any colony (not being a colony for whose external relations a country other than the United Kingdom is responsible),

(b)   any country outside Her Majesty's dominions in which Her Majesty has jurisdiction in right of Her Majesty's Government of the United Kingdom.

(2) An Order in Council under this section may contain such transitional and other consequential and incidental provisions as appear to Her Majesty to be expedient, including provisions amending or repealing any legislation about the carriage of goods by sea forming part of the law of any of the territories mentioned in paragraphs (a) and (b) above.

(3) An Order in Council under this section may be varied or revoked by a subsequent Order in Council.

5. Extension of application of Rules to carriage from ports in British possessions, etc—(1) Her Majesty may by Order in Council provide that section 1(3) of this Act shall have effect as if the reference therein to the United Kingdom included a reference to all or any of the following territories, that is—

(a)   the Isle of Man;

(b)   any of the Channel Islands specified in the Order;

(c)   any colony specified in the Order (not being a colony for whose external relations a country other than the United Kingdom is responsible);

(d)   …

(e)   any country specified in the Order, being a country outside Her Majesty's domains in which Her Majesty has jurisdiction in right of Her Majesty's Government of the United Kingdom.

(2) An Order in Council under this section may be varied or revoked by a subsequent Order in Council.

6. Supplemental.—(1) This Act may be cited as the Carriage of Goods by Sea Act 1971.

(2) It is hereby declared that this Act extends to Northern Ireland.

(3) The following enactments shall be repealed, that is—

(a)   the Carriage of Goods by Sea Act 1924,

(b) section 12(4)(a) of the Nuclear Installations Act 1965,

and without prejudice to section 17(2)(a) of the Interpretation Act 1978, the reference to the said Act of 1924 in section 1(1)(i)(ii) of the Hovercraft Act 1968 shall include a reference to this Act.

(4) It is hereby declared that for the purposes of Article VIII of the Rules section 18 of the Merchant Shipping Act 1979 (which entirely exempts shipowners and others in certain circumstances from liability for loss of, or damage to, goods) is a provision relating to limitation of liability.

(5) This Act shall come into force on such day as Her Majesty may by Order in Council appoint, and, for the purposes of the transition from the law in force immediately before the day appointed under this subsection to the provisions of this Act, the Order appointing the day may provide that those provisions shall have effect subject to such transitional provisions as may be contained in the Order.

SCHEDULE
THE HAGUE RULES
AS AMENDED BY THE BRUSSELS PROTOCOL 1968

Article 1

In these Rules the following words are employed, with the meanings set out below:—

(a) 'Carrier' includes the owner or the charterer who enters into a contract of carriage with a shipper.

(b) 'Contract of carriage' applies only to contracts of carriage covered by a bill of lading or any similar document of title, in so far as such document relates to the carriage of goods by sea, including any bill of lading or any similar document as aforesaid issued under or pursuant to a charter-party from the moment at which such bill of lading or similar document of title regulates the relations between a carrier and a holder of the same.

(c) 'Goods' includes goods, wares, merchandise, and articles of every kind whatsoever except live animals and cargo which by the contract of carriage is stated as being carried on deck and is so carried.

(d) 'Ship' means any vessel used for the carriage of goods by sea.

(e) 'Carriage of goods' covers the period from the time when the goods are loaded on to the time they are discharged from the ship.

Article *II*

Subject to the provisions of Article VI, under every contract of carriage of goods by sea the carrier, in relation to the loading, handling, stowage, carriage, custody, care and discharge of such goods, shall be subject to the responsibilities and liabilities, and entitled to the rights and immunities hereinafter set forth.

Article *III*

1. The carrier shall be bound before and at the beginning of the voyage to exercise due diligence to—
(a) Make the ship seaworthy.
(b) Properly man, equip and supply the ship.
(c) Make the holds, refrigerating and cool chambers, and all other parts of the ship in which goods are carried, fit and safe for their reception, carriage and preservation.

2. Subject to the provisions of Article IV, the carrier shall properly and carefully load, handle, stow, carry, keep, care for, and discharge the goods carried.

3. After receiving the goods into his charge the carrier or the master or agent of the carrier shall, on demand of the shipper, issue to the shipper a bill of lading showing among other things—
(a) The leading marks necessary for identification of the goods as the same are furnished in writing by the shipper before the loading of such goods starts, provided such marks are stamped or otherwise shown clearly upon the goods if uncovered, or on the cases or coverings in which such goods are contained, in such a manner as should ordinarily remain legible until the end of the voyage.
(b) Either the number of packages or pieces, or the quantity, or weight, as the case may be, as furnished in writing by the shipper.
(c) The apparent order and condition of the goods.

Provided that no carrier, master or agent of the carrier shall be bound to state or show in the bill of lading any marks, number quantity or weight which he has reasonable ground for suspecting not accurately to represent the goods actually received, or which he has had no reasonable means of checking.

4. Such a bill of lading shall be prima facie evidence of the receipt by the carrier of the goods as therein described in accordance with paragraph 3

(a), (b) and (c). However, proof to the contrary shall not be admissible when the bill of lading has been transferred to a third party acting in good faith.

5. The shipper shall be deemed to have guaranteed to the carrier the accuracy at the time of shipment of the marks, number, quantity and weight, as furnished by him, and the shipper shall indemnify the carrier against all loss, damages and expenses arising or resulting from inaccuracies in such particulars. The right of the carrier to such indemnity shall in no way limit his responsibility and liability under the contract of carriage to any person other than the shipper.

6. Unless notice of loss or damage and the general nature of such loss or damage be given in writing to the carrier or his agent at the port of discharge before or at the time of the removal of the goods into the custody of the person entitled to delivery thereof under the contract of carriage, or, if the loss or damage be not apparent, within three days, such removal shall be prima facie evidence of the delivery by the carrier of the goods as described in the bill of lading.

The notice in writing need not be given if the state of the goods has, at the time of their receipt, been the subject of joint survey of inspection.

Subject to paragraph 6 *bis* the carrier and the ship shall in any event be discharged from all liability whatsoever in respect of the goods, unless suit is brought within one year of their delivery or of the date when they should have been delivered. This period may, however, be extended if the parties so agree after the cause of action has arisen.

In the case of any actual or apprehended loss or damage the carrier and the receiver shall give all reasonable facilities to each other for inspecting and tallying the goods.

6 *bis*. An action for indemnity against a third person may be brought even after the expiration of the year provided for in the preceding paragraph if brought within the time allowed by the law of the Court seized of the case. However, the time allowed shall be not less than three months, commencing from the day when the person bringing such action for indemnity has settled the claim or has been served with process in the action against himself.

7. After the goods are loaded the bill of lading to be issued by the carrier, master, or agent of the carrier, to the shipper shall, if the shipper so demands, be a 'shipped' bill of lading, provided that if the shipper shall have previously

taken up any document of title to such goods, he shall surrender the same as against the issue of the 'shipped' bill of lading, but at the option of the carrier such document of title may be noted at the port of shipment by the carrier, master, or agent with the name or names of the ship or ships upon which the goods have been shipped and the date or dates of shipment, and when so noted, if it shows the particulars mentioned in paragraph 3 of Article III, shall for the purpose of this article be deemed to constitute a 'shipped' bill of lading.

8. Any clause, covenant, or agreement in a contract of carriage relieving the carrier or the ship from liability for loss or damage to, or in connection with, goods arising from negligence, fault, or failure in the duties and obligations provided in this article or lessening such liability otherwise than as provided in these Rules, shall be null and void and of no effect. A benefit of insurance in favour of the carrier or similar clause shall be deemed to be a clause relieving the carrier from liability.

Article *IV*

1. Neither the carrier nor the ship shall be liable for loss or damage arising or resulting from unseaworthiness unless caused by want of due diligence on the part of the carrier to make the ship seaworthy, and to secure that the ship is properly manned, equipped and supplied, and to make the holds, refrigerating and cool chambers and all other parts of the ship in which goods are carried fit and safe for their reception, carriage and preservation in accordance with the provisions of paragraph 1 of Article III. Whenever loss or damage has resulted from unseaworthiness the burden of proving the exercise of due diligence shall be on the carrier or other person claiming exemption under this article.

2. Neither the carrier nor the ship shall be responsible for loss or damage arising or resulting from—
(a) Act, neglect, or default of the master, mariner, pilot, or the servants of the carrier in the navigation or in the management of the ship.
(b) Fire, unless caused by the actual fault or privity of the carrier.
(c) Perils, dangers and accidents of the sea or other navigable waters.
(d) Act of God.
(e) Act of war.
(f) Act of public enemies.
(g) Arrest or restraint of princes, rulers or people, or seizure under legal process.

(h) Quarantine restrictions.

(i) Act or omission of the shipper or owner of the goods, his agent or representative.

(j) Strikes or lockouts or stoppage or restraint of labour from whatever cause, whether partial or general.

(k) Riots and civil commotions.

(l) Saving or attempting to save life or property at sea.

(m) Wastage in bulk or weight or any other loss or damage arising from inherent defect, quality or vice of the goods.

(n) Insufficiency of packing.

(o) Insufficiency or inadequacy of marks.

(p) Latent defects not discoverable by due diligence.

(q) Any other cause arising without the actual fault or privity of the carrier, or without the fault or neglect of the agents or servants of the carrier, but the burden of proof shall be on the person claiming the benefit of this exception to show that neither the actual fault or privity of the carrier nor the fault or neglect of the agents or servants of the carrier contributed to the loss or damage.

3. The shipper shall not be responsible for loss or damage sustained by the carrier or the ship arising or resulting from any cause without the act, fault or neglect of the shipper, his agents or his servants.

4. Any deviation in saving or attempting to save life or property at sea or any reasonable deviation shall not be deemed to be an infringement or breach of these Rules or of the contract of carriage, and the carrier shall not be liable for any loss or damage resulting therefrom.

5. (a) Unless the nature and value of such goods have been declared by the shipper before shipment and inserted in the bill of lading, neither the carrier nor the ship shall in any event be or become liable for any loss or damage to or in connection with the goods in an amount exceeding the equivalent of 10,000 francs per package or unit of 30 francs per kilo of gross weight of the goods lost or damaged, whichever is the higher.

(b) The total amount recoverable shall be calculated by reference to the value of such goods at the place and time at which the goods are discharged from the ship in accordance with the contract or should have been so discharged.

The value of the goods shall be fixed according to the commodity exchange price, or, if there be no such price, according to the current market price, or, if there be no commodity exchange price or current market price, by reference to the normal value of goods of the same kind and quality.

(c) Where a container, pallet or similar article of transport is used to consolidate goods, the number of packages or units enumerated in the bill of lading as packed in such article of transport shall be deemed the number of packages or units for the purpose of this paragraph as far as these packages or units are concerned. Except as aforesaid such article of transport shall be considered the package or unit.

(d) A franc means a unit consisting of 65.5 milligrammes of gold of millesimal fineness 900. The date of conversion of the sum awarded into national currencies shall be governed by the law of the Court seized of the case.

(e) Neither the carrier nor the ship shall be entitled to the benefit of the limitation of liability provided for in this paragraph if it is proved that the damage resulted from an act or omission of the carrier done with intent to cause damage, or recklessly and with knowledge that damage would probably result.

(f) The declaration mentioned in sub-paragraph (a) of this paragraph, if embodied in the bill of lading, shall be prima facie evidence, but shall not be binding or conclusive on the carrier.

(g) By agreement between the carrier, master or agent of the carrier and the shipper other maximum amounts than those mentioned in sub-paragraph (a) of this paragraph may be fixed, provided that no maximum amount so fixed shall be less than the appropriate maximum mentioned in that sub-paragraph.

(h) Neither the carrier nor the ship shall be responsible in any event for loss or damage to, or in connection with, goods if the nature or value thereof has been knowingly mis-stated by the shipper in the bill of lading.

6. Goods of an inflammable, explosive or dangerous nature to the shipment whereof the carrier, master or agent of the carrier has not consented with knowledge of their nature and character, may at any time before discharge be landed at any place, or destroyed or rendered innocuous by the carrier without compensation and the shipper of such goods shall be liable for all damages and expenses directly or indirectly arising out of or resulting from such shipment. If any such goods shipped with such knowledge and consent shall become a danger to the ship or cargo, they may in like manner be landed at any place, or destroyed or rendered innocuous by the

carrier without liability on the part of the carrier except to general average, if any.

Article *IV* Bis

1. The defences and limits of liability provided for in these Rules shall apply in any action against the carrier in respect of loss or damage to goods covered by a contract of carriage whether the action be founded in contract or in tort.

2. If such an action is brought against a servant or agent of the carrier (such servant or agent not being an independent contractor), such servant or agent shall be entitled to avail himself of the defences and limits of liability which the carrier is entitled to invoke under these Rules.

3. The aggregate of the amounts recoverable from the carrier, and such servants and agents, shall in no case exceed the limit provided for in these Rules.

4. Nevertheless, a servant or agent of the carrier shall not be entitled to avail himself of the provisions of this article, if it is proved that the damage resulted from an act or omission of the servant or agent done with intent to cause damage or recklessly and with knowledge that damage would probably result.

Article V

A carrier shall be at liberty to surrender in whole or in part all or any of his rights and immunities or to increase any of his responsibilities and obligations under these Rules, provided such surrender or increase shall be embodied in the bill of lading issued to the shipper. The provisions of these Rules shall not be applicable to charter-parties, but if bills of lading are issued in the case of a ship under a charter-party they shall comply with the terms of these Rules. Nothing in these Rules shall be held to prevent the insertion in a bill of lading of any lawful provision regarding general average.

Article VI

Notwithstanding the provisions of the preceding articles, a carrier, master or agent of the carrier and a shipper shall in regard to any particular goods be at liberty to enter into any agreement in any terms as to the responsibility and liability of the carrier for such goods, and as to the rights and immunities of the carrier in respect of such goods, or his obligation as to seaworthiness, so far as this stipulation is not contrary to public policy, or the care or diligence of his servants or agents in regard to the loading, handling, stowage, carriage, custody, care and discharge of the goods carried by sea, provided that in this case no bill of lading has been or shall be issued and that the terms agreed shall be embodied in a receipt which shall be a non-negotiable document and shall be marked as such.

Any agreement so entered into shall have full legal effect.

Provided that this article shall not apply to ordinary commercial shipments made in the ordinary course of trade, but only to other shipments where the character or condition of the property to be carried or the circumstances, terms and conditions under which the carriage is to be performed are such as reasonably to justify a special agreement.

Article *VII*

Nothing herein contained shall prevent a carrier or a shipper from entering into any agreement, stipulation, condition, reservation or exemption as to the responsibility and liability of the carrier or the ship for the loss or damage to, or in connection with, the custody and care and handling of goods prior to the loading on, and subsequent to the discharge from, the ship on which the goods are carried by sea.

Article *VIII*

The provisions of these Rules shall not affect the rights and obligations of the carrier under any statute for the time being in force relating to the limitation of the liability of owners of sea-going vessels.

Article *IX*

These Rules shall not affect the provisions of any international Convention or national law governing liability for nuclear damage.

Article *X*

The provisions of these Rules shall apply to every bill of lading relating to the carriage of goods between ports in two different States if:

(a)   the bill of lading is issued in a contracting State, or

(b)   the carriage is from a port in a contracting State, or

(c)   the contract contained in or evidenced by the bill of lading provides that these Rules or legislation of any State giving effect to them are to govern the contract,

whatever may be the nationality of the ship, the carrier, the shipper, the consignee, or any other interested person.

Appendix 4
The Hamburg Rules

UNITED NATIONS CONVENTION ON THE CARRIAGE OF GOODS BY SEA 1978

Preamble

The states parties to this convention,

Having recognized the desirability of determining by agreement certain rules relating to the carriage of goods by sea,

Have decided to conclude a Convention for this purpose and have thereto agreed as follows:

PART I. GENERAL PROVISIONS

Article 1. Definitions

In this Convention:

1. 'Carrier' means any person by whom or in whose name a contract of carriage of goods by sea has been concluded with a shipper.

2. 'Actual carrier' means any person to whom the performance of the carriage of the goods, or of part of the carriage, has been entrusted by the carrier, and includes any other person to whom such performance has been entrusted.

3. 'Shipper' means any person by whom or in whose name or on whose behalf a contract of carriage of goods by sea has been concluded with a

carrier, or any person by whom or in whose name or on whose behalf the goods are actually delivered to the carrier in relation to the contract of carriage by sea.

4. 'Consignee' means the person entitled to take delivery of the goods.

5. 'Goods' includes live animals; where the goods are consolidated in a container, pallet or similar article of transport or where they are packed, 'goods' includes such article of transport or packaging if supplied by the shipper.

6. 'Contract of carriage by sea' means any contract whereby the carrier undertakes against payment of freight to carry goods by sea from one port to another; however, a contract which involves carriage by sea and also carriage by some other means is deemed to be a contract of carriage by sea for the purposes of this Convention only in so far as it relates to the carriage by sea.

7. 'Bill of lading' means a document which evidences a contract of carriage by sea and taking over or loading of the goods by the carrier, and by which the carrier undertakes to deliver the goods against surrender of the document. A provision in the document that the goods are to be delivered to the order of a named person, or to order, or to bearer, constitutes such an undertaking.

8. 'Writing' includes, inter alia, telegram and telex.

Article 2. Scope of application

1. The provisions of this Convention are applicable to all contracts of carriage by sea between two different States, if:
(a) the port of loading as provided for in the contract of carriage by sea is located in a Contracting State, or
(b) the port of discharge as provided for in the contract of carriage by sea is located in a Contracting State, or
(c) one of the optional ports of discharge provided for in the contract of carriage by sea is the actual port of discharge and such port is located in a Contracting State, or
(d) the bill of lading or other document evidencing the contract of carriage by sea is issued in a Contracting State, or
(e) the bill of lading or other document evidencing the contract of carriage by sea provides that the provisions of this Convention or the legislation of any State giving effect to them are to govern the contract.

2. The provisions of this Convention are applicable without regard to the nationality of the ship, the carrier, the actual carrier, the shipper, the consignee or any other interested person.

3. The provisions of this Convention are not applicable to charter-parties. However, where a bill of lading is issued pursuant to a charter-party, the provisions of the Convention apply to such a bill of lading if it governs the relation between the carrier and the holder of the bill of lading, not being the charterer.

4. If a contract provides for future carriage of goods in a series of shipments during an agreed period, the provisions of this Convention apply to each shipment. However, where a shipment is made under a charter-party, the provisions of para 3 of this Article apply.

Article 3. Interpretation of the Convention

In the interpretation and application of the provisions of this Convention regard shall be had to its international character and to the need to promote uniformity.

PART II. LIABILITY OF THE CARRIER

Article 4. Period of responsibility

1. The responsibility of the carrier for the goods under this Convention covers the period during which the carrier is in charge of the goods at the port of loading, during the carriage and at the port of discharge.

2. For the purpose of para 1 of this Article, the carrier is deemed to be in charge of the goods
(a)   from the time he has taken over the goods from:
    (i)   the shipper, or a person acting on his behalf; or
    (ii) an authority or other third party to whom, pursuant to law or regulations applicable at the port of loading, the goods must be handed over for shipment;
(b)   until the time he has delivered the goods:
    (i)   by handing over the goods to the consignee; or
    (ii) in cases where the consignee does not receive the goods from the carrier, by placing them at the disposal of the consignee in accordance with the contract or with the law or with the usage of the particular trade, applicable at the port of discharge; or

(iii) by handing over the goods to an authority or other third party to whom, pursuant to law or regulations applicable at the port of discharge, the goods must be handed over.

3. In paras 1 and 2 of this Article, reference to the carrier or to the consignee means, in addition to the carrier or the consignee, the servants or agents, respectively, of the carrier or the consignee.

Article 5. Basis of liability

1. The carrier is liable for loss resulting from loss of or damage to the goods, as well as from delay in delivery, if the occurrence which caused the loss, damage or delay took place while the goods were in his charge as defined in art 4, unless the carrier proves that he, his servants or agents took all measures that could reasonably be required to avoid the occurrence and its consequences.

2. Delay in delivery occurs when the goods have not been delivered at the port of discharge provided for in the contract of carriage by sea within the time expressly agreed upon or, in the absence of such agreement, within the time which it would be reasonable to require of a diligent carrier, having regard to the circumstances of the case.

3. The person entitled to make a claim for the loss of goods may treat the goods as lost if they have not been delivered as required by art 4 within 60 consecutive days following the expiry of the time for delivery according to para 2 of this Article.

4. (a) The carrier is liable
    (i) for loss of or damage to the goods or delay in delivery caused by fire, if the claimant proves that the fire arose from fault or neglect on the part of the carrier, his servants or agents;
    (ii) for such loss, damage or delay in delivery which is proved by the claimant to have resulted from the fault or neglect of the carrier, his servants or agents, in taking all measures that could reasonably be required to put out the fire and avoid or mitigate its consequences.

  (b) In case of fire on board the ship affecting the goods, if the claimant or the carrier so desires, a survey in accordance with shipping practices must be held into the cause and circumstances of the fire, and a copy of the surveyor's report shall be made available on demand to the carrier and the claimant.

5. With respect to live animals, the carrier is not liable for loss, damage or delay in delivery resulting from any special risks inherent in that kind of carriage. If the carrier proves that he has complied with any special instructions given to him by the shipper respecting the animals and that, in the circumstances of the case, the loss, damage or delay in delivery could be attributed to such risks, it is presumed that the loss, damage or delay in delivery was so caused, unless there is proof that all or a part of the loss, damage or delay in delivery resulted from fault or neglect on the part of the carrier, his servants or agents.

6. The carrier is not liable, except in general average, where loss, damage or delay in delivery resulted from measures to save life or from reasonable measures to save property at sea.

7. Where fault or neglect on the part of the carrier, his servants or agents combines with another cause to produce loss, damage or delay in delivery the carrier is liable only to the extent that the loss, damage or delay in delivery is attributable to such fault or neglect, provided that the carrier proves the amount of the loss, damage or delay in delivery not attributable thereto.

Article 6. Limits of liability

1.(a) The liability of the carrier for loss resulting from loss of or damage to goods according to the provisions of art 5 is limited to an amount equivalent to 835 units of account per package or other shipping unit or 2.5 units of account per kilogramme of gross weight of the goods lost or damaged, whichever is the higher.

(b) The liability of the carrier for delay in delivery according to the provisions of art 5 is limited to an amount equivalent to two and a half times the freight payable for the goods delayed, but not exceeding the total freight payable under the contract of carriage of goods by sea.

(c) In no case shall the aggregate liability of the carrier, under both subparas (a) and (b) of this paragraph, exceed the limitation which would be established under subpara (a) of this paragraph for total loss of the goods with respect to which such liability was incurred.

2. For the purpose of calculating which amount is the higher in accordance with para 1 (a) of this Article the following rules apply:

(a) Where a container, pallet or similar article of transport is used to consolidate goods, the package or other shipping units enumerated in the bill of lading, if issued, or otherwise in any other document evidencing the contract of carriage by sea, as packed in such article of transport are deemed packages or shipping units. Except as aforesaid the goods in such article of transport are deemed one shipping unit.

(b) In cases where the article of transport itself has been lost of damaged, that article of transport, if not owned or otherwise supplied by the carrier, is considered one separate shipping unit.

3. Unit of account means the unit of account mentioned in art 26.

4. By agreement between the carrier and the shipper, limits of liability exceeding those provided for in para 1 may be fixed.

Article 7. Application to non-contractual claims

1. The defences and limits of liability provided for in this Convention apply in any action against the carrier in respect of loss or damage to the goods covered by the contract of carriage by sea, as well as of delay in delivery whether the action is founded in contract, in tort of otherwise.

2. If such an action is brought against a servant or agent of the carrier, such servant or agent, if he proves that he acted within the scope of his employment, is entitled to avail himself of the defences and limits of liability which the carrier is entitled to invoke under this Convention.

3. Except as provided in art 8, the aggregate of the amounts recoverable from the carrier and from any persons referred to in para 2 of this Article shall not exceed the limits of liability provided for in this Convention.

Article 8. Loss of right to limit responsibility

1. The carrier is not entitled to the benefit of the limitation of liability provided for in art 6 if it is proved that the loss, damage or delay in delivery resulted from an act or omission of the carrier done with the intent to cause such loss, damage or delay, or recklessly and with knowledge that such loss, damage or delay would probably result.

2. Notwithstanding the provisions of para 2 of art 7, a servant or agent of the carrier is not entitled to the benefit of the limitation of liability provided for in art 6 if it is proved that the loss, damage or delay in delivery resulted from an act or omission of such servant or agent, done with the intent to

cause such loss, damage or delay, or recklessly and with knowledge that such loss, damage or delay would probably result.

Article 9. Deck cargo

1. The carrier is entitled to carry the goods on deck only if such carriage is in accordance with an agreement with the shipper or with the usage of the particular trade or is required by statutory rules or regulations.

2. If the carrier and the shipper have agreed that the goods shall or may be carried on deck, the carrier must insert in the bill of lading or other document evidencing the contract of carriage by sea a statement to that effect. In the absence of such a statement the carrier has the burden of proving that an agreement for carriage on deck has been entered into; however, the carrier is not entitled to invoke such an agreement against a third party, including a consignee, who has acquired the bill of lading in good faith.

3. Where the goods have been carried on deck contrary to the provisions of para 1 of this Article or where the carrier may not under para 2 of this Article invoke an agreement for carriage on deck, the carrier, notwithstanding the provisions of para 1 of art 5, is liable for loss of or damage to the goods, as well as for delay in delivery, resulting solely from the carriage on deck, and the extent of his liability is to be determined in accordance with the provisions of art 6 or art 8 of this Convention as the case may be.

4. Carriage of goods on deck contrary to express agreement for carriage under deck is deemed to be an act or omission of the carrier within the meaning of art 8.

Article 10. Liability of the carrier and actual carrier

1. Where the performance of the carriage or part thereof has been entrusted to an actual carrier, whether or not in pursuance of a liberty under the contract of carriage by sea to do so, the carrier nevertheless remains responsible for the entire carriage according to the provisions of this Convention. The carrier is responsible, in relation to the carriage performed by the actual carrier, for the acts and omissions of the actual carrier and of his servants and agents acting within the scope of their employment.

2. All the provisions of this Convention governing the responsibility of the carrier also apply to the responsibility of the actual carrier for the carriage performed by him. The provisions of paras 2 and 3 of art 7 and of

para 2 of art 8 apply if an action is brought against a servant or agent of the actual carrier.

3. Any special agreement under which the carrier assumes obligations not imposed by this Convention or waives rights conferred by this Convention affects the actual carrier only if agreed to by him expressly and in writing. Whether or not the actual carrier has so agreed, the carrier nevertheless remains bound by the obligations or waivers resulting from such special agreement.

4. Where and to the extent that both the carrier and the actual carrier are liable, their liability is joint and several.

5. The aggregate of the amounts recoverable from the carrier, the actual carrier and their servants and agents shall not exceed the limits of liability provided for in this Convention.

6. Nothing in this Article shall prejudice any right of recourse as between the carrier and the actual carrier.

Article 11. Through carriage

1. Notwithstanding the provisions of para 1 of art 10, where a contract of carriage by sea provides explicitly that a specified part of the carriage covered by the said contract is to be performed by a named person other than the carrier, the contract may also provide that the carrier is not liable for loss, damage or delay in delivery caused by an occurrence which takes place while the goods are in the charge of the actual carrier during such part of the carriage. Nevertheless, any stipulation limiting or excluding such liability is without effect if no judicial proceedings can be instituted against the actual carrier in a court competent under para 1 or 2 of art 21. The burden of proving that any loss, damage or delay in delivery has been caused by such an occurrence rests upon the carrier.

2. The actual carrier is responsible in accordance with the provisions of para 2 of art 10 for loss, damage or delay in delivery caused by an occurrence which takes place while the goods are in his charge.

PART III. LIABILITY OF THE SHIPPER

Article 12. General rule

The shipper is not liable for loss sustained by the carrier or the actual carrier, or for damage sustained by the ship, unless such loss or damage was caused by the fault or neglect of the shipper, his servants or agents. Nor is any servant or agent of the shipper liable for such loss or damage unless the loss or damage was caused by fault or neglect on his part.

Article 13. Special rules on dangerous goods

1. The shipper must mark or label in a suitable manner dangerous goods as dangerous.

2. Where the shipper hands over dangerous goods to the carrier or an actual carrier, as the case may be, the shipper must inform him of the dangerous character of the goods and, if necessary, of the precautions to be taken. If the shipper fails to do so and such carrier or actual carrier does not otherwise have knowledge of their dangerous character:
(a) the shipper is liable to the carrier and any actual carrier for the loss resulting from the shipment of such goods, and
(b) the goods may at any time be unloaded, destroyed or rendered innocuous, as the circumstances may require, without payment of compensation.

3. The provisions of para 2 of this Article may not be invoked by any person if during the carriage he has taken the goods in his charge with knowledge of their dangerous character.

4. If, in cases where the provisions of para 2, subpara (b), of this Article do not apply or may not be invoked, dangerous goods become an actual danger to life or property, they may be unloaded, destroyed or rendered innocuous, as the circumstances may require, without payment of compensation except where there is an obligation to contribute in general average or where the carrier is liable in accordance with the provisions of art 5.

PART IV. TRANSPORT DOCUMENTS

Article 14. Issue of bill of lading

1. When the carrier or the actual carrier takes the goods in his charge, the carrier must, on demand of the shipper, issue to the shipper a bill of lading.

2. The bill of lading may be signed by a person having authority from the carrier. A bill of lading signed by the master of the ship carrying the goods is deemed to have been signed on behalf of the carrier.

3. The signature on the bill of lading may be in handwriting, printed in facsimile, perforated, stamped, in symbols, or made by any other mechanical or electronic means, if not inconsistent with the law of the country where the bill of lading is issued.

Article 15. Contents of bill of lading

1. The bill of lading must include, inter alia, the following particulars:
(a) the general nature of the goods, the leading marks necessary for identification of the goods, an express statement, if applicable, as to the dangerous character of the goods, the number of packages or pieces, and the weight of the goods or their quantity otherwise expressed, all such particulars as furnished by the shipper;
(b) the apparent condition of the goods;
(c) the name and principal place of business of the carrier;
(d) the name of the shipper;
(e) the consignee if named by the shipper;
(f) the port of loading under the contract of carriage by sea and the date on which the goods were taken over by the carrier at the port of loading;
(g) the port of discharge under the contract of carriage by sea;
(h) the number of originals of the bill of lading, if more than one;
(i) the place of issuance of the bill of lading;
(j) the signature of the carrier or a person acting on his behalf;
(k) the freight to the extent payable by the consignee or other indication that freight is payable by him;
(l) the statement referred to in para 3 of art 23;
(m) the statement, if applicable, that the goods shall or may be carried on deck;
(n) the date or the period of delivery of the goods at the port of discharge if expressly agreed upon between the parties; and
(o) any increased limit or limits of liability where agreed in accordance with para 4 of art 6.

2. After the goods have been loaded on board, if the shipper so demands, the carrier must issue to the shipper a 'shipped' bill of lading which, in addition to the particulars required under para 1 of this Article, must state that the goods are on board a named ship or ships, and the date or dates of loading. If the carrier has previously issued to the shipper a bill of lading or other document of title with respect to any of such goods, on request of the carrier, the shipper must surrender such document in exchange for a 'shipped' bill of lading. The carrier may amend any previously

issued document in order to meet the shipper's demand for a 'shipped' bill of lading if, as amended, such document includes all the information required to be contained in a 'shipped' bill of lading.

3. The absence in the bill of lading of one or more particulars referred to in this Article does not affect the legal character of the document as a bill of lading provided that it nevertheless meets the requirements set out in para 7 of art 1.

Article 16. Bills of lading: reservations and evidentiary effect

1. If the bill of lading contains particulars concerning the general nature, leading marks, number of packages or pieces, weight or quantity of the goods which the carrier or other person issuing the bill of lading on his behalf knows or has reasonable grounds to suspect do not accurately represent the goods actually taken over or, where a 'shipped' bill of lading is issued, loaded, or if he had no reasonable means of checking such particulars, the carrier or such other person must insert in the bill of lading a reservation specifying these inaccuracies, grounds of suspicion or the absence of reasonable means of checking.

2. If the carrier or other person issuing the bill of lading on his behalf fails to note on the bill of lading the apparent condition of the goods, he is deemed to have noted on the bill of lading that the goods were in apparent good condition.

3. Except for particulars in respect of which and to the extent to which a reservation permitted under para 1 of this Article has been entered:
(a) the bill of lading is prima facie evidence of the taking over or, where a 'shipped' bill of lading is issued, loading, by the carrier of the goods as described in the bill of lading; and
(b) proof to the contrary by the carrier is not admissible if the bill of lading has been transferred to a third party, including a consignee, who in good faith has acted in reliance on the description of the goods therein.

4. A bill of lading which does not, as provided in para 1, subpara (k) of art 15, set forth the freight or otherwise indicate that freight is payable by the consignee or does not set forth demurrage incurred at the port of loading payable by the consignee, is prima facie evidence that no freight or such demurrage is payable by him. However, proof to the contrary by the carrier is not admissible when the bill of lading has been transferred to a third party, including a consignee, who in good faith has acted in reliance on the absence in the bill of lading of any such indication.

Article 17. Guarantees by the shipper

1. The shipper is deemed to have guaranteed to the carrier the accuracy of particulars relating to the general nature of the goods, their marks, number, weight and quantity as furnished by him for insertion in the bill of lading. The shipper must indemnify the carrier against the loss resulting from inaccuracies in such particulars. The shipper remains liable even if the bill of lading has been transferred by him. The right of the carrier to such indemnity in no way limits his liability under the contract of carriage by sea to any person other than the shipper.

2. Any letter of guarantee or agreement by which the shipper undertakes to indemnify the carrier against loss resulting from the issuance of the bill of lading by the carrier, or by a person acting on his behalf, without entering the reservation relating to particulars furnished by the shipper for insertion in the bill of lading, or to the apparent condition of the goods, is void and of no effect as against any third party, including a consignee, to whom the bill of lading has been transferred.

3. Such letter of guarantee or agreement is valid as against the shipper unless the carrier or the person acting on his behalf, by omitting the reservation referred to in para 2 of this Article, intends to defraud a third party, including a consignee, who acts in reliance on the description of the goods in the bill of lading. In the latter case, if the reservation omitted relates to particulars furnished by the shipper for insertion in the bill of lading, the carrier has no right of indemnity from the shipper pursuant to para 1 of this Article.

4. In the case of intended fraud referred to in para 3 of this Article the carrier is liable, without the benefit of the limitation of liability provided for in this Convention, for the loss incurred by a third party, including a consignee, because he has acted in reliance on the description of the goods in the bill of lading.

Article 18. Documents other than bills of lading

Where a carrier issues a document other than a bill of lading to evidence the receipt of the goods to be carried, such a document is prima facie evidence of the conclusion of the contract of carriage by sea and the taking over by the carrier of the goods as therein described.

PART V. CLAIMS AND ACTIONS

Article 19. Notice of loss, damage or delay

1. Unless notice of loss or damage, specifying the general nature of such loss or damage, is given in writing by the consignee to the carrier not later than the working day after the day when the goods were handed over to the consignee, such handing over is prima facie evidence of the delivery by the carrier of the goods as described in the document of transport or, if no such document has been issued, in good condition.

2. Where the loss or damage is not apparent, the provisions of para 1 of this Article apply correspondingly if notice in writing is not given within 15 consecutive days after the day when the goods were handed over to the consignee.

3. If the state of the goods at the time they were handed over to the consignee has been the subject of a joint survey or inspection by the parties, notice in writing need not be given of loss or damage ascertained during such survey or inspection.

4. In the case of any actual or apprehended loss or damage the carrier and the consignee must give all reasonable facilities to each other for inspecting and tallying the goods.

5. No compensation shall be payable for loss resulting from delay in delivery unless a notice has been given in writing to the carrier within 60 consecutive days after the day when the goods were handed over to the consignee.

6. If the goods have been delivered by an actual carrier, any notice given under this Article to him shall have the same effect as if it had been given to the carrier, and any notice given to the carrier shall have effect as if given to such actual carrier.

7. Unless notice of loss or damage, specifying the general nature of the loss or damage, is given in writing by the carrier or actual carrier to the shipper not later than 90 consecutive days after the occurrence of such loss or damage or after the delivery of the goods in accordance with para 2 of art 4, whichever is later, the failure to give such notice is prima facie evidence that the carrier or the actual carrier has sustained no loss or damage due to the fault or neglect of the shipper, his servants or agents.

8. For the purpose of this Article, notice given to a person acting on the carrier's or the actual carrier's behalf, including the master or the officer in

The Hamburg Rules

charge of the ship, or to a person acting on the shipper's behalf is deemed to have been given to the carrier, to the actual carrier or to the shipper, respectively.

Article 20. Limitation of actions

1. Any action relating to carriage of goods under this Convention is time-barred if judicial or arbitral proceedings have not been instituted within a period of two years.

2. The limitation period commences on the day on which the carrier has delivered the goods or part thereof or, in cases where no goods have been delivered, on the last day on which the goods should have been delivered.

3. The day on which the limitation period commences is not included in the period.

4. The person against whom a claim is made may at any time during the running of the limitation period extend that period by a declaration in writing to the claimant. This period may be further extended by another declaration or declarations.

5. An action for indemnity by a person held liable may be instituted even after the expiration of the limitation period provided for in the preceding paragraphs if instituted within the time allowed by the law of the State where proceedings are instituted. However, the time allowed shall not be less than 90 days commencing from the day when the person instituting such action for indemnity has settled the claim or has been served with process in the action against himself.

Article 21. Jurisdiction

1. In judicial proceedings relating to carriage of goods under this Convention the plaintiff, at his option, may institute an action in a court which, according to the law of the State where the court is situated, is competent and within the jurisdiction of which is situated one of the following places:
(a) the principal place of business or, in the absence thereof, the habitual residence of the defendant; or
(b) the place where the contract was made provided that the defendant has there a place of business, branch or agency through which the contract was made; or

(c) the port of loading or the port of discharge; or

(d) any additional place designated for that purpose in the contract of carriage by sea.

2. (a) Notwithstanding the preceding provisions of this Article, an action may be instituted in the courts of any port or place in a Contracting State at which the carrying vessel or any other vessel of the same ownership may have been arrested in accordance with applicable rules of the law of that State and of international law. However, in such a case, at the petition of the defendant, the claimant must remove the action, at this choice, to one of the jurisdictions referred to in para 1 of this Article for the determination of the claim, but before such removal the defendant must furnish security sufficient to ensure payment of any judgment that may subsequently be awarded to the claimant in the action.

(b) All questions relating to the sufficiency or otherwise of the security shall be determined by the court of the port or place of the arrest.

3. No judicial proceedings relating to carriage of goods under this Convention may be instituted in a place not specified in para 1 or 2 of this Article. The provisions of this paragraph do not constitute an obstacle to the jurisdiction of the Contracting States for provisional or protective measures.

4. (a) Where an action has been instituted in a court competent under para 1 or 2 of this Article or where judgment has been delivered by such a court, no new action may be started between the same parties on the same grounds unless the judgment of the court before which the first action was instituted is not enforceable in the country in which the new proceedings are instituted;

(b) for the purpose of this Article the institution of measures with a view to obtaining enforcement of a judgment is not to be considered as the starting of a new action;

(c) for the purpose of this Article, the removal of an action to a different court within the same country, or to a court in another country, in accordance with para 2 (a) of this Article, is not to be considered as the starting of a new action.

5. Notwithstanding the provisions of the preceding paragraphs, an agreement made by the parties, after a claim under the contract of carriage by sea has arisen, which designates the place where the claimant may institute an action, is effective.

Article 22. Arbitration

1. Subject to the provisions of this Article, parties may provide by agreement evidenced in writing that any dispute that may arise relating to carriage of goods under this Convention shall be referred to arbitration.

2. Where a charter-party contains a provision that disputes arising thereunder shall be referred to arbitration and a bill of lading issued pursuant to the charter-party does not contain a special annotation providing that such provision shall be binding upon the holder of the bill of lading, the carrier may not invoke such provision as against a holder having acquired the bill of lading in good faith.

3. The arbitration proceedings shall, at the option of the claimant, be instituted at one of the following places:
(a) any place in a State within whose territory is situated:
   (i) the principal place of business of the defendant or, in the absence thereof, the habitual residence of the defendant; or
   (ii) the place where the contract was made, provided that the defendant has there a place of business, branch or agency through which the contract was made; or
   (iii) the port of loading or the port of discharge; or
(b) any place designated for that purpose in the arbitration clause or agreement.

4. The arbitrator or arbitration tribunal shall apply the rules of this Convention.

5. The provisions of paras 3 and 4 of this Article are deemed to be part of every arbitration clause or agreement, and any term of such clause or agreement which is inconsistent therewith is null and void.

6. Nothing in this Article affects the validity of an agreement relating to arbitration made by the parties after the claim under the contract of carriage by sea has arisen.

PART VI. SUPPLEMENTARY PROVISIONS

Article 23. Contractual stipulations

1. Any stipulation in a contract of carriage by sea, in a bill of lading, or in any other document evidencing the contract of carriage by sea is null and void to the extent that it derogates, directly or indirectly, from the provisions

of this Convention. The nullity of such a stipulation does not affect the validity of the other provisions of the contract or document of which it forms a part. A clause assigning benefit of insurance of the goods in favour of the carrier, or any similar clause, is null and void.

2. Notwithstanding the provisions of para 1 of this Article, a carrier may increase his responsibilities and obligations under this Convention.

3. Where a bill of lading or any other document evidencing the contract of carriage by sea is issued, it must contain a statement that the carriage is subject to the provisions of this Convention which nullify any stipulation derogating therefrom to the detriment of the shipper or the consignee.

4. Where the claimant in respect of the goods has incurred loss as a result of a stipulation which is null and void by virtue of the present Article, or as a result of the omission of the statement referred to in para 3 of this Article, the carrier must pay compensation to the extent required in order to give the claimant compensation in accordance with the provisions of this Convention for any loss of or damage to the goods as well as for delay in delivery. The carrier must, in addition, pay compensation for costs incurred by the claimant for the purpose of exercising his right, provided that costs incurred in the action where the foregoing provision is invoked are to be determined in accordance with the law of the State where proceedings are instituted.

Article 24. General average

1. Nothing in this Convention shall prevent the application of provisions in the contract of carriage by sea or national law regarding the adjustment of general average.

2. With the exception of art 20, the provisions of this Convention relating to the liability of the carrier for loss of or damage to the goods also determine whether the consignee may refuse contribution in general average and the liability of the carrier to indemnify the consignee in respect of any such contribution made or any salvage paid.

Article 25. Other conventions

1. This Convention does not modify the rights or duties of the carrier, the actual carrier and their servants and agents, provided for in international conventions or national law relating to the limitation of liability of owners of seagoing ships.

2. The provisions of arts 21 and 22 of this Convention do not prevent the application of the mandatory provisions of any other multilateral convention already in force at the date of this Convention relating to matters dealt with in the said Articles, provided that the dispute arises exclusively between parties having their principal place of business in States members of such other convention. However, this paragraph does not affect the application of para 4 of art 22 of this Convention.

3. No liability shall arise under the provisions of this Convention for damage caused by a nuclear incident if the operator of a nuclear installation is liable for such damage:

(a)   under either the Paris Convention of July 29, 1960, on Third Party Liability in the Field of Nuclear Energy as amended by the Additional Protocol of January 28, 1964, or the Vienna Convention of May 21, 1963, on Civil Liability for Nuclear Damage, or

(b)   by virtue of national law governing the liability for such damage, provided that such law is in all respects as favourable to persons who may suffer damage as either the Paris or Vienna Conventions.

4. No liability shall arise under the provisions of this Convention for any loss of or damage to or delay in delivery of luggage for which the carrier is responsible under any international convention or national law relating to the carriage of passengers and their luggage by sea.

5. Nothing contained in this Convention prevents a Contracting State from applying any other international convention which is already in force at the date of this Convention and which applies mandatorily to contracts of carriage of goods primarily by a mode of transport other than transport by sea. This provision also applies to any subsequent revision or amendment of such international convention.

Article 26. Unit of account

1. The unit of account referred to in art 6 of this Convention is the Special Drawing Right as defined by the International Monetary Fund. The amounts mentioned in art 6 are to be converted into the national currency of a State according to the value of such currency at the date of judgment or the date agreed upon by the parties. The value of a national currency, in terms of the Special Drawing Right, of a Contracting State which is a member of the International Monetary Fund is to be calculated in accordance with the method of valuation applied by the International Monetary Fund in effect at the date in question for its operations and transactions. The value of a

national currency in terms of the Special Drawing Eight of a Contracting State which is not a member of the International Monetary Fund is to be calculated in a manner determined by that State.

2. Nevertheless, those States which are not members of the International Monetary Fund and whose law does not permit the application of the provisions of para 1 of this Article may, at the time of signature, or at the time of ratification, acceptance, approval or accession or at any time thereafter, declare that the limits of liability provided for in this Convention to be applied in their territories shall be fixed as:

12,500 monetary units per package or other shipping unit or 37.5 monetary units per kilogramme of gross weight of the goods.

3. The monetary unit referred to in para 2 of this Article corresponds to sixty-five and a half milligrammes of gold of millesimal fineness nine hundred. The conversion of the amounts referred to in para 2 into the national currency is to be made according to the law of the State concerned.

4. The calculation mentioned in the last sentence of para 1 and the conversion mentioned in para 3 of this Article is to be made in such a manner as to express in the national currency of the Contracting State as far as possible the same real value for the amounts in art 6 as is expressed there in units of account. Contracting States must communicate to the depositary the manner of calculation pursuant to para 1 of this Article, or the result of the conversion mentioned in para 3 of this Article, as the case may be, at the time of signature or when depositing their instruments of ratification, acceptance, approval or accession, or when availing themselves of the option provided for in para 2 of this Article and whenever there is a change in the manner of such calculation or in the result of such conversion.

ANNEX II
COMMON UNDERSTANDING ADOPTED BY THE UNITED NATIONS CONFERENCE ON THE CARRIAGE OF GOODS BY SEA

It is the common understanding that the liability of the carrier under this Convention is based on the principle of presumed fault or neglect. This means that, as a rule, the burden of proof rests on the carrier but, with respect to certain cases, the provisions of the Convention modify this rule.

The Warsaw Conventions

CHAPTER I
SCOPE.—DEFINITIONS

Article I

(1) This Convention applies to all international carriage of persons, luggage or goods performed by aircraft for reward. It applies equally to gratuitous carriage by aircraft performed by an air transport undertaking.

(2) For the purposes of this Convention the expression 'international carriage' means any carriage in which, according to the contract made by the parties, the place of departure and the place of destination, whether or not there be a break in the carriage or a transhipment, are situated either within the territories of two High Contracting Parties, or within the territory of a single High Contracting party, if there is an agreed stopping place within a territory subject to the sovereignty, suzerainty, mandate or authority of another Power, even though that Power is not a party to this Convention. A carriage without such an agreed stopping place between territories subject to the sovereignty, suzerainty, mandate or authority of the same High Contracting party is not deemed to be international for the purposes of this Convention.

(3) A carriage to be performed by several successive air carriers is deemed, for the purposes of this Convention, to be one undivided carriage, if it has

been regarded by the parties as a single operation, whether it had been agreed upon under the form of a single contract or of a series of contracts, and it does not lose its international character merely because one contract or a series of contracts is to be performed entirely within a territory subject to the sovereignty, suzerainty, mandate or authority of the same High Contracting Party.

Article 2

(1) This Convention applies to carriage performed by the State or by legally constituted public bodies provided it falls within the conditions laid down in Article 1.

(2) This Convention does not apply to carriage performed under the terms of any international postal Convention.

...

[*Articles* 3 *and* 4 *of the Convention are not concerned with the carriage of goods.*]

...

Section 3.—Air consignment note

Article 5

(1) Every carrier of goods has the right to require the consignor to make out and hand over to him a document called an 'air consignment note'; every consignor has the right to require the carrier to accept this document.

(2) The absence, irregularity or loss of this document does not affect the existence or the validity of the contract of carriage which shall, subject to the provisions of Article 9, be none the less governed by the rules of this Convention.

Article 6

(1) The air consignment note shall be made out by the consignor in three original parts and be handed over with the goods.

(2) The first part shall be marked 'for the carrier', and shall be signed by the consignor. The second part shall be marked 'for the consignee', it shall be

signed by the consignor and by the carrier and shall accompany the goods. The third part shall be signed by the carrier and handed by him to the consignor after the goods have been accepted.

(3) The carrier shall sign on acceptance of the goods.

(4) The signature of the carrier may be stamped; that of the consignor may be printed or stamped.

(5) If, at the request of the consignor, the carrier makes out the air consignment note, he shall be deemed, subject to proof to the contrary, to have done so on behalf of the consignor.

Article 7

The carrier of goods has the right to require the consignor to make out separate consignment notes when there is more than one package.

Article 8

The air consignment note shall contain the following particulars:—
(a) the place and date of its execution;
(b) the place of departure and of destination;
(c) the agreed stopping places, provided that the carrier may reserve the right to alter the stopping places in case of necessity, and that if he exercises that right the alteration shall not have the effect of depriving that right, the alteration shall not have the effect of depriving the carriage of its international character;
(d) the name and address of the consignor;
(e) the name and address of the first carrier;
(f) the name and address of the consignee, if the case so requires;
(g) the nature of the goods;
(h) the number of the packages, the method of packing and the particular marks or numbers upon them;
(i) the weight, the quantity and the volume or dimensions of the goods;
(j) the apparent condition of the goods and of the packing;
(k) the freight, if it has been agreed upon, the date and place of payment, and the person who is to pay it;
(l) if the goods are sent for payment on delivery, the price of the goods, and, if the case so requires, the amount of the expenses incurred;

(m) the amount of the value declared in accordance with Article 22 (2);

(n) the number of parts of the air consignment note;

(o) the documents handed to the carrier to accompany the air consignment note;

(p) the time fixed for the completion of the carriage and a brief note of the route to be followed, if these matters have been agreed upon;

(q) a statement that the carriage is subject to the rules relating to liability established by this Convention.

Article 9

If the carrier accepts goods without an air consignment note having been made out, or if the air consignment note does not contain all the particulars set out in Article 8 (a) to (i) inclusive and (q), the carrier shall not be entitled to avail himself of the provisions of this Convention which exclude or limit his liability.

Article 10

(1) The consignor is responsible for the correctness of the particulars and statements relating to the goods which he inserts in the air consignment note.

(2) The consignor will be liable for all damage suffered by the carrier or any other person by reason of the irregularity, incorrectness or incompleteness of the said particulars and statements.

Article 11

(1) The air consignment note is prima facie evidence of the conclusion of the contract, of the receipt of the goods and of the conditions of carriage.

(2) The statements in the air consignment note relating to the weight, dimensions and packing of the goods, as well as those relating to the number of packages, are prima facie evidence of the facts stated; those relating to the quantity, volume and condition of the goods do not constitute evidence against the carrier except so far as they both have been, and are stated in the air consignment note to have been, checked by him in the presence of the consignor, or relate to the apparent condition of the goods.

Article 12

(1) Subject to his liability to carry out all his obligations under the contract of carriage, the consignor has the right to dispose of the goods by withdrawing them at the aerodrome of departure or destination, or by stopping them in the course of the journey on any landing, or by calling for them to be delivered at the place of destination or in the course of the journey to a person other than the consignee named in the air consignment note, or by requiring them to be returned to the aerodrome of departure. He must not exercise this right of disposition in such a way as to prejudice the carrier or other consignors and he must repay any expenses occasioned by the exercise of this right.

(2) If it is impossible to carry out the orders of the consignor the carrier must so inform him forthwith.

(3) If the carrier obeys the orders of the consignor for the disposition of the goods without requiring the production of the part of the air consignment note delivered to the latter, he will be liable, without prejudice to his right of recovery from the consignor, for any damage which may be caused thereby to any person who is lawfully in possession of that part of the air consignment note.

(4) The right conferred on the consignor ceases at the moment when that of the consignee begins in accordance with Article 13. Nevertheless, if the consignee declines to accept the consignment note or the goods, or if he cannot be communicated with, the consignor resumes his right of disposition.

Article 13

(1) Except in the circumstances set out in the preceding Article, the consignee is entitled, on arrival of the goods at the place of destination, to require the carrier to hand over to him the air consignment note and to deliver the goods to him, on payment of the charges due and on complying with the conditions of carriage set out in the air consignment note.

(2) Unless it is otherwise agreed, it is the duty of the carrier to give notice to the consignee as soon as the goods arrive.

(3) If the carrier admits the loss of the goods, or if the goods have not arrived at the expiration of seven days after the date on which they ought to have arrived, the consignee is entitled to put into force against the carrier the rights which flow from the contract of carriage.

Article 14

The consignor and the consignee can respectively enforce all the rights given them by Articles 12 and 13, each in his own name, whether he is acting in his own interest or in the interest of another, provided that he carries out the obligations imposed by the contract.

Article 15

(1) Articles 12, 13 and 14 do not affect either the relations of the consignor or the consignee with each other or the mutual relations of third parties whose rights are derived either from the consignor or from the consignee.

(2) The provisions of Articles 12, 13 and 14 can only be varied by express provision in the air consignment note.

Article 16

(1) The consignor must furnish such information and attach to the air consignment note such documents as are necessary to meet the formalities of customs, octroi or police before the goods can be delivered to the consignee. The consignor is liable to the carrier for any damage occasioned by the absence, insufficiency or irregularity of any such information or documents, unless the damage is due to the fault of the carrier or his agents.

(2) The carrier is under no obligation to enquire into the correctness or sufficiency of such information or documents.

CHAPTER III
LIABILITY OF THE CARRIER

Article 17

The carrier is liable for damage sustained in the event of the death or wounding of a passenger or any other bodily injury suffered by a passenger, if the accident which caused the damage so sustained took place on board the aircraft or in the course of any of the operations of embarking or disembarking.

Article 18

(1) The carrier is liable for damage sustained in the event of the destruction or loss of, or of damage to, any registered luggage or any goods, if the occurrence which caused the damage so sustained took place during the carriage by air.

(2) The carriage by air within the meaning of the preceding paragraph comprises the period during which the luggage of goods are in charge of the carrier, whether in an aerodrome or on board an aircraft, or, in the case of a landing outside an aerodrome, in any place whatsoever.

(3) The period of the carriage by air does not extend to any carriage by land, by sea or by river performed outside an aerodrome. If, however, such a carriage takes place in the performance of a contract for carriage by air, for the purpose of loading, delivery or transhipment, any damage is presumed, subject to proof to the contrary, to have been the result of an event which took place during the carriage by air.

Article 19

The carrier is liable for damage occasioned by delay in the carriage by air of passengers, luggage or goods.

Article 20

(1) The carrier is not liable if he proves that he and his agents have taken all necessary measures to avoid the damage or that it was impossible for him or them to take such measures.

(2) In the carriage of goods and luggage the carrier is not liable if he proves that the damage was occasioned by negligent pilotage or negligence in the handling of the aircraft or in navigation and that, in all other respects, he and his agents have taken all necessary measures to avoid the damage.

Article 21

If the carrier proves that the damage was caused by or contributed to by the negligence of the injured person the Court may, in accordance with the provision of its own law, exonerate the carrier wholly or partly from his liability.

Article 22

(1) In the carriage of passengers the liability of the carrier for each passenger is limited to the sum of 125,000 francs. Where, in accordance with the law of the Court seised of the case, damages may be awarded in the form of periodical payments, the equivalent capital value of the said payments shall not exceed 125,000 francs. Nevertheless, by special contract, the carrier and the passenger may agree to a higher limit of liability.

(2) In the carriage of registered luggage and of goods, the liability of the carrier is limited to a sum of 250 francs per kilogram, unless the consignor has made, at the time when the package was handed over to the carrier, a special declaration of the value at delivery and has paid a supplementary sum if the case so requires. In that case the carrier will be liable to pay a sum not exceeding the declared sum, unless he proves that that sum is greater than the actual value to the consignor at delivery.

(3) As regards objects of which the passenger takes charge himself the liability of the carrier is limited to 5,000 francs per passenger.

(4) The sums mentioned above shall be deemed to refer to the French franc consisting of 65½ milligrams gold of millesimal fineness 900. These sums may be converted into any national currency in round figures.

Article 23

Any provision tending to relieve the carrier of liability or to fix a lower limit than that which is laid down in this Convention shall be null and void, but the nullity of any such provision does not involve the nullity of the whole contract, which shall remain subject to the provisions of this Convention.

Article 24

(1) In the cases covered by Articles 18 and 19 any action for damages, however founded, can only be brought subject to the conditions and limits set out in this Convention.

(2) In the cases covered by Article 17 the provisions of the preceding paragraph also apply, without prejudice to the questions as to who are the persons who have the right to bring suit and what are their respective rights.

Article 25

(1) The carrier shall not be entitled to avail himself of the provisions of this Convention which exclude or limit his liability, if the damage is caused by his wilful misconduct or by such default on his part as, in accordance with the law of the Court seised of the case, is considered to be equivalent to wilful misconduct.

(2) Similarly the carrier shall not be entitled to avail himself of the said provisions, if the damage is caused as aforesaid by any agent of the carrier acting within the scope of his employment.

Article 26

(1) Receipt by the person entitled to delivery of luggage or goods without complaint is prima facie evidence that the same have been delivered in good condition and in accordance with the document of carriage.

(2) In the case of damage, the person entitled to delivery must complain to the carrier forthwith after the discovery of the damage, and, at the latest, within three days from the date of receipt in the case of luggage and seven days from the date of receipt in the case of goods. In the case of delay the complaint must be made at the latest within fourteen days from the date on which the luggage or goods have been placed at his disposal.

(3) Every complaint must be made in writing upon the document or carriage or by separate notice in writing despatched within the times aforesaid.

(4) Failing complaint within the times aforesaid, no action shall lie against the carrier, save in the case of fraud on his part.

Article 27

In the case of the death of the person liable, an action for damages lies in accordance with the terms of this Convention against those legally representing his estate.

Article 28

(1) An action for damages must be brought, at the option of the plaintiff, in the territory of one of the High Contracting Parties, either before the Court

having jurisdiction where the carrier is ordinarily resident, or has his principal place of business, or has an establishment by which the contract has been made or before the Court having jurisdiction at the place of destination.

(2) Questions of procedure shall be governed by the law of the Court seised of the case.

Article 29

(1) The right to damages shall be extinguished if an action is not brought within two years, reckoned from the date of arrival at the destination, or from the date on which the aircraft ought to have arrived, or from the date on which the carriage stopped.

(2) The method of calculating the period of limitation shall be determined by the law of the Court seised of the case.

Article 30

(1) In the case of carriage to be performed by various successive carriers and falling within the definition set out in the third paragraph of Article 1, each carrier who accepts passengers, luggage or goods is subjected to the rules set out in this Convention, and is deemed to be one of the contracting parties to the contract of carriage in so far as the contract deals with that part of the carriage which is performed under his supervision.

(2) In the case of carriage of this nature, the passenger or his representative can take action only against the carrier who performed the carriage during which the accident or the delay occurred, save in the case where, by express agreement, the first carrier has assumed liability for the whole journey.

(3) As regards luggage or goods, the passenger or consignor will have a right of action against the first carrier, and the passenger or consignee who is entitled to delivery will have a right of action against the last carrier, and further, each may take action against the carrier who performed the carriage during which the destruction, loss, damage or delay took place. These carriers will be jointly and severally liable to the passenger or to the consignor or consignee.

CHAPTER IV
PROVISIONS RELATING TO COMBINED CARRIAGE

Article 31

(1) In the case of combined carriage performed partly by air and partly by any other mode of carriage, the provisions of this Convention apply only to the carriage by air, provided that the carriage by air falls within the terms of Article 1.

(2) Nothing in this Convention shall prevent the parties in the case of combined carriage from inserting in the document of air carriage conditions relating to other modes of carriage, provided that the provisions of this Convention are observed as regards the carriage by air.

CHAPTER V
GENERAL AND FINAL PROVISIONS

Article 32

Any clause contained in the contract and all special agreements entered into before the damage occurred by which the parties purport to infringe the rules laid down by this Convention, whether by deciding the law to be applied, or by altering the rules as to jurisdiction, shall be null and void. Nevertheless for the carriage of goods arbitration clauses are allowed, subject to this Convention, if the arbitration is to take place within one of the jurisdictions referred to in the first paragraph of Article 28.

Article 33

Nothing contained in this Convention shall prevent the carrier either from refusing to enter into any contract of carriage, or from making regulations which do not conflict with the provisions of this Convention.

Article 34

This Convention does not apply to international carriage by air performed by way of experimental trial by air navigation undertakings with the view to the establishment of a regular line of air navigation, nor does it apply to carriage performed in extraordinary circumstances outside the normal scope of an air carrier's business.

[*The remaining articles of the Convention are administrative only.*]

THE WARSAW CONVENTION 1955

[*The following articles deal with the main points on which this Convention differs from that of 1929.*]

Article 8

The air waybill shall contain:

(a) an indication of the places of departure and destination;

(b) if the places of departure and destination are within the territory of a single High Contracting Party, one or more agreed stopping places being within the territory of another State, an indication of at least one such stopping place;

(c) a notice to the consignor to the effect that, if the carriage involves an ultimate destination or stop in a country other than the country of departure, the Warsaw Convention may be applicable and that the Convention governs and in most cases limits the liability of carriers in respect of loss or damage to cargo.

...

Article 25

The limits of liability specified in Article 22 shall not apply, if it is proved that the damage resulted from an act or omission of the carrier, his servants or agents, done with intent to cause damage or recklessly and with knowledge that damage would probably result; provided that, in the case of such act or omission of a servant or agent, it is also proved that he was acting within the scope of his employment.

Article 25A

(1) If an action is brought against a servant or agent of the carrier arising out of damage to which this Convention relates, such servant or agent, if he proves that he acted within the scope of his employment, shall be

entitled to avail himself of the limits of liability which that carrier himself is entitled to invoke under Article 22.

(2) The aggregate of the amounts recoverable from the carrier, his servants and agents, in that case, shall not exceed the said limits.

(3) The provisions of paragraphs (1) and (2) of this Article shall not apply if it is proved that the damage resulted from an act or omission of the servant or agent done with intent to cause damage or recklessly and with knowledge that damage would probably result.

Article 26

(1) Receipt by the person entitled to delivery of baggage or cargo without complaint is prima facie evidence that the same has been delivered in good condition and in accordance with the document or carriage.

(2) In the case of damage the person entitled to delivery must complain to the carrier forthwith after the discovery of the damage, and, at the latest, within seven days from the date of receipt in the case of baggage and fourteen days from the date of receipt in the case of cargo. In the case of delay the complaint must be made at the latest within twenty-one days from the date on which the baggage or cargo have been placed at his disposal.

(3) Every complaint must be made in writing upon the document of carriage of by separate notice in writing despatched within the times aforesaid.

(4) Failing complaint within the times aforesaid, no action shall lie against the carrier, save in the case of fraud on his part.

...

Appendix 6
UNCTAD/ICC Rules for multimodal transport documents

I APPLICABILITY

1.1. These Rules apply when they are incorporated, however this is made, in writing, orally or otherwise, into a contract of carriage by reference to the UNCTAD/ICC Rules for multimodal transport documents, irrespective of whether there is a unimodal or a multimodal transport contract involving one or several modes of transport or whether a document has been issued or not.

1.2. Whenever such a reference is made, the parties agree that these Rules shall supersede any additional terms of the multimodal transport contract which are in conflict with these Rules, except insofar as they increase the responsibility or obligations of the multimodal transport operator.

2 DEFINITIONS

2.1. *Multimodal transport contract* means a single contract for the carriage of goods by at least two different modes of transport.

2.2. *Multimodal transport operator* (MTO) means any person who concludes a multimodal transport contract and assumes responsibility for the performance thereof as a carrier.

2.3. *Carrier* means the person who actually performs or undertakes to perform the carriage, or part thereof, whether he is identical with the multimodal transport operator or not.

2.4. *Consignor* means the person who concludes the multimodal transport contract with the multimodal transport operator.

2.5. *Consignee* means the person entitled to receive the goods from the multimodal transport operator.

2.6. *Multimodal transport document* (MT document) means a document evidencing a multimodal transport contract and which can be replaced by electronic data interchange messages insofar as permitted by applicable law and be:
(a)   issued in a negotiable form; or
(b)   issued in a non-negotiable form indicating a named consignee.

2.7. *Taken in charge* means that the goods have been handed over to and accepted for carriage by the MTO.

2.8. *Delivery* means:
(a)   the handing over of the goods to the consignee; or
(b)   the placing of the goods at the disposal of the consignee in accordance with the multimodal transport contract or with the law or usage of the particular trade applicable at the place of delivery; or
(c)   the handing over of the goods to an authority or other third party to whom, pursuant to the law or regulations applicable at the place of delivery, the goods must be handed over.

2.9. *Special Drawing Right* (SDR) means the unit of account as defined by the International Monetary Fund.

2.10. *Goods* means any property including live animals as well as containers, pallets or similar articles of transport or packaging not supplied by the MTO, irrespective of whether such property is to be or is carried on or under deck.

3   EVIDENTIARY EFFECT OF THE INFORMATION CONTAINED IN THE MULTIMODAL TRANSPORT DOCUMENT

The information in the *MT document* shall be prima facie evidence of the taking in charge by the MTO of the goods as described by such information unless a contrary indication, such as 'shipper's weight, load and count', 'shipper-packed container' or similar expression, has been made in the printed text or superimposed on the document.

Proof to the contrary shall not be admissible when the MT document has been transferred, or the equivalent electronic data interchange message has been transmitted to and acknowledged by the consignee who in good faith has relied and acted thereon.

4   RESPONSIBILITIES OF THE MULTIMODAL TRANSPORT OPERATOR

4.1.   *Period of responsibility*

The responsibility of the MTO for the goods under these Rules covers the period from the time the MTO has taken the goods in his charge to the time of their delivery.

4.2.   *The liability of the MTO for his servants, agents and other persons*

The multimodal transport operator shall be responsible for the acts and omissions of his servants or agents, when any such servant or agent is acting within the scope of his employment, or of any other person of whose services he makes use for the performance of the contract, as if such acts and omissions were his own.

4.3.   *Delivery of the goods to the consignee*

The MTO undertakes to perform or to procure the performance of all acts necessary to ensure delivery of the goods:
(a)   when the *MT document* has been issued in a negotiable form 'to bearer', to the person surrendering one original of the document; or
(b)   when the *MT document* has been issued in a negotiable form 'to order', to the person surrendering one original of the document duly endorsed; or
(c)   when the *MT document* has been issued in a negotiable form to a named person, to that person upon proof of his identity and surrender of one original document; if such document has been transferred 'to order' or in blank the provisions of (b) above apply; or
(d)   when the *MT document* has been issued in a non-negotiable form, to the person named as consignee in the document upon proof of his identity; or
(e)   when no document has been issued, to a person as instructed by the consignor or by a person who has acquired the consignor's or the consignee's rights under the multimodal transport contract to give such instructions.

5   LIABILITY OF THE MULTIMODAL TRANSPORT OPERATOR

5.1.   *Basis of liability*

Subject to the defences set forth in Rule 5.4 and Rule 6, the MTO shall be liable for loss of or damage to the goods, as well as for delay in delivery, if the occurrence which caused the loss, damage or delay in delivery took place while the goods were in his charge as defined in Rule 4.1, unless the MTO proves that no fault or neglect of his own, his servants or agents or any other person referred to in Rule 4 has caused or contributed to the loss, damage or delay in delivery. However, the MTO shall not be liable for loss following from delay in delivery unless the consignor has made a declaration of interest in timely delivery which has been accepted by the MTO.

5.2. *Delay in delivery*

Delay in delivery occurs when the goods have not been delivered within the time expressly agreed upon or, in the absence of such agreement, within the time which it would be reasonable to require of a diligent MTO, having regard to the circumstances of the case.

5.3. *Conversion of delay into final loss*

If the goods have not been delivered within ninety consecutive days following the date of delivery determined according to Rule 5.2, the claimant may, in the absence of evidence to the contrary, treat the goods as lost.

5.4. *Defences of carriage by sea or inland waterways*

Notwithstanding the provisions of Rule 5.1 the MTO shall not be responsible for loss, damage or delay in delivery with respect to goods carried by sea or inland waterways when such loss, damage or delay during such carriage has been caused by:

- act, neglect, or default of the master, mariner, pilot or the servants of the carrier in the navigation or in the management of the ship;
- fire, unless caused by the actual fault or privity of the carrier;

however, always provided that whenever loss or damage has resulted from unseaworthiness of the ship, the MTO can prove that due diligence has been exercised to make the ship seaworthy at the commencement of the voyage.

5.5. *Assessment of compensation*

5.5.1. Assessment of compensation for loss of or damage to the goods shall be made by reference to the value of such goods at the place and time they are delivered to the consignee or at the place and time when, in accordance with the multimodal transport contract, they should have been so delivered.

5.5.2. The value of the goods shall be determined according to the current commodity exchange price or, if there is no such price, according to the current market price or, if there is no commodity exchange price or current market price, by reference to the normal value of goods of the same kind and quality.

6   LIMITATION OF LIABILITY OF THE MULTIMODAL TRANSPORT OPERATOR

6.1.   Unless the nature and value of the goods have been declared by the consignor before the goods have been taken in charge by the MTO and inserted in the *MT document*, the MTO shall in no event be or become liable for any loss of or damage to the goods in an amount exceeding the equivalent of 666.67 SDR per package or unit or 2 SDR per kilogramme of gross weight of the goods lost or damaged, whichever is the higher.

6.2.   Where a container, pallet or similar article of transport is loaded with more than one package or unit, the packages or other shipping units enumerated in the *MT document* as packed in such article of transport are deemed packages or shipping units. Except as aforesaid, such article of transport shall be considered the package or unit.

6.3.   Notwithstanding the above-mentioned provisions, if the multimodal transport does not, according to the contract, include carriage of goods by sea or by inland waterways, the liability of the MTO shall be limited to an amount not exceeding 8.33 SDR per kilogramme of gross weight of the goods lost or damaged.

6.4.   When the loss of or damage to the goods occurred during one particular stage of the multimodal transport, in respect of which an applicable international convention or mandatory national law would have provided another limit of liability if a separate contract of carriage had been made for that particular stage of transport, then the limit of the MTO's liability for such loss or damage shall be determined by reference to the provisions of such convention or mandatory national law.

6.5.   If the MTO is liable in respect of loss following from delay in delivery, or consequential loss or damage other than loss of or damage to the goods, the liability of the MTO shall be limited to an amount not exceeding the equivalent of the freight under the multimodal transport contract for the multimodal transport.

6.6.   The aggregate liability of the MTO shall not exceed the limits of liability for total loss of the goods.

7 LOSS OF THE RIGHT OF THE MULTIMODAL TRANSPORT OPERATOR TO LIMIT LIABILITY

The MTO is not entitled to the benefit of the limitation of liability if it is proved that the loss, damage or delay in delivery resulted from a personal act or omission of the MTO done with the intent to cause such loss, damage or delay, or recklessly and with knowledge that such loss, damage or delay would probably result.

8 LIABILITY OF THE CONSIGNOR

8.1. The consignor shall be deemed to have guaranteed to the MTO the accuracy, at the time the goods were taken in charge by the MTO, of all particulars relating to the general nature of the goods, their marks, number, weight, volume and quantity and, if applicable, to the dangerous character of the goods, as furnished by him or on his behalf for insertion in the *MT document*.

8.2. The consignor shall indemnify the MTO against any loss resulting from inaccuracies in or inadequacies of the particulars referred to above.

8.3. The consignor shall remain liable even if the *MT document* has been transferred by him.

8.4. The right of the MTO to such indemnity shall in no way limit his liability under the multimodal transport contract to any person other than the consignor.

9 NOTICE OF LOSS OF OR DAMAGE TO THE GOODS

9.1. Unless notice of loss of or damage to the goods, specifying the general nature of such loss or damage, is given in writing by the consignee to the MTO when the goods are handed over to the consignee, such handing over is prima facie evidence of the delivery by the MTO of the goods as described in the *MT document*.

9.2. Where the loss or damage is not apparent, the same prima facie effect shall apply if notice in writing is not given within 6 consecutive days after the day when the goods were handed over to the consignee.

10 TIME-BAR

The MTO shall, unless otherwise expressly agreed, be discharged of all liability under these Rules unless suit is brought within 9 months after the delivery of the goods, or the date when the goods should have been delivered, or the date when, in accordance with Rule 5.3, failure to deliver the goods would give the consignee the right to treat the goods as lost.

11 APPLICABILITY OF THE RULES TO ACTIONS IN TORT

These Rules apply to all claims against the MTO relating to the performance of the multimodal transport contract, whether the claim be founded in contract or in tort.

12 APPLICABILITY OF THE RULES TO THE MULTIMODAL TRANSPORT OPERATOR'S SERVANTS, AGENTS AND OTHER PERSONS EMPLOYED BY HIM

These Rules apply whenever claims relating to the performance of the multimodal transport contract are made against any servant, agent or other person whose services the MTO has used in order to perform the multimodal transport contract, whether such claims are founded in contract or in tort, and the aggregate liability of the MTO and such servants, agents or other persons shall not exceed the limits in Rule 6.

13 MANDATORY LAW

These Rules shall only take effect to the extent that they are not contrary to the mandatory provisions of international conventions or national law applicable to the multimodal transport contract.

Acknowledgment

Copyright © 1992, International Chamber of Commerce (Publication no 481). The official version is the English one. These, and other publications of the International Chamber of Commerce in the fields of arbitration, banking and transport techniques are available from ICC Publishing SA, 38 Cours Albert ler, 75008 Paris, France.

UNCTAD/ICC Rules for multimodal transport documents

Appendix 7
Sale of Goods Act 1979

PART III. EFFECTS OF THE CONTRACT

Transfer of property as between seller and buyer

16. Goods must be ascertained. Where there is a contract for the sale of unascertained goods no property in the goods is transferred to the buyer unless and until the goods are ascertained.

17. Property passes when intended to pass.—(1) Where there is a contract for the sale of specific or ascertained goods the property in them is transferred to the buyer at such time as the parties to the contract intend it to be transferred.

(2) For the purpose of ascertaining the intention of the parties regard shall be had to the terms of the contract, the conduct of the parties and the circumstances of the case.

18. Rules for ascertaining intention. Unless a different intention appears, the following are rules for ascertaining the intention of the parties as to the buyer at which the property in the goods is to pass to the buyer.

Rule 1.—Where there is an unconditional contract for the sale of specific goods in a deliverable state the property in the goods passes to the buyer when the contract is made, and it is immaterial whether the time of payment or the time of delivery, or both, be postponed.

Rule 2.—Where there is a contract for the sale of specific goods and the seller is bound to do something to the goods for the purpose of putting them into a deliverable state, the property does not pass until the thing is done and the buyer has notice that it has been done.

Rule 3.—Where there is a contract for the sale of specific goods in a deliverable state but the seller is bound to weigh, measure, test, or do some other act or thing with reference to the goods for the purpose of ascertaining the price, the property does not pass until the act or thing is done and the buyer has notice that it has been done.

Rule 4.—When goods are delivered to the buyer on approval or on sale or return or other similar terms the property in the goods passes to the buyer—

(a) when he signifies his approval or acceptance to the seller or does any other act adopting the transaction;

(b) if he does not signify his approval or acceptance to the seller but retains the goods without giving notice of rejection, then, if a time has been fixed for the return of the goods, on the expiration of that time, and, if no time had been fixed, on the expiration of a reasonable time.

Rule 5.—(1) Where there is a contract for the sale of unascertained or future goods by description, and goods of that description and in a deliverable state are unconditionally appropriated to the contract, either by the seller with the assent of the buyer or by the buyer with the assent of the seller, the property in the goods then passes to the buyer; and the assent may be expressed or implied, and may be given either before or after the appropriation is made.

(2) Where, in pursuance of the contract, the seller delivers the goods to the buyer or to a carrier or other bailee or custodier (whether named by the buyer or not) for the purpose of transmission to the buyer, and does not reserve the right of disposal, he is to be taken to have unconditionally appropriated the goods to the contract.

19. Reservation of right of disposal. —(1) Where there is a contract for the sale of specific goods or where goods are subsequently appropriated to the contract, the seller may, by the terms of the contract or appropriation, reserve the right of disposal of the goods until certain conditions are fulfilled; and in such a case, notwithstanding the delivery of the goods to the buyer, or to a carrier or other bailee or custodier for the purpose of transmission to the buyer, the property in the goods does not pass to the buyer until the conditions imposed by the seller are fulfilled.

(2) Where goods are shipped, and by the bill of lading the goods are deliverable to the order of the seller or his agent, the seller is prima facie to be taken to reserve the right of disposal.

(3) Where the seller of goods draws on the buyer for the price, and transmits the bill of exchange and bill of lading to the buyer together to

secure acceptance or payment of the bill of exchange, the buyer is bound to return the bill of lading if he does not honour the bill of exchange, and if he wrongfully retains the bill of lading the property in the goods does not pass to him.

20. Risk prima facie passes with property. —(1) Unless otherwise agreed, the goods remain at the seller's risk until the property in them is transferred to the buyer, but when the property in them is transferred to the buyer the goods are at the buyer's risk whether delivery has been made or not.

(2) But where delivery has been delayed through the fault of either buyer or seller the goods are at the risk of the party at fault as regards any loss which might not have occurred but for such fault.

(3) Nothing in this section affects the duties or liabilities of either seller or buyer as a bailee or custodier of the goods of the other party.

Transfer of title

21. Sale by person not the owner. —(1) Subject to this Act, where goods are sold by a person who is not their owner, and who does not sell them under the authority or with the consent of the owner, the buyer acquires no better title to the goods than the seller had, unless the owner of the goods is by his conduct precluded from denying the seller's authority to sell.

(2) Nothing in this Act affects—
(a) the provisions of the Factors Acts or any enactment enabling the apparent owner of goods to dispose of them as if he were their true owner;
(b) the validity of any contract of sale under any special common law or statutory power of sale or under the order of a court of competent jurisdiction.

22. Market overt. —(1) Where goods are sold in market overt, according to the usage of the market, the buyer acquires a good title to the goods, provided he buys them in good faith and without notice of any defect or want of title on the part of the seller.

(2) This section does not apply to Scotland.

(3) Paragraph 8 of Schedule 1 below applies in relation to a contract under which goods were sold before 1 January 1968 or (in the application of this Act to Northern Ireland) 29 August 1967.

23. Sale under voidable title. When the seller of goods has a voidable title to them, but his title has not been avoided at the time of the sale, the buyer acquires a good title to the goods, provided he buys them in good faith and without notice of the seller's defect of title.

24. Seller in possession after sale. Where a person having sold goods continues or is in possession of the goods, or of the documents of title to the goods, the delivery or transfer by that person, or by a mercantile agent acting for him, of the goods or documents of title under any sale, pledge, or other disposition thereof, to any person receiving the same in good faith and without notice of the previous sale, has the same effect as if the person making the delivery or transfer were expressly authorised by the owner of the goods to make the same.

25. Buyer in possession after sale. —(1) Where a person having bought or agreed to buy goods obtains, with the consent of the seller, possession of the goods or the documents of title to the goods, the delivery or transfer by that person, or by a mercantile agent acting for him, of the goods or documents of title, under any sale, pledge, or other disposition thereof, to any person receiving the same in good faith and without notice of any lien or other right of the original seller in respect of the goods, has the same effect as if the person making the delivery or transfer were a mercantile agent in possession of the goods or documents of title with the consent of the owner.

(2) For the purposes of subsection (1) above—
(a)   the buyer under a conditional sale agreement is to be taken not to be a person who has bought or agreed to buy goods, and
(b)   'conditional sale agreement' means an agreement for the sale of goods which is a consumer credit agreement within the meaning of the Consumer Credit Act 1974 under which the purchase price or part of it is payable by instalments, and the property in the goods is to remain in the seller (notwithstanding that the buyer is to be in possession of the goods) until such conditions as to the payment of instalments or otherwise as may be specified in the agreement are fulfilled.

(3) Paragraph 9 of Schedule 1 below applies in relation to a contract under which a person buys or agrees to buy goods and which is made before the appointed day.

(4) In subsection (3) above and paragraph 9 of Schedule 1 below references to the appointed day are to the day appointed for the purposes of those

provisions by an order of the Secretary of State made by statutory instrument.

26. Supplementary to sections 24 and 25. In sections 24 and 25 above 'mercantile agent' means a mercantile agent having in the customary course of his business as such agent authority either—

(a) to sell goods, or

(b) to consign goods for the purpose of sale, or

(c) to buy goods, or

(d) to raise money on the security of goods.

Appendix 8

Sale of Goods (Amendment) Act 1995

1 Unascertained goods forming part of an identified bulk

(1)   At the beginning of section 16 of the Sale of Goods Act 1979 ('the 1979 Act') there shall be added the words 'Subject to section 20A below'.

(2)   In section 18 of the 1979 Act, at the end of rule 5 there shall be added the following—

'(3) Where there is a contract for the sale of a specified quantity of unascertained goods in a deliverable state forming part of a bulk which is identified either in the contract or by subsequent agreement between the parties and the bulk is reduced to (or to less than) that quantity, then, if the buyer under that contract is the only buyer to whom goods are then due out of the bulk—
(a)   the remaining goods are to be taken as appropriated to that contract at the time when the bulk is so reduced, and
(b)   the property in those goods then passes to that buyer.

(4) Paragraph (3) above applies also (with the necessary modifications) where a bulk is reduced to (or to less than) the aggregate of the quantities due to a single buyer under separate contracts relating to that bulk and he is the only buyer to whom goods are then due out of that bulk.'

(3)   After section 20 of the 1979 Act there shall be inserted the following—

'20A.—Undivided shares in goods forming part of a bulk.

(1)   This section applies to a contract for the sale of a specified quantity of unascertained goods if the following conditions are met—
(a)   the goods or some of them form part of a bulk which is identified either in the contract or by subsequent agreement between the parties; and
(b)   the buyer has paid the price for some or all of the goods which are the subject of the contract and which form part of the bulk.

(2)   Where this section applies, then (unless the parties agree otherwise), as soon as the conditions specified in paragraphs (a) and (b) of subsection (1) above are met or at such later time as the parties may agree—

(a)   property in an undivided share in the bulk is transferred to the buyer, and

(b)   the buyer becomes an owner in common of the bulk.

(3)   Subject to subsection (4) below, for the purposes of this section, the undivided share of a buyer in a bulk at any time shall be such share as the quantity of goods paid for and due to the buyer out of the bulk bears to the quantity of goods in the bulk at that time.

(4)   Where the aggregate of the undivided shares of buyers in a bulk determined under subsection (3) above would at any time exceed the whole of the bulk at that time, the undivided share in the bulk of each buyer shall be reduced proportionately so that the aggregate of the undivided shares is equal to the whole bulk.

(5)   Where a buyer has paid the price for only some of the goods due to him out of a bulk, any delivery to the buyer out of the bulk shall, for the purposes of this section, be ascribed in the first place to the goods in respect of which payment has been made.

(6)   For the purposes of this section payment of part of the prices for any goods shall be treated as payment for a corresponding part of the goods.

20B.—Deemed consent by co-owner to dealings in bulk goods.

(1)   A person who has become an owner in common of a bulk by virtue of section 20A above shall be deemed to have consented to—

(a)   any delivery of goods out of the bulk to any other owner in common of the bulk, being goods which are due to him under his contract;

(b)   any dealing with or removal, delivery or disposal of goods in the bulk by any other person who is an owner in common of the bulk in so far as the goods fall within that co-owner's undivided share in the bulk at the time of the dealing, removal, delivery or disposal.

(2)   No cause of action shall accrue to anyone against a person by reason of that person having acted in accordance with paragraph (a) or (b) of subsection (1) above in reliance on any consent deemed to have been given under that subsection.

(3)   Nothing in this section or section 20A above shall—

(a)   impose an obligation on a buyer of goods out of a bulk to compensate any other buyer of goods out of that bulk for any shortfall in the goods received by that other buyer;

(b)   affect any contractual arrangement between buyers of goods out of a bulk for adjustments between themselves; or

(c)   affect the rights of any buyers under his contract.'.

2 Additional provisions

In section 61(1) of the 1979 Act—

(a) after the definition of 'action' there shall be inserted the following definition—

'"bulk" means a mass or collection of goods of the same kind which—
(a) is contained in a defined space or area; and
(b) is such that any goods in the bulk are interchangeable with any other goods therein of the same number or quantity;';

(b) at the end of the definition of 'delivery' there shall be added the words 'except that in relation to sections 20A and 20B above it includes such appropriation of goods to the contract as results in property in the goods being transferred to the buyer;';

(c) at the end of the definition of 'goods' there shall be added the words 'and includes an undivided share in goods;';

(d) at the end of the definition of 'specific goods' there shall be added the words 'and includes an undivided share, specified as a fraction or percentage, of goods identified and agreed on as aforesaid'.

Appendix 9

The Institute Cargo Clauses*

INSTITUTE CARGO CLAUSES (C)

Risks covered

1   This insurance covers, except as provided in Clauses 4, 5, 6 and 7 below,

1.1   loss of or damage to the subject-matter insured reasonably attributable to

1.1.1   fire or explosion

1.1.2   vessel or craft being stranded grounded sunk or capsized

1.1.3   overturning or derailment of land conveyance

1.1.4   collision or contact of vessel craft or conveyance with any external object other than water

1.1.5   discharge of cargo at a port of distress

1.2   loss of or damage to the subject-matter insured caused by

1.2.1   general average sacrifice

1.2.2   jettison

2   This insurance covers general average and salvage charges, adjusted or determined according to the contract of affreightment and/or the governing law and practice, incurred to avoid or in connection with the avoidance of loss from any cause except those excluded in Clauses 4, 5, 6 and 7 or elsewhere in this insurance.

3   This insurance is extended to indemnify the Assured against such proportion of liability under the contract of affreightment 'Both to Blame Collision' Clause as is in respect of a loss recoverable hereunder. In the

*   Reproduced by kind permission of the Institute of London Underwriters.

event of any claim by shipowners under the said Clause the Assured agree to notify the Underwriters who shall have the right, at their own cost and expense, to defend the Assured against such claim.

Exclusions

4   In no case shall this insurance cover

4.1   loss damage or expense attributable to wilful misconduct of the Assured

4.2   ordinary leakage, ordinary loss in weight or volume, or ordinary wear and tear of the subject-matter insured

4.3   loss damage or expense caused by insufficiency or unsuitability of packing or preparation of the subject-matter insured (for the purpose of this Clause 4.3 'packing' shall be deemed to include stowage in a container or liftvan but only when such stowage is carried out prior to attachment of this insurance or by the Assured or their servants)

4.4   loss damage or expense caused by inherent vice or nature of the subject-matter insured

4.5   loss damage or expense proximately caused by delay, even though the delay be caused by a risk insured against (except expenses payable under Clause 2 above)

4.6   loss damage or expense arising from insolvency or financial default of the owners managers charterers or operators of the vessel

4.7   deliberate damage to or deliberate destruction of the subject-matter insured or any part thereof by the wrongful act of any person or persons

4.8   loss damage or expense arising from the use of any weapon of war employing atomic or nuclear fission and/or fusion or other like reaction or radioactive force or matter.

5

5.1   In no case shall this insurance cover loss damage or expense arising from

unseaworthiness of vessel or craft,

unfitness of vessel craft conveyance container or liftvan for the safe carriage of the subject-matter insured,

where the Assured or their servants are privy to such unseaworthiness or unfitness, at the time the subject-matter insured is loaded therein.

5.2   The Underwriters waive any breach of the implied warranties of seaworthiness of the ship and fitness of the ship to carry the subject-matter insured to destination, unless the Assured or their servants are privy to such unseaworthiness or unfitness.

6 In no case shall this insurance cover loss damage or expense caused by

6.1 war civil war revolution rebellion insurrection, or civil strife arising therefrom, or any hostile act by or against a belligerent power

6.2 capture seizure arrest restraint or detainment, and the consequences thereof or any attempt thereat

6.3 derelict mines torpedoes bombs or other derelict weapons of war.

7 In no case shall this insurance cover loss damage or expense

7.1 caused by strikers, locked-out workmen, or persons taking part in labour disturbances, riots or civil commotions

7.2 resulting from strikes, lock-outs, labour disturbances, riots or civil commotions

7.3 caused by any terrorist or any person acting from a political motive.

Duration

8

8.1 This insurance attaches from the time the goods leave the warehouse or place of storage at the place named herein for the commencement of the transit, continues during the ordinary course of transit and terminates either

    8.1.1 on delivery to the Consignees; or other final warehouse or place of storage at the destination named herein,

    8.1.2 on delivery to any other warehouse or place of storage, whether prior to or at the destination named herein, which the Assured elect to use either

        8.1.2.1 for storage other than in the ordinary course of transit or

        8.1.2.2 for allocation or distribution,

    or

    8.1.3 on the expiry of 60 days after completion of discharge overside of the goods hereby insured from the oversea vessel at the final port of discharge,

whichever shall first occur.

8.2 If, after discharge overside from the oversea vessel at the final port of discharge, but prior to termination of this insurance, the goods are to be forwarded to a destination other than that to which they are insured

The Institute Cargo Clauses

hereunder, this insurance, whilst remaining subject to termination as provided for above, shall not extend beyond the commencement of transit to such other destination.

8.3 This insurance shall remain in force (subject to termination as provided for above and to the provisions of Clause 9 below) during delay beyond the control of the Assured, any deviation, forced discharge, reshipment or transhipment and during any variation of the adventure arising from the exercise of a liberty granted to shipowners or charterers under the contract of affreightment.

9 If owing to circumstances beyond the control of the Assured either the contract of carriage is terminated at a port or place other than the destination named therein or the transit is otherwise terminated before delivery of the goods as provided for in Clause 8 above, then this insurance shall also terminate *unless prompt notice is given to the Underwriters and continuation of cover is requested when the insurance shall remain in force subject to an additional premium if required by the Underwriters*, either

9.1 until the goods are sold and delivered at such port or place, or, unless otherwise specially agreed, until the expiry of 60 days after arrival of the goods hereby insured at such port or place, whichever shall first occur,

or

9.2 if the goods are forwarded within the said period of 60 days (or any agreed extension thereof) to the destination named herein or to any other destination, until terminated in accordance with the provisions of Clause 8 above.

10 Where, after attachment of this insurance, the destination is changed by the Assured, *held covered at a premium and on conditions to be arranged subject to prompt notice being given to the Underwriters*,

Claims

11

11.1 In order to recover under this insurance the Assured must have an insurable interest in the subject-matter insured at the time of the loss.

11.2 Subject to 11.1 above, the Assured shall be entitled to recover for insured loss occurring during the period covered by this insurance, notwithstanding that the loss occurred before the contract of insurance was concluded, unless the Assured were aware of the loss and the Underwriters were not.

12   Where, as a result of the operation of a risk covered by this insurance, the insured transit is terminated at a port or place other than that to which the subject-matter is covered under this insurance, the Underwriters will reimburse the Assured for any extra charges properly and reasonably incurred in unloading storing and forwarding the subject-matter to the destination to which it is insured hereunder.

This Clause 12, which does not apply to general average or salvage charges, shall be subject to the exclusions contained in Clauses 4, 5, 6 and 7 above, and shall not include charges arising from the fault negligence insolvency or financial default of the Assured or their servants.

13   No claim for Constructive Total Loss shall be recoverable hereunder unless the subject-matter insured is reasonably abandoned either on account of its actual total loss appearing to be unavoidable or because the cost of recovering, reconditioning and forwarding the subject-matter to the destination to which it is insured would exceed its value on arrival.

14

14.1 If any Increased Value insurance is effected by the Assured on the cargo insured herein the agreed value of the cargo shall be deemed to be increased to the total amount insured under this insurance and all Increased Value insurances covering the loss, and liability under this insurance shall be in such proportion as the sum insured herein bears to such total amount insured.

In the event of claim the Assured shall provide the Underwriters with evidence of the amounts insured under all other insurances.

14.2 Where this insurance is on Increased Value the following clause shall apply:

The agreed value of the cargo shall be deemed to be equal to the total amount insured under the primary insurance and all Increased Value insurances covering the loss and effected on the cargo by the Assured, and liability under this insurance shall be in such proportion as the sum insured herein bears to such total amount insured.

In the event of claim the Assured shall provide the Underwrites with evidence of the amounts insured under all other insurances.

Benefit of insurance

15   This insurance shall not inure to the benefit of the carrier or other bailee.

Minimising losses

16 It is the duty of the Assured and their servants and agents in respect of loss recoverable hereunder
16.1 to take such measures as may be reasonable for the purpose of averting or minimising such loss, and
16.2 to ensure that all rights against carriers, bailees or other third parties are properly preserved and exercised

and the Underwriters will, in addition to any loss recoverable hereunder, reimburse the Assured for any charges properly and reasonably incurred in pursuance of these duties.

17 Measures taken by the Assured or the Underwriters with the object of saving, protecting or recovering the subject-matter insured shall not be considered as a waiver or acceptance of abandonment or otherwise prejudice the rights of either party.

Avoidance of delay

18 It is a condition of this insurance that the Assured shall act with reasonable despatch in all circumstances within their control.

Law and practice

19 This insurance is subject to English law and practice.

Note:—It is necessary for the Assured when they become aware of an event which is 'held covered' under this insurance to give prompt notice to the Underwriters and the right to such cover is dependent upon compliance with this obligation.

INSTITUTE CARGO CLAUSES (B)

Risks covered

1 This insurance covers, except as provided in Clauses 4, 5, 6 and 7 below,
1.1 loss of or damage to the subject-matter insured reasonably attributable to
1.1.1. fire or explosion

1.1.2 vessel or craft being stranded grounded sunk or capsized

1.1.3 overturning or derailment of land conveyance

1.1.4 collision or contact of vessel craft or conveyance with any external object other than water

1.1.5 discharge of cargo at a port of distress

1.1.6 earthquake volcanic eruption or lightning,

1.2 loss of or damage to the subject-matter insured caused by

1.2.1 general average sacrifice

1.2.2 jettison or washing overboard

1.2.3 entry of sea lake or river water into vessel craft hold conveyance container liftvan or place of storage,

1.3 total loss of any package lost overboard or dropped whilst loading on to, or unloading from, vessel or craft.

2   This insurance covers general average and salvage charges, adjusted or determined according to the contract of affreightment and/or the governing law and practice, incurred to avoid or in connection with the avoidance of loss from any cause except those excluded in Clauses 4, 5, 6 and 7 or elsewhere in this insurance.

3   This insurance is extended to indemnify the Assured against such proportion of liability under the contract of affreightment 'Both to Blame Collision' Clause as is in respect of a loss recoverable hereunder. In the event of any claim by shipowners under the said Clause the Assured agree to notify the Underwriters who shall have the right, at their own cost and expense, to defend the Assured against such claim.

Exclusions

4   In no case shall this insurance cover

4.1   loss damage or expense attributable to wilful misconduct of the Assured

4.2   ordinary leakage, ordinary loss in weight or volume, or ordinary wear and tear of the subject-matter insured

4.3   loss damage or expense caused by insufficiency or unsuitability of packing or preparation of the subject-matter insured (for the purpose of this Clause 4.3 'packing' shall be deemed to include stowage in a container or liftvan but only when such stowage is carried out prior to attachment of this insurance or by the Assured or their servants)

4.4   loss damage or expense caused by inherent vice or nature of the subject-matter insured

4.5 loss damage or expense proximately caused by delay, even though the delay be caused by a risk insured against (except expenses payable under Clause 2 above)

4.6 loss damage or expense arising from insolvency or financial default of the owners managers charterers or operators of the vessel

4.7 deliberate damage to or deliberate destruction of the subject-matter insured or any part thereof by the wrongful act of any person or persons

4.8 loss damage or expense arising from the use of any weapon of war employing atomic or nuclear fission and/or fusion or other like reaction or radioactive force or matter.

5

5.1 In no case shall this insurance cover loss damage or expense arising from

unseaworthiness of vessel or craft,

unfitness of vessel craft conveyance container or liftvan for the safe carriage of the subject-matter insured,

where the Assured or their servants are privy to such unseaworthiness or unfitness, at the time the subject-matter insured is loaded therein.

5.2 The Underwriters waive any breach of the implied warranties of seaworthiness of the ship and fitness of the ship to carry the subject-matter insured to destination, unless the Assured or their servants are privy to such unseaworthiness or unfitness.

6 In no case shall this insurance cover loss damage or expense caused by

6.1 war civil war revolution rebellion insurrection, or civil strife arising therefrom, or any hostile act by or against a belligerent power

6.2 capture seizure arrest restraint or detainment, and the consequences thereof or any attempt thereat

6.3 derelict mines torpedoes bombs or other derelict weapons of war.

7 In no case shall this insurance cover loss damage or expense

7.1 caused by strikers, locked-out workmen, or persons taking part in labour disturbances, riots or civil commotions

7.2 resulting from strikes, lock-outs, labour disturbances, riots or civil commotions

7.3 caused by any terrorist or any person acting from a political motive.

(The remaining clauses are as for the C clauses.)

INSTITUTE CARGO CLAUSES (A)

Risks covered

1 This insurance covers all risks of loss of or damage to the subject-matter insured except as provided in Clauses 4, 5, 6 and 7 below.

2 This insurance covers general average and salvage charges, adjusted or determined according to the contract of affreightment and/or the governing law and practice, incurred to avoid or in connection with the avoidance of loss from any cause except those excluded in Clauses 4, 5, 6 and 7 or elsewhere in this insurance.

3 This insurance is extended to indemnify the Assured against such proportion of liability under the contract of affreightment 'Both to Blame Collision' Clause as is in respect of a loss recoverable hereunder. In the event of any claim by shipowners under the said Clause and Assured agree to notify the Underwriters who shall have the right, at their own cost and expense, to defend the Assured against such claim.

Exclusions

4 In no case shall this insurance cover
4.1 loss damage or expense attributable to wilful misconduct of the Assured
4.2 ordinary leakage, ordinary loss in weight or volume, or ordinary wear and tear of the subject-matter insured
4.3 loss damage or expense caused by insufficiency or unsuitability of packing or preparation of the subject-matter insured (for the purpose of this Clause 4.3 'packing' shall be deemed to include stowage in a container or liftvan but only when such stowage is carried out prior to attachment of this insurance or by the Assured or their servants)
4.4 loss damage or expense caused by inherent vice or nature of the subject-matter insured
4.5 loss damage or expense proximately caused by delay, even though the delay be caused by a risk insured against (except expenses payable under Clause 2 above)
4.6 loss damage or expense arising from insolvency or financial default of the owners managers charterers or operators of the vessel
4.7 loss damage or expense arising from the use of any weapon of war employing atomic or nuclear fission and/or fusion or other like reaction or radioactive force or matter.

5

5.1 In no case shall this insurance cover loss damage or expense arising from

unseaworthiness of vessel or craft,

unfitness of vessel craft conveyance container or liftvan for the safe carriage of the subject-matter insured,

where the Assured or their servants are privy to such unseaworthiness or unfitness, at the time the subject-matter insured is loaded therein.

5.2 The Underwriters waive any breach of the implied warranties of seaworthiness of the ship and fitness of the ship to carry the subject-matter insured to destination, unless the Assured or their servants are privy to such unseaworthiness or unfitness.

6 In no case shall this insurance cover loss damage or expense caused by

6.1 war civil war revolution rebellion insurrection, or civil strife arising therefrom, or any hostile act by or against a belligerent power

6.2 capture seizure arrest restraint or detainment (piracy excepted), and the consequences thereof or any attempt thereat

6.3 derelict mines torpedoes bombs or other derelict weapons of war.

7 In no case shall this insurance cover loss damage or expense

7.1 caused by strikers, locked-out workmen, or persons taking part in labour disturbances, riots or civil commotions

7.2 resulting from strikes, lock-outs, labour disturbances, riots or civil commotions

7.3 caused by any terrorist or any person acting from a political motive.

(The remaining clauses are as for the C clauses.)

ICC Uniform Customs and Practice for Documentary Credits

A. GENERAL PROVISIONS AND DEFINITIONS

Article 1 Application of UCP

The Uniform Customs and Practice for Documentary Credits, 1993 Revision, ICC Publication No 500, shall apply to all Documentary Credits (including to the extent to which they may be applicable, Standby Letter(s) of Credit) where they are incorporated into the text of the Credit. They are binding on all parties thereto, unless otherwise expressly stipulated in the Credit.

Article 2 Meaning of Credit

For the purposes of these Articles, the expressions 'Documentary Credit(s)' and 'Standby Letter(s) of Credit' (hereinafter referred to as 'Credit(s)'), mean any arrangement, however named or described, whereby a bank (the 'Issuing Bank') acting at the request and on the instructions of a customer (the 'Applicant') or on its own behalf,

i.   is to make a payment to or to the order of a third party (the 'Beneficiary'), or is to accept and pay bills of exchange (Draft(s)) drawn by the Beneficiary),
     or
ii. authorises another bank to effect such payment, or to accept and pay such bills of exchange (Draft(s)),
     or
iii. authorises another bank to negotiate,
     against stipulated document(s), provided that the terms and conditions of the Credit are complied with.

For the purposes of these Articles, branches of a bank in different countries are considered another bank.

Article 3   Credits v Contracts

a)   Credits, by their nature, are separate transactions from the sales or other contract(s) on which they may be based and banks are in no way concerned with or bound by such contract(s), even if any reference whatsoever to such contract(s) is included in the Credit. Consequently, the undertaking of a bank to pay, accept and pay Draft(s) or negotiate and/or to fulfil any other obligation under the Credit, is not subject to claims or defences by the Applicant resulting from his relationships with the Issuing Bank or the Beneficiary.

b)   A Beneficiary can in no case avail himself of the contractual relationships existing between the banks or between the Applicant and the issuing Bank.

Article 4   Documents v Goods/Services/Performances

In Credit operations all parties concerned deal with documents, and not with goods, services and/or other performances to which the documents may relate.

Article 5   Instructions to Issue/Amend Credits

a)   Instructions for the issuance of a Credit, the Credit itself, instructions for an amendment thereto, and the amendment itself, must be complete and precise.

In order to guard against confusion and misunderstanding, banks should discourage any attempt:

i.   to include excessive detail in the Credit or in any amendment thereto;

ii.   to give instructions to issue, advise or confirm a Credit by reference to a Credit previously issued (similar Credit) where such previous Credit has been subject to accepted amendment(s), and/or unaccepted amendment(s).

b)   All instructions for the issuance of a Credit and the Credit itself and, where applicable, all instructions for an amendment thereto and the amendment itself, must state precisely the document(s) against which payment, acceptance or negotiation is to be made.

B. FORM AND NOTIFICATION OF CREDITS

Article 6   Revocable v Irrevocable Credits
a)   A Credit may be either
            revocable,
            or
            irrevocable.
b)   The Credit, therefore, should clearly indicate whether it is revocable or irrevocable.
c)   In the absence of such indication the Credit shall be deemed to be irrevocable.

Article 7   Advising Bank's Liability
a)   A Credit may be advised to a Beneficiary through another bank (the 'Advising Bank') without engagement on the part of the Advising Bank, but that bank, if it elects to advise the Credit, shall take reasonable care to check the apparent authenticity of the Credit which it advises. If the bank elects not to advise the Credit, it must so inform the issuing Bank without delay.
b)   If the Advising Bank cannot establish such apparent authenticity it must inform, without delay, the bank from which the instructions appear to have been received that is has been unable to establish the authenticity of the Credit and if it elects nonetheless to advise the Credit is must inform the Beneficiary that it has not been able to establish the authenticity of the Credit.

Article 8   Revocation of a Credit
a)   A revocable Credit may be amended or cancelled by the Issuing Bank at any moment and without prior notice to the Beneficiary.
b)   However, the Issuing Bank must:
    i.   reimburse another bank with which a revocable Credit has been made available for sight payment, acceptance or negotiation – for any payment, acceptance or negotiation made by such bank – prior to receipt by it of notice of amendment or cancellation, against documents which appear on their face to be in compliance with the terms and conditions of the Credit;
    ii.   reimburse another bank with which a revocable Credit has been made available for deferred payment, if such a bank has, prior to

receipt by it of notice of amendment or cancellation, taken up documents which appear on their face to be in compliance with the terms and conditions of the Credit.

Article 9   Liability of Issuing and Confirming Banks

a)   An irrevocable Credit constitutes a definite undertaking of the Issuing Bank, provided that the stipulated documents are presented to the Nominated Bank or to the Issuing Bank and that the terms and conditions of the Credit are complied with:

   i.   if the Credit provides for sight payment – to pay at sight;

   ii.   if the Credit provides for deferred payment – to pay on the maturity date(s) determinable in accordance with the stipulations of the Credit;

   iii.   if the Credit provides for acceptance:

      a)   by the Issuing Bank – to accept Draft(s) drawn by the Beneficiary on the Issuing Bank and pay them at maturity,

      or

      b)   by another drawee bank – to accept and pay at maturity Draft(s) drawn by the Beneficiary on the Issuing Bank in the event the drawee bank stipulated in the Credit does not accept Draft(s) drawn on it, or to pay Draft(s) accepted but not paid by such drawee bank at maturity;

   iv.   if the Credit provides for negotiation – to pay without recourse to drawers and/or bona fide holders. Draft(s) drawn by the Beneficiary and/or document(s) presented under the Credit. A Credit should not be issued available by Draft(s) on the Applicant. If the Credit nevertheless calls for Draft(s) on the Applicant, banks will consider such Draft(s) as an additional document(s).

b)   A confirmation of an irrevocable Credit by another bank (the 'Confirming Bank') upon the authorisation or request of the Issuing Bank, constitutes a definite undertaking of the Confirming Bank, in addition to that of the Issuing Bank, provided that the stipulated documents are presented to the Confirming Bank or to any other Nominated Bank and that the terms and conditions of the Credit are complied with:

   i.   if the Credit provides for sight payment – to pay at sight;

   ii.   if the Credit provides for deferred payment – to pay on the maturity date(s) determinable in accordance with the stipulations of the Credit;

iii. if the Credit provides for acceptance:
  a) by the Confirming Bank – to accept Draft(s) drawn by the Beneficiary on the Confirming Bank and pay them at maturity,

  or

  b) by another drawee bank – to accept and pay at maturity Draft(s) drawn by the Beneficiary on the Confirming Bank, in the event the drawee bank stipulated in the Credit does not accept Draft(s) drawn on it, or to pay Draft(s) accepted but not paid by such drawee bank at maturity;

iv. if the Credit provides for negotiation – to negotiate without recourse to drawers and/or bona fide holders, Draft(s) drawn by the Beneficiary and/or document(s) presented under the Credit. A Credit should not be issued available by Draft(s) on the Applicant. If the Credit nevertheless calls for Draft(s) on the Applicant, banks will consider such Draft(s) as an additional document(s).

c) i. If another bank is authorised or requested by the Issuing Bank to add its confirmation to a Credit but is not prepared to do so, it must so inform the Issuing Bank without delay.

  iii. Unless the Issuing Bank specifies otherwise in its authorisation or request to add confirmation, the Advising Bank may advise the Credit to the Beneficiary without adding its confirmation.

d) i. Except as otherwise provided by Article 48, an irrevocable Credit can neither be amended nor cancelled without the agreement of the Issuing Bank, the Confirming Bank, if any, and the Beneficiary.

  ii. The Issuing Bank shall be irrevocably bound by an amendment(s) issued by it from the time of the issuance of such amendment(s). A Confirming Bank may extend its confirmation to an amendment and shall be irrevocably bound as of the time of its advice of the amendment. A Confirming Bank may, however, choose to advise an amendment to the Beneficiary without extending its confirmation and if so, must inform the Issuing Bank and the Beneficiary without delay.

  iii. The terms of the original Credit (or a Credit incorporating previously accepted amendment(s)) will remain in force for the Beneficiary until the Beneficiary communicates his acceptance of the amendment to the bank that advised such amendment. The Beneficiary should give notification of acceptance of the amendment to the bank that advised such amendment. The Beneficiary should give notification of acceptance or rejection of amendment(s). If the Beneficiary fails to give such notification, the tender of documents to the Nominated Bank or Issuing Bank, that conform to the Credit and to not yet accepted amendment(s), will be deemed to be notification of acceptance by the Beneficiary of such amendment(s) and as of that moment that Credit will be amended.

iv. Partial acceptance of amendments contained in one and the same advice of amendment is not allowed and consequently will not be given any effect.

Article 10　Types of Credit

a) All Credits must clearly indicate whether they are available by sight payment, by deferred payment, by acceptance or by negotiation.

b) i. Unless the Credit stipulates that it is available only with the Issuing Bank, all Credits must nominate the bank (the 'Nominated Bank') which is authorised to pay, to incur a deferred payment undertaking, to accept Draft(s) or to negotiate. In a freely negotiable Credit, any bank is a Nominated Bank.

Presentation of documents must be made to the Issuing Bank of the Confirming Bank, if any, or any other Nominated Bank.

ii. Negotiation means the giving of value for Draft(s) and/or document(s) by the bank authorised to negotiate. Mere examination of the documents without giving of value does not constitute a negotiation.

c) Unless the Nominated Bank is the Confirming Bank, nomination by the Issuing Bank does not constitute any undertaking by the Nominated Bank to pay, to incur a deferred payment undertaking, to accept Draft(s), or to negotiate. Except where expressly agreed to by the Nominated Bank and so communicated to the Beneficiary, the Nominated Bank's receipt of and/or examination and/or forwarding of the documents does not make that bank liable to pay, to incur a deferred payment undertaking, to accept Draft(s), or to negotiate.

d) By nominating another bank, or by allowing for negotiation by any bank, or by authorising or requesting another bank to add its confirmation, the Issuing Bank authorises such bank to pay, accept Draft(s) or negotiate as the case may be, against documents which appear on their face to be in compliance with the terms and conditions of the Credit and undertakes to reimburse such bank in accordance with the provisions of these Articles.

Article 11   Teletransmitted and Pre-Advised Credits

a) i.   When an Issuing Bank instructs an Advising Bank by an authenticated teletransmission to advise a Credit or an amendment to a Credit, the teletransmission will be deemed to be the operative Credit instrument or the operative amendment, and no mail confirmation should be sent. Should a mail confirmation nevertheless be sent, it will have no effect and the Advising Bank will have no obligation to check such mail confirmation against the operative Credit instrument or the operative amendment received by teletransmission.

   ii.   If the teletransmission states 'full details to follow' (or words of similar effect) or states that the mail confirmation is to be the operative Credit instrument or the operative amendment, then the teletransmission will not be deemed to be the operative Credit instrument or the operative amendment. The Issuing Bank must forward the operative Credit instrument or the operative amendment to such Advising Bank without delay.

b) If a bank uses the services of an Advising Bank to have the Credit advised to the Beneficiary, it must also use the services of the same bank for advising an amendment(s).

c) A preliminary advice of the issuance or amendment of an irrevocable Credit (pre-advice), shall only be given by an Issuing Bank if such bank is prepared to issue the operative Credit instrument or the operative amendment thereto. Unless otherwise stated in such preliminary advice by the Issuing Bank, an Issuing Bank having given such pre-advice shall be irrevocably committed to issue or amend the Credit, in terms not inconsistent with the pre-advice, without delay.

Article 12   Incomplete or Unclear Instructions

If incomplete or unclear instructions are received to advise, confirm or amend a Credit, the bank requested to act on such instructions may give preliminary notification to the Beneficiary for information only and without responsibility. This preliminary notification should state clearly that the notification is provided for information only and without the responsibility of the Advising Bank. In any event, the Advising Bank must inform the Issuing Bank of the action taken and request it to provide the necessary information.

The Issuing Bank must provide the necessary information without delay. The Credit will be advised, confirmed or amended, only when complete and clear instructions have been received and if the Advising Bank is then prepared to act on the instructions.

C. LIABILITIES AND RESPONSIBILITIES

Article 13   Standard for Examination of Documents

a)   Banks must examine all documents stipulated in the Credit with reasonable care, to ascertain whether or not they appear, on their face, to be in compliance with the terms and conditions of the Credit. Compliance of the stipulated documents on their face with the terms and conditions of the Credit, shall be determined by international standard banking practice as reflected in these Articles. Documents which appear on their face to be inconsistent with one another will be considered as not appearing on their face to be in compliance with the terms and conditions of the Credit.

Documents not stipulated in the Credit will not be examined by banks. If they receive such documents, they shall return them to be presented or pass them on without responsibility.

b)   The Issuing Bank, the Confirming Bank, if any, or a Nominated Bank acting on their behalf, shall each have a reasonable time, not to exceed seven banking days following the day of receipt of the documents, to examine the documents and determine whether to take up or refuse the documents and to inform the party from which it received the documents accordingly.

c)   If a Credit contains conditions without stating the document(s) to be presented in compliance therewith, banks will deem such conditions as not stated and will disregard them.

Article 14   Discrepant Documents and Notice

a)   When the Issuing Bank authorises another bank to pay, incur a deferred payment undertaking, accept Draft(s), or negotiate against documents which appear on their face to be in compliance with the terms and conditions of the Credit, the Issuing Bank and the Confirming Bank, if any, are bound:

   i.   to reimburse the Nominated Bank which has paid, incurred a deferred payment undertaking, accepted Draft(s), or negotiated;

   ii.   to take up the documents.

b) Upon receipt of the documents the Issuing Bank and/or Confirming Bank, if any, or a Nominated Bank acting on their behalf, must determine on the basis of the documents alone whether or not they appear on their face to be in compliance with the terms and conditions of the Credit. If the documents appear on their face not to be in compliance with the terms and conditions of the Credit, such banks may refuse to take up the documents.

c) If the Issuing Bank determines that the documents appear on their face not to be in compliance with the terms and conditions of the Credit, it may in its sole judgment approach the Applicant for a waiver of the discrepancy(ies). This does not, however, extend the period mentioned in sub-Article 13(b).

d) i. If the Issuing Bank and/or Confirming Bank, if any, or a Nominated Bank acting on their behalf, decides to refuse the documents, it must give notice to that effect by telecommunications or, if that is not possible, by other expeditious means, without delay but not later than the close of the seventh banking day following the day of receipt of the documents. Such notice shall be given to the bank from which it received the documents, or to the Beneficiary, if it received the documents directly from him.

   ii. Such notice must state all discrepancies in respect of which the bank refuses the documents and must also state whether it is holding the documents at the disposal of, or is returning them to, the presenter.

   iii. The Issuing Bank and/or Confirming Bank, if any, shall then be entitled to claim from the remitting bank refund, with interest, of any reimbursement which has been made to that bank.

e) If the Issuing Bank and/or Confirming Bank, if any, fails to act in accordance with the provisions of this Article and/or fails to hold the documents at the disposal of, or return them to the presenter, the Issuing Bank and/or Confirming Bank, if any, shall be precluded from claiming that the documents are not in compliance with the terms and conditions of the Credit.

f) If the remitting bank draws the attention of the Issuing Bank and/or Confirming Bank, if any, to any discrepancy(ies) in the document(s) or advises such banks that it has paid, incurred a deferred payment undertaking, accepted Draft(s) or negotiated under reserve or against an indemnity in respect of such discrepancy(ies), the Issuing Bank and/or Confirming Bank, if any, shall not be thereby relieved from any of their obligations under any provision of this Article. Such reserve or indemnity concerns only the relations between the remitting bank and the party towards whom the reserve was made, or from whom, or on whose behalf, the indemnity was obtained.

Article 15   Disclaimer on Effectiveness of Documents

Banks assume no liability or responsibility for the form, sufficiency, accuracy, genuineness, falsification or legal effect of any document(s), or for the general and/or particular conditions stipulated in the document(s) or superimposed thereon; nor do they assume any liability or responsibility for the description, quantity, weight, quality, condition, packing, delivery, value or existence of the goods represented by any document(s), or for the good faith or acts and/or omissions, solvency, performance or standing of the consignors, the carriers, the forwarders, the consignees or the insurers of the goods, or any other person whomsoever.

Article 16   Disclaimer on the Transmission of Messages

Banks assume no liability or responsibility for the consequences arising out of delay and/or loss in transit or any message(s), letter(s) or document(s), or for delay, mutilation or other error(s) arising in the transmission of any telecommunication. Banks assume no liability or responsibility for errors in translation and/or interpretation of technical terms, and reserve the right to transmit Credit terms without translating them.

Article 17   Force Majeure

Banks assume no liability or responsibility for the consequences arising out of the interruption of their business by Acts of God, riots, civil commotions, insurrections, wars or any other causes beyond their control, or by any strikes or lockouts. Unless specifically authorised, banks will not, upon resumption of their business, pay, incur a deferred payment undertaking, accept Draft(s) or negotiate under Credits which expired during such interruption of their business.

Article 18   Disclaimer for Acts of an Instructed Party
a)   Banks utilising the services of another bank or other banks for the purpose of giving effect to the instructions of the Applicant do so for the account and at the risk of such Applicant.

b) Banks assume no liability or responsibility should the instructions they transmit not be carried out, even if they have themselves taken the initiative in the choice of such other bank(s).

c) i. A party instructing another party to perform services is liable for any charges, including commissions, fees, costs or expenses incurred by the instructed party in connection with its instructions.

   ii. Where a Credit stipulates that such charges are for the account of a party other than the instructing party, and charges cannot be collected, the instructing party remains ultimately liable for the payment thereof.

d) The Applicant shall be bound by and liable to indemnify the banks against all obligations and responsibilities imposed by foreign laws and usages.

Article 19   Bank-to-Bank Reimbursement Arrangements

a) If an Issuing Bank intends that the reimbursement to which a paying, accepting or negotiating bank is entitled, shall be obtained by such bank (the 'Claiming Bank'), claiming on another party (the 'Reimbursing Bank'), it shall provide such Reimbursing Bank in good time with the proper instructions or authorisation to honour such reimbursement claims.

b) Issuing Banks shall not require a Claiming Bank to supply a certificate of compliance with the terms and conditions of the Credit to the Reimbursing Bank.

c) An Issuing Bank shall not be relieved from any of its obligations to provide reimbursement if and when reimbursement is not received by the Claiming Bank from the Reimbursing Bank.

d) The Issuing Bank shall be responsible to the Claiming Bank for any loss of interest if reimbursement is not provided by the Reimbursing Bank on first demand, or as otherwise specified in the Credit, or mutually agreed, as the case may be.

e) The Reimbursing Bank charges should be for the account of the Issuing Bank. However, in cases where the charges are for the account of another party, it is the responsibility of the Issuing Bank to so indicate in the original Credit and in the reimbursement authorisation. In cases where the Reimbursing Bank's charges are for the account of another party they shall be collected from the Claiming bank when the Credit is drawn under. In cases where the Credit is not drawn under, the Reimbursing Bank's charges remain the obligation of the Issuing Bank.

D. DOCUMENTS

Article 20   Ambiguity as to the Issuers of Documents

a) Terms such as 'first class', 'well known', 'qualified', 'independent', 'official', 'competent', 'local' and the like, shall not be used to describe the issuers of any document(s) to be presented under a Credit. If such terms are incorporated in the Credit, banks will accept the relative document(s) as presented, provided that it appears on its face to be in compliance with the other terms and conditions of the Credit and not to have been issued by the Beneficiary.

b) Unless otherwise stipulated in the Credit, banks will also accept as an original document(s), a document(s) produced or appearing to have been produced:

   i.   by reprographic, automated or computerised systems;

   ii.   as carbon copies;

   provided that it is marked as original and, where necessary, appears to be signed.

   A document may be signed by handwriting, by facsimile signature, by perforated signature, by stamp, by symbol, or by any other mechanical or electronic method of authentication.

c) i.   Unless otherwise stipulated in the Credit, banks will accept as a copy(ies), a document(s) either labelled copy or not marked as an original – a copy(ies) need not be signed.

   ii.   Credits that require multiple document(s) such as 'duplicate', 'two fold', 'two copies' and the like, will be satisfied by the presentation of one original and the remaining number in copies except where the document itself indicates otherwise.

d) Unless otherwise stipulated in the Credit, a condition under a Credit calling for a document to be authenticated, validated, legalised, visaed, certified or indicating a similar requirement, will be satisfied by any signature, mark, stamp or label on such document that on its face appear to satisfy the above condition.

Article 21   Unspecified Issuers or Contents of Documents

When documents other than transport documents, insurance documents and commercial invoices are called for, the Credit should stipulate by whom such documents are to be issued and their wording or data content. If the Credit does not so stipulate, banks will accept such documents as presented, provided that their data content is not inconsistent with any other stipulated document presented.

Article 22 Issuance Date of Documents v Credit Date

Unless otherwise stipulated in the Credit, banks will accept a document bearing a date of issuance prior to that of the Credit, subject to such document being presented within the time limits set out in the Credit and these Articles.

Article 23 Marine/Ocean Bill of Lading

a) If a credit calls for a bill of lading covering a port-to-port shipment, banks will, unless otherwise stipulated in the Credit, accept a document, however named, which:

i. appears on its face to indicate the name of the carrier and to have been signed or otherwise authenticated by:
- the carrier or a named agent for or on behalf of the carrier, or
- the master or a named agent for or on behalf of the master.

Any signature or authentication of the carrier or master must be identified as a carrier or master, as the case may be. An agent signing or authenticating for the carrier or master must also indicate the name and capacity of the party, ie carrier or master, on whose behalf that agent is acting,

and

ii. indicates that the goods have been loaded on board, or shipped on a named vessel.

Loading on board or shipment on a named vessel may be indicated by pre-printed wording on the bill of lading that the goods have been loaded on board a named vessel or shipped on a named vessel, in which case the date of issuance of the bill of lading will be deemed to be the date of loading on board and the date of shipment.

In all other cases loading on board a named vessel must be evidenced by a notation on the bill of lading which gives the date on which the goods have been loaded on board, in which the case the date of the on board notification will be deemed to be the date of shipment.

If the bill of lading contains the indication 'intended vessel', or similar qualification in relation to the vessel, loading on board a named vessel must be evidenced by an on board notation on the bill of lading which, in addition to the date on which the goods have been loaded on board, also includes the name of the vessel on which the goods have been loaded, even if they have been loaded on the vessel named as the 'intended vessel'.

If the bill of lading indicates a place of receipt or taking in charge different from the port of loading, the on board notation must also include the port of loading stipulated in the Credit and the name of the vessel on which the goods have been loaded, even if they have been loaded on the vessel named in the bill of lading. This provision also applied whenever loading on board the vessel is indicated by pre-printed wording on the bill of lading,

and

iii. indicates the port of loading and the port of discharge stipulated in the Credit, notwithstanding that it:

    a) indicates a place of taking in charge different from the port of loading, and/or a place of final destination different from the port of discharge,

         and/or

    b) contains the indication 'intended' or similar qualification in relation to the port of loading and/or port of discharge, as long as the document also states the ports of loading and/or discharge stipulated in the Credit,

         and

iv. consists of a sole original bill of lading or, if issued in more than one original, the full set as so issued,

and

v. appears to contain all of the terms and conditions of carriage, or some of such terms and conditions by reference to a source or document other than the bill of lading (short form/blank back of bill of lading); banks will not examine the contents of such terms and conditions,

and

vi. contains no indication that it is subject to a charter party and/or no indication that the carrying vessel is propelled by sail only,

and

vii. in all other respects meets the stipulations of the Credit.

b) For the purpose of this Article, transhipment means unloading and reloading from one vessel to another vessel during the course of ocean carriage from the port of loading to the port of discharge stipulated in the Credit.

c)   Unless transhipment is prohibited by the terms of the Credit, banks will accept a bill of lading which indicates that the goods will be transhipped, provided that the entire ocean carriage is covered by one and the same bill of lading.

d)   Even if the Credit prohibits transhipment, banks will accept a bill of lading which:

i.   indicates that transhipment will take place as long as the relevant cargo is shipped in Container(s), Trailer(s) and/or 'LASH' barge(s) as evidenced by the bill of lading, provided that the entire ocean carriage is covered by one and the same bill of lading, and/or

ii. incorporates clauses stating that the carrier reserves the right to tranship.

Article 24   Non-Negotiable Sea Waybill

a)   If a Credit calls for a non-negotiable sea waybill covering a port-to-port shipment, banks will, unless otherwise stipulated in the Credit, accept a document, however named, which:

i.   appears on its face to indicate the name of the carrier and to have been signed or otherwise authenticated by:

-   the carrier or a named agent for or on behalf of the carrier, or
-   the master or a named agent for or on behalf of the master,

Any signature or authentication of the carrier or master must be identified as carrier or master, as the case may be. An agent signing or authenticating for the carrier or master must also indicate the name and the capacity of the party, ie carrier or master, on whose behalf that agent is acting.

and

ii. indicates that the goods have been loaded on board, or shipped on a named vessel.

Loading on board or shipment on a named vessel may be indicated by pre-printed wording on the non-negotiable sea waybill that the goods have been loaded on board a named vessel or shipped on a named vessel, in which case the date of issuance of the non-negotiable sea waybill will be deemed to be the date of loading on board and the date of shipment.

In all other cases loading on board a named vessel must be evidenced by a notation on the non-negotiable sea waybill which gives the date on which the goods have been loaded on board, in which case the date of the on board notation will be deemed to be the date of shipment.

If the non-negotiable sea waybill contains the indication 'intended vessel', of similar qualification in relation to the vessel, loading on board a named vessel must be evidenced by an on board notation on the non-negotiable sea waybill which, in addition to the date on which the goods have been loaded on board, includes the name of the vessel on which the goods have been loaded, even if they have been loaded on the vessel named as the 'intended vessel'.

If the non-negotiable sea waybill indicates a place of receipt or taking in charge different from the port of loading, the on board notation must also include the port of loading stipulated in the Credit and the name of the vessel on which the goods have been loaded, event if they have been loaded on a vessel names in the non-negotiable sea waybill. This provision also applied whenever loading on board the vessel is indicated by pre-printed wording on the non-negotiable sea waybill,

and

iii. indicates the port of loading and the port of discharge stipulated in the Credit, notwithstanding that it:

a) indicates a place of taking charge different from the port of loading, and/or a place of final destination different from the port of discharge,

and/or

b) contains the indication 'Intended' or similar qualification in relation to the port of loading and/or port of discharge, as long as the document also states the ports of loading and/or discharge stipulated in the Credit,

and

iv. consists of a sole original non-negotiable sea waybill, or if issued in more than one original, the full set as so issued,

and

v. appears to contain all of the terms and conditions of carriage, or some of such terms and conditions by reference to a source or document other than the non-negotiable sea waybill (short form/blank back non-negotiable sea waybill); banks will not examine the contents of such terms and conditions,

and

vi. contains no indication that it is subject to a charterparty and/or no indication that the carrying vessel is propelled by sail only, and

vii.   in all other respects meets the stipulations of the Credit.

b)   For the purposes of this Article, transhipment means unloading and reloading from one vessel to another vessel during the course of ocean carriage from the port of loading to the port of discharge stipulated in the Credit.

c)   Unless transhipment is prohibited by the terms of the Credit, banks will accept a non-negotiable sea waybill which indicates that the goods will be transhipped, provided that the entire ocean carriage is covered by one and the same non-negotiable sea waybill.

d)   Even if the Credit prohibits transhipment, banks will accept a non-negotiable sea waybill which:

i.   indicates that transhipment will take place as long as the relevant cargo is shipped in Container(s), Trailer(s) and/or 'LASH' barge(s) as evidenced by the non-negotiable sea waybill, provided that the entire ocean carriage is covered by one and the same non-negotiable sea waybill,
and/or

ii.   incorporates clauses stating that the carrier reserves the right to tranship.

Article 25   Charter Party Bill of Lading

a)   If a Credit calls for or permits a charter party bill of lading, banks will, unless otherwise stipulated in the Credit, accept a document, however named, which:

i.   contains any indication that it is subject to a charter party, and

ii.   appears on its face to have been signed or otherwise authenticated by:
-   the master or a named agent for or on behalf of the master, or
-   the owner or a named agent for or on behalf of the owner.

Any signature or authentication of the master or owner must be identified as master or owner as the case may be. An agent signing or authenticating for the master or owner must also indicate the name and the capacity of the party, ie master or owner, on whose behalf that agent is acting,
and

iii.   does or does not indicate the name of the carrier, and

iv.   indicates that the goods have been loaded on board or shipped on a named vessel.

Loading on board or shipment on a named vessel may be indicated by pre-printed wording on the bill of lading that the goods have been loaded on board a named vessel or shipped on a named vessel, in which case the date of issuance of the bill of lading will be deemed to be the date of loading on board and the date of shipment.

In all other cases loading on board a named vessel must be evidenced by a notation on the bill of lading which gives the date on which the goods have been loaded on board, in which case the date of the on board notation will be deemed to be the date of shipment,

and

v.   indicates the port of loading and the port of discharge stipulated in the Credit,

and

vi.   consists of a sole original bill of lading or, if issued in more than one original, the full set as so issued,

and

vii.   contains no indication that the carrying vessel is propelled by sail only,

and

viii. in all other respects meets the stipulations of the Credit.

b)   Even if the Credit requires the presentation of a charter party contract in connection with a charter party bill of lading, banks will not examine such charter party contract, but will pass it without responsibility on their part.

Article 26   Multimodal Transport Document

a)   If a Credit calls for a transport document covering at least two different modes of transport (multimodal transport), banks will, unless otherwise stipulated in the Credit, accept a document, however named, which:

i.   appears on its face to indicate the name of the carrier or multimodal transport operator and to have been signed or otherwise authenticated by:

–   the carrier or multimodal transport operator or a named agent for or on behalf of the carrier or multimodal transport operator,

or

–   the master or named agent for or on behalf of the master.

Any signature or authentication of the carrier, multimodal transport operator or master must be identified as carrier, multimodal transport operator or master, as the case may be. An agent signing or authenticating for the carrier, multimodal transport operator or master must also indicate the name and the capacity of the party, ie carrier, multimodal transport operator or master, on whose behalf that agent is acting,

and

ii.   indicates that the goods have been dispatched, taken in charge or loaded on board.

Dispatch, taking in charge or loading on board may be indicated by wording to that effect on the multimodal transport document and the date of issuance will be deemed to be the date of dispatch, taking in charge or loading on board and the date of shipment. However, if the document indicates, by stamp or otherwise, a date of dispatch, taking in charge or loading on board, such date will be deemed to be the date of shipment,

and

iii.   a)   indicates the place of taking in charge stipulated in the Credit which may be different from the port, airport or place of loading, and the place of final destination stipulated in the Credit which may be different from the port, airport or place of discharge,

and/or

b)   contains the indication 'intended' or similar qualification in relation to the vessel and/or port of loading and/or port of discharge,

and

iv.   consists of a sole original multimodal transport document or, if issued in more than one original, the full set as so issued,

and

v.   appears to contain all of the terms and conditions of carriage, or some of such terms and conditions by reference to a source or document other than the multimodal transport document (short form/blank back multimodal transport document); banks will not examine the contents of such terms and conditions,

and

vi.   contains no indication that it is subject to a charter party and/or no indication that the carrying vessel is propelled by sail only,

and

vii. in all other respects meets the stipulations of the Credit.

b) Even if the Credit prohibits transhipment, banks will accept a
    multimodal transport document which indicates that transhipment
    will or may take place, provided that the entire carriage is covered by
    one and the same multimodal transport document.

Article 27 Air Transport Document

a) If a Credit calls for an air transport document, banks will, unless
    otherwise stipulated in the Credit, accept a document, however named,
    which:

    i.   appears on its face to indicate the name of the carrier and to have
           been signed or otherwise authenticated by:
- the carrier, or
- a named agent for or on behalf of the carrier.

           Any signature of authentication of the carrier must be identified
           as carrier. An agent signing or authenticating for the carrier must
           also indicate the name and the capacity of the party, ie carrier, on
           whose behalf that agent is acting,
           and

    ii. indicates that the goods have been accepted for carriage,
           and

    iii. where the Credit calls for an actual date of dispatch, indicates a
           specific notation of such date, the date of dispatch so indicated
           on the air transport document will be deemed to be the date of
           shipment.

           For the purpose of this Article, the information appearing in the
           box on the air transport document (marked 'For Carrier Use Only'
           or similar expression) relative to the flight number and date will
           not be considered as a specific notation of such date of dispatch.
           In all other cases, the date of issuance of the air transport
           document will be deemed to be the date of shipment,
           and

    iv. indicates the airport of departure and the airport of destination
           stipulated in the Credit,
           and

    v.   appears to be the original for consignor/shipper even if the Credit
           stipulates a full set of originals, or similar expressions,
           and

    vi. appears to contain all of the terms and conditions of carriage, or
           some of such terms and conditions, by reference to a source or
           document other than the air transport document; banks will not

examine the contents of such terms and conditions, and

vii. in all other respects meets the stipulations of the Credit.

b) For the purpose of this Article, transhipment means unloading and reloading from one aircraft to another aircraft during the course of carriage from the airport of departure to the airport of destination stipulated in the Credit.

c) Even if the Credit prohibits transhipment, banks will accept an air transport document which indicates that transhipment will or may take place, provided that the entire carriage is covered by one and the same air transport document.

Article 28   Road, Rail or Inland Waterway Transport Documents

a) If a Credit calls for a road, rail or inland waterway transport document, banks will, unless otherwise stipulated in the Credit, accept a document of the type called for, however named, which:

i. appears on its face to indicate the name of the carrier and to have been signed or otherwise authenticated by the carrier or a named agent for or on behalf of the carrier and/or to bear a reception stamp or other indication of receipt by the carrier or a named agent for or on behalf of the carrier.

Any signature, authentication, reception stamp or other indication of receipt of the carrier, must be identified on its face as that of the carrier. An agent signing or authenticating for the carrier, must also indicate the name and the capacity of the party, ie carrier, on whose behalf that agent is acting, and

ii. indicates that the goods have been received for shipment, dispatch or carriage or wording to this effect. The date of issuance will be deemed to be the date of shipment unless the transport document contains a reception stamp, in which case the date of the reception stamp will be deemed to be the date of shipment, and

iii. indicates the place of shipment and the place of destination stipulated in the Credit, and

iv. in all other respects meets the stipulations of the Credit.

b) In the absence of any indication on the transport document as to the numbers issued, banks will accept the transport document(s) presented as constituting a full set. Banks will accept as original(s) the transport document(s) whether marked as original(s) or not.

c) For the purposes of this Article, transhipment means unloading and reloading from one means of conveyance to another means of conveyance, in different modes of transport, during the course of carriage from the place of shipment to the place of destination stipulated in the Credit.

d) Even if the Credit prohibits transhipment, banks will accept a road, rail, or inland waterway transport document which indicates that transhipment will or may take place, provided that the entire carriage is covered by one and the same transport document and within the same mode of transport.

Article 29   Courier and Post Receipts

a) If a Credit calls for a post receipt or certificate of posting, banks will, unless otherwise stipulated in the Credit, accept a post receipt or certificate of posting which:

   i. appears on its face to have been stamped or otherwise authenticated and dated in the place from which the Credit stipulates the goods are to be shipped or dispatched and such date will be deemed to be the date of shipment or dispatch, and

   ii. in all other respects meets the stipulations of the Credit.

b) If a Credit calls for a document issued by a courier or expedited delivery service evidencing receipt of the goods for delivery, banks will, unless otherwise stipulated in the Credit, accept a document, however named, which:

   i. appears on its face to indicate the name of the courier/service, and to have been stamped, signed or otherwise authenticated by such named courier/service (unless the Credit specifically calls for a document issued by a named Courier/Service, banks will accept a document issued by any Courier/Service), and

   ii. indicates a date of pick-up or of receipt or wording to this effect, such date being deemed to be the date of shipment or dispatch, and

   iii. in all other respects meets the stipulations of the Credit.

Article 30 Transport Documents issued by Freight Forwarders

Unless otherwise authorised in the Credit, banks will only accept a transport document issued by a freight forwarder if it appears on its face to indicate:

i.   the name of the freight forwarder as a carrier or multimodal transport operator and to have been signed or otherwise authenticated by the freight forwarder as carrier or multimodal transport operator,

or

ii.   the name of the carrier or multimodal transport operator and to have been signed or otherwise authenticated by the freight forwarder as a named agent for or on behalf of the carrier or multimodal transport operator.

Article 31 'On Deck', 'Shipper's Load and Count', Name of Consignor

Unless otherwise stipulated in the Credit, banks will accept a transport document which:

i.   does not indicate, in the case of carriage by sea or by more than one means of conveyance including carriage by sea, that the goods are or will be loaded on deck. Nevertheless, banks will accept a transport document which contains a provision that the goods may be carried on deck, provided that it does not specifically state that they are or will be loaded on deck,

and/or

ii.   bears a clause on the face thereof such as 'shipper's load and count' or 'said by shipper to contain' or words to similar effect,

and/or

iii.   indicates as the consignor of the goods a party other than the Beneficiary of the Credit.

Article 32 Clean Transport Documents

a)   A clean transport document is one which bears no clause or notation which expressly declares a defective condition of the goods and/or the packaging.

b)   Banks will not accept transport documents bearing such clauses or notations unless the Credit expressly stipulates the clauses or notations which may be accepted.

c) Banks will regard a requirement in a Credit for a transport document to bear the clause 'clean on board' as complied with if such transport document meets the requirements of this Article and or Articles 23, 24, 25, 26, 27, 28 or 30.

Article 33   Freight Payable/Prepaid Transport Documents

a) Unless otherwise stipulated in the Credit, or inconsistent with any of the documents presented under the Credit, banks will accept transport documents stating that freight or transportation charges (hereafter referred to as 'freight') have still to be paid.

b) If a Credit stipulates that the transport document has to indicate that freight has been paid or prepaid, banks will accept a transport document on which words clearly indicating payment or prepayment of freight appear by stamp or otherwise, or on which payment or prepayment of freight is indicated by other means. If the Credit requires courier charges to be paid or prepaid banks will also accept a transport document issued by a courier or expedited delivery service evidencing that courier charges are for the account of a party other than the consignee.

c) The words 'freight prepayable' or 'freight to be prepaid' or words of similar effect, if appearing on transport documents, will not be accepted as constituting evidence of the payment of freight.

d) Banks will accept transport documents bearing reference by stamp or otherwise to costs additional to the freight, such as costs of, or disbursements incurred in connection with, loading, unloading or similar operations, unless the conditions of the Credit specifically prohibit such reference.

Article 34   Insurance Documents

a) Insurance documents must appear on their face to be issued and signed by insurance companies or underwriters or their agents.

b) If the insurance document indicates that it has been issued in more than one original, all the originals must be presented unless otherwise authorised in the Credit.

c) Cover notes issued by brokers will not be accepted, unless specifically authorised in the Credit.

d) Unless otherwise stipulated in the Credit, banks will accept an insurance certificate or a declaration of an open cover presigned by insurance companies or underwriters or their agents. If a Credit specifically calls for an insurance certificate or a declaration under an open cover, banks will accept, in lieu thereof, an insurance policy.

e) Unless otherwise stipulated in the Credit, or unless it appears from the insurance document that the cover is effective at the latest from the date of loading on board or dispatch or taking in charge the goods, banks will not accept an insurance document which bears a date of issuance later than the date of loading on board or dispatch or taking in charge as indicated in such transport document.

f) i. Unless otherwise stipulated in the Credit, the insurance document must be expressed in the same currency as the Credit.

iii. Unless otherwise stipulated in the Credit, the minimum amount for which the insurance document must indicate the insurance cover to have been effected is the CIF (cost, insurance and freight (…'named port of destination')) or CIP (carriage and insurance paid to (…'named place of destination')) value of the goods, as the case may be, plus 10%, but only when the CIF or CIP value can be determined from the documents on their face. Otherwise, banks will accept as such minimum amount 110% of the amount for which payment, acceptance or negotiation is requested under the Credit, or 110% of the gross amount of the invoice, whichever is the greater.

Article 35   Type of Insurance Cover

a) Credits should stipulate the type of insurance required and, if any, the additional risks which are to be covered. Imprecise terms such as 'usual risks' or 'customary risks' shall not be used; if they are used, banks will accept insurance documents as presented, without responsibility for any risks not being covered.

b) Failing specific stipulations in the Credit, banks will accept insurance documents as presented, without responsibility for any risks not being covered.

c) Unless otherwise stipulated in the Credit, banks will accept an insurance document which indicates that the cover is subject to a franchise or an excess (deductible).

Article 36   All Risks Insurance Cover

Where a Credit stipulates 'insurance against all risks', banks will accept an insurance document which contains any 'all risks' notation or clause, whether or not bearing the heading 'all risks', even if the insurance document indicates that certain risks are excluded, without responsibility for any risk(s) not being covered.

Article 37   Commercial Invoices

a)   Unless otherwise stipulated in the Credit, commercial invoices;

   i.   must appear on their face to be issued by the Beneficiary named in the Credit (except as provided in Article 48); and

   ii.   must be made out in the name of the Applicant (except as provided in sub-Article 48); and

   iii.   need not be signed.

b)   Unless otherwise stipulated in the Credit, banks may refuse commercial invoices issued for amounts in excess of the amount permitted by the Credit. Nevertheless, if a bank authorised to pay, incur a deferred payment undertaking, accept Draft(s), or negotiate under a Credit accepts such invoices, its decision will be binding on all parties, provided that such bank has not paid, incurred a deferred payment undertaking, accepted Draft(s) or negotiated for an amount in excess for the amount permitted by the Credit.

c)   The description of the goods in the commercial invoice must correspond with the description in the Credit. In all other documents, the goods may be described in general terms not inconsistent with the description of goods in the Credit.

Article 38   Other documents

If a credit calls for an attestation or certification of weight in the case of transport other than by sea, banks will accept a weight stamp or declaration of weight which appears to have been superimposed on the transport document by the carrier or his agent unless the Credit specifically stipulates that the attestation or certification of weight must be by means of a separate document.

E.   MISCELLANEOUS PROVISIONS

Article 39   Allowances in Credit Amount, Quantity and Unit Price

a)   The words 'about', 'approximately', 'circa' or similar expressions used in connection with the amount of the Credit or the quantity or the unit price stated in the Credit are to be construed as allowing a difference of not more than 10% less than the amount of the quantity or the unit price to which they refer.

b) Unless a Credit stipulates that the quantity of the goods specified must not be exceeded or reduced, a tolerance of 5% more or 5% less will be permissible, always provided that the amount of the drawings does not exceed the amount of the Credit. This tolerance does not apply when the Credit stipulates the quantity in terms of a stated number of packing units or individual items.

c) Unless a Credit which prohibits partial shipments stipulates otherwise, or unless sub-Article (b) above is applicable, a tolerance of 5% less in the amount of the drawing will be permissible, provided that the Credit stipulates the quantity of the goods, such quantity of goods is shipped in full, and if the Credit stipulates a unit price, such price is not reduced. This provision does not apply when expressions referred to sub-Article (a) above are used in the Credit.

Article 40   Partial Shipments/Drawings

a) Partial shipments and/or drawings are allowed, unless the Credit stipulates otherwise.

b) Transport documents which appear on their face to indicate that shipment has been made on the same means of conveyance and for the same journey, provided they indicate the same destination, will not be regarded as covering partial shipments, even if the transport documents indicate different dates of shipment and/or different ports of loading, places of taking in charge, or despatch.

c) Shipments made by post or by courier will not be regarded as partial shipments if the post receipts or certificates of posting or courier's receipts or despatch notes appear to have been stamped, signed or otherwise authenticated in the place from which the Credit stipulates the goods are to be despatched, and on the same date.

Article 41   Instalments Shipments/Drawings

If drawings and/or shipments within given periods are stipulated in the Credit and any instalment is not drawn and/or shipped within the period allowed for that instalment, the Credit ceases to be available for that and any subsequent instalments, unless otherwise stipulated in the Credit.

Article 42   Expiry Date and Place for Presentation of Documents

a)   All Credits must stipulate an expiry date and a place for presentation of documents for payment, acceptance, or with the exception of freely negotiable Credits, a place for presentation of documents for negotiation. An expiry date stipulated for payment, acceptance or negotiation will be construed to express an expiry date for presentation of documents.

b)   Except as provided in sub-Article 44(a), documents must be presented on or before such expiry date.

c)   If an Issuing Bank states that the credit is to be available 'for one month', 'for six months', or the like, but does not specify the date from which the time is to run, the date of issuance of the Credit by the Issuing Bank will be deemed to be the first day from which such time is to be run. Banks should discourage indication of the expiry date of the Credit in this manner.

Article 43   Limitation on the Expiry Date

a)   In addition to stipulating an expiry date for presentation of documents, every Credit which calls for a transport document(s)should also stipulate a specified period of time after the date of shipment during which presentation must be made on compliance with the terms and conditions of the Credit. If no such period of time is stipulated, banks will not accept documents presented to them later than 21 days after the date of shipment. In any event, documents must be presented not later than the expiry date of the Credit.

b)   In cases in which sub-Article 40(b) applies, the date of shipment will be considered to be the latest shipment date on any of the transport documents presented.

Article 44   Extension of Expiry Date

a)   If the expiry date of the Credit and/or the last day of the period of time for presentation of documents stipulated by the Credit or applicable by virtue of Article 43 falls on the day on which the bank to which presentation has to be made is closed for reasons other than those referred to in Article 17, the stipulated expiry date and/or the last day of the period of time after the date of shipment for presentation of documents, as the case may be, shall be extended to the first following day on which such bank is open.

b) The latest date of shipment shall not be extended by reason of the extension of the expiry date and/or the period of time after the date of shipment for presentation of documents in accordance with sub-Article (a) above. If no such latest date for shipment is stipulated in the Credit or amendments thereto, banks will not accept transport documents indicating a date of shipment later than the expiry date stipulated in the Credit or amendments thereto.

c) The bank to which presentation is made on such first following business day must provide a statement that the documents were presented within the time limits extended in accordance with sub-Article 44(a) of the Uniform Customs and Practice for Documentary Credits, 1993 Revision, ICC Publication No 500.

Article 45 Hours of Presentation

Banks are under no obligation to accept presentation of documents outside their banking hours.

Article 46 General Expressions as to Dates for Shipment

a) Unless otherwise stipulated in the Credit, the expression 'shipment' used in stipulating an earliest and/or a latest date for shipment will be understood to include expressions such as 'loading on board', 'dispatch', 'accepted for carriage', 'date of post receipt', 'date of pick up', and the like, and in the case of a Credit calling for a multimodal transport document the expression 'taking in charge'.

b) Expressions such as 'prompt', 'immediately', 'as soon as possible', and the like should not be used. If they are used banks will disregard them.

c) If the expression 'on or about' or similar expressions are used, banks will interpret them as a stipulation that shipment is to be made during the period from five days before to five days after the specified date, both end days included.

Article 47 Date Terminology for Periods of Shipment

a) The words 'to', 'until', 'till', 'from' and words of similar import applying to any date or period in the Credit referring to shipment will be understood to include the date mentioned.

b) The word 'after' will be understood to exclude the date mentioned.

c) The terms 'first half', 'second half' of the month shall be construed respectively as the 1st to the 15th, and the 16th to the last day of such month, all dates inclusive.

d) The terms 'beginning', 'middle', or 'end' of a month shall be construed respectively as the 1st to the 10th, the 11th to the 20th, and the 21st to the last day of such month, all dates inclusive.

F. TRANSFERABLE CREDIT

Article 48   Transferable Credit

a) A transferable Credit is a Credit under which the beneficiary (First Beneficiary) may request the bank authorised to pay, incur a deferred payment undertaking, accept or negotiate (the 'Transferring Bank'), or in the case of a freely negotiable Credit, the Bank specifically authorised in the Credit as a Transferring Bank, to make the Credit available in whole or in part to one or more other Beneficiary(ies) (Second Beneficiary(ies)).

b) A Credit can be transferred only if it is expressly designated as 'transferable' by the Issuing Bank. Terms such as 'divisible', 'fractionable', 'assignable' and 'transmissible' do not render the Credit transferable. If such terms are used they shall be disregarded.

c) The Transferring Bank shall be under no obligation to effect such transfer except to the extent and in the manner expressly consented to by such bank.

d) At the time of making a request for transfer and prior to transfer of the Credit, the First Beneficiary must irrevocably instruct the Transferring Bank whether or not he retains the right to refuse to allow the Transferring Bank to advise amendments to the Second Beneficiary(ies). If the Transferring Bank consents to the transfer under these conditions, it must, at the time of transfer, advise the Second Beneficiary(ies) of the First Beneficiary(ies) instructions regarding amendments.

e) If a Credit is transferred to more than one Second Beneficiary(ies) refusal of an amendment from one or more Second Beneficiary(ies) does not invalidate the acceptance(s) by the other Second Beneficiary(ies) with respect to whom the Credit will be amended accordingly. With respect to the Second Beneficiary(ies) who reject the amendment, the Credit will remain unamended.

f)   Transferring Bank charges in respect of transfers including commissions, fees, costs or expenses are payable by the First Beneficiary, unless otherwise agreed. If the Transferring Bank agrees to transfer the Credit it shall be under no obligation to effect the transfer until such charges are paid.

g)   Unless otherwise stated in the Credit, a transferable Credit can be transferred once only. Consequently the Credit cannot be transferred at the request of a Second Beneficiary to any subsequent Third Beneficiary. For the purpose of this Article, a retransfer to the First Beneficiary does not constitute a prohibited transfer.

Fractions of a transferable Credit (not exceeding in the aggregate the amount of the Credit) can be transferred separately, provided partial shipments/drawings are not prohibited, and the aggregate of such transfers will be considered as constituting only one transfer of the Credit.

h)   The Credit can be transferred only on the terms and conditions specified in the Original Credit, with the exception of:
-   the amount of the Credit,
-   any unit price stated therein,
-   the expiry date,
-   the last day for presentation of documents in accordance with Article 43,
-   the period of shipment,
any or all of which may be reduced or curtailed.

The percentage of which insurance cover must be effected may be increased in such a way as to provide the amount of cover stipulated in the original Credit, or these Articles.

In addition the name of the First Beneficiary can be substituted for that of the Applicant, but if the name of the Applicant is specifically required by the original Credit to appear in any document(s) other than the invoice, such requirement must be fulfilled.

i)   The First Beneficiary has the right to substitute his own invoice(s) (and Draft(s)) for these and the Second Beneficiary(ies), for amounts not in excess of the original amount stipulated in the Credit, and upon such substitution of invoice(s) (and Draft(s)) the First Beneficiary can draw under Credit for the difference, if any, between his invoice(s) and the Second Beneficiary's(ies) invoice(s).

When a Credit has been transferred and the First Beneficiary is to supply his own invoice(s) (and Draft(s)) in exchange for the Second Beneficiary's(ies) invoice(s) (and Draft(s))but fails to do so on first demand, the Transferring Bank has the right to deliver to the Issuing Bank the documents received under the transferred Credit, including the Second Beneficiary's(ies) invoice(s) (and Draft(s)) without further responsibility to the First Beneficiary.

j) The First Beneficiary may request the payment or negotiation be effected to the Second Beneficiary(ies) at the place to which the Credit has been transferred up to and including the expiry date of the Credit, unless the original Credit expressly states that it may not be made available for payment and negotiation at a place other than that stipulated in the Credit. This is without prejudice to the First Beneficiary's right to substitute subsequently his own invoice(s) (and Draft(s)) for those of the Second Beneficiary(ies) and to claim any difference due to him.

G. ASSIGNMENT OF PROCEEDS

Article 49   Assignment of Proceeds

The fact that a Credit is not stated to be transferable shall not affect the Beneficiary's right to assign any proceeds to which he may be, or may become, entitled under such Credit, in accordance with the provisions of the applicable law. This Article relates only to the assignment of proceeds and not to the assignment of the right to perform under the Credit itself.

Index

Index

Index

Index

Rob
Cas